Brent A. Calloway

CPH Christian Living Commentary

THE BOOK OF JAMES

THE BOOK OF JAMES

CPH CHRISTIAN LIVING COMMENTARY

Brent A. Calloway

Christian Publishing House

Cambridge, Ohio

Christian Publishing House
Professional Christian Publishing of the Good News

A special thanks to Mrs. Nancy D. Swank for editing efforts.

THE BOOK OF JAMES (CPH CHRISTIAN LIVING COMMENTARY)

ISBN-13: 978-0692411698

ISBN-10: 0692411690

INTRODUCTION The Letter of James

Before beginning this commentary, it is highly recommended that you read Appendices A, B, and C at the end, as they will enable you to better understand what lies ahead. If you do not, some comments may be difficult to understand.

The book of James is one of the easiest to read and applicable books in the New Testament Canon. James is an essential book for any Christian to read, as it contains within it, principles for Christian living and many practical applications that serve as expectations for the life of the Christian. James deals with a variety of topics throughout his letter to these Christians. In chapter one, James deals with issues such as trials, nature of temptation, application of God's word, and authentic religion. In chapter two James deals with issues such as favoritism, and what true saving faith looks like. In chapter three, James deals with the proper use of the tongue and danger of an uncontrolled tongue and heavenly wisdom compared with demonic wisdom. In chapter four James discusses issues of quarreling and fighting, repentance, speaking against one's brother and making plans apart from God. Then, in chapter five James warns the rich against coming destruction and calls upon the Christian to be patient in light of their afflictions, and the ministry responsibilities of the spiritually sick person and elders they call upon. James throughout his letter often asks his audience questions to challenge their Christian walk and relationship with God.

Authorship

James who is the author of this book is one of at least four James' who is mentioned in the New Testament. The four are as follows:

(1) James, who is the father of the apostle Judas (not Judas Iscariot) Lu 6:16; Ac 1:13

(2) James, who is the Son of Zebedee; brother of John and one of the 12 apostles of Jesus Christ Matt 10:2

(3) James was the son of Alphaeus, who was also another apostle of Jesus Christ. (Matt 10:2, 3; Mark 3:18; Lu 6:15; Ac 1:13) Some scholars believe that Alphaeus was the same person as Clopas. Therefore, James' mother would have been Mary, which would be the same "Mary the mother of James the Less and Joses, and Salome." (John 19:25; Mark

15:40; Matt 27:56) He might have been called "James the Less," because he was younger or smaller physically than James, the son of Zebedee was. If these scholars are wrong; then, there are five James in the New Testament.

(4) James, the son of Joseph and Mary, who was a half-brother of Jesus. (Mark 6:3; Gal. 1:19) He was not an apostle, but he was the overseer of the church at Jerusalem (Ac 12:17), as well as the author of the book bearing his name.

The author of our letter simply writes of himself, "James, a slave[1] of God and of the Lord Jesus Christ." (Jam 1:1) As we can see from our list of four in the above, Jesus had two apostles named James. (Matt 10:2-3) However, these are unlikely candidates as authors. One James, who was one of the 12 apostles, the son of Zebedee, was the first of the 12 to be martyred (Acts 12:2). He was executed about 44 C.E.[2] This is far too early of a date for the book of James to have been penned by James, the son of Zebedee. The other James, who was an apostle, the son of Alphaeus, was not that well known in the Bible record, so we do not know hardly anything about him. When we think of the James, who wrote the letter bearing his name, it is of an outspoken person, who was crucial and influential in early Christianity. Moreover, being that there were two apostles named James, the son of Alphaeus, would have likely mentioned himself in some way to differentiate himself. The James of our book had no need to identify himself.

Therefore, the evidence points to the only true candidate as the author of the book of James, the half-brother of Jesus, as he was well-known enough to go by "James." He was visited by the apostle Paul (Gal. 1:18-19) and referred to as "the Lord's brother" (v. 19). He was a "pillar" in the Jerusalem congregation (2:9). He presided over the Jerusalem council in Acts 15:13-19. Yes, this unbelieving half-brother of Jesus was moved by the resurrection and the special appearance from his brother, he became the most prominent James of the New Testament and could go by "James" alone. (Matt. 13:55; Ac 21:15-25; 1 Cor. 15:7; Ga 2:9)

Again, the author of our book identifies himself as "James, a slave of God and of the Lord Jesus Christ," which is very similar to Jude and his letter, the other half-brother of Jesus Christ, who wrote, "Jude, a servant

---

[1] Or *servant*

[2] In this publication, instead of the traditional "A.D." and "B.C.," the more accurate "C.E." (Common Era) and "B.C.E." (before the Common Era) are used.

2

of Jesus Christ and brother of James." (Jam. 1:1; Jude 1:1) Finally, the salutation to the book of James has the term "Greetings!" in the same way as the council in Jerusalem's letter to Gentile believers.--Acts 15:13, 22, and 23.

Historical Setting (Bible Background)

James does not give us much information into the historical context of which he is writing, but rather gives principles and imperatives for his readers. We know from James 1:1 that James is writing to Christians that have been scattered. This has been taken to refer to the scattering of Christians that took place after the stoning of Stephen (Acts 8:1). If this were the case, it could indicate that James is writing to believers that were undergoing persecutions for their faith. James makes mention of how the Christians were being mistreated in the fact that they were not being paid their wages by their laborers (James 5:1-6). James also writes to his readers that they are to remain patient in their suffering in light of the Lord's return (James 5:9-11). James mentions that the trials were various that these believers were enduring and not just limited to persecutions (James 1:2-4). Therefore, we know that James' audience was going through trials in whatever capacity those might have been: whether physical persecution, financial oppression or whatever they may have been facing.

When James speaks of "the twelve tribes in the Dispersion," he is not referring to the 12 tribes of literal Israel, as the Jews, who made up Judaism were not his "brothers" that were 'holding the faith in our Lord Jesus Christ.' (See James 1:2; 2:1, 5) Before Jesus' execution, He made it clear that the 12 tribes of literal Israel had been rejected. He said, "the kingdom of God will be taken away from you and given to a people producing its fruits." (Matt. 21:43) Who are these people that would produce fruit? It was "the Israel of God." (Gal 6:16) After Jesus' ransom sacrifice, those who entered the Christian congregation, were not Jews in a fleshly way, but were the Israel of God in an inward way, a spiritual Israel, open to both Jew and Gentile. (Rom. 2:29; 4:16, 17; 9:6-8; Gal. 3:7, 29; 4:21-31; Phil. 3:3) These spiritual Israelites were dispersed throughout the then known world. "There arose on that day a great persecution against the church in Jerusalem, and they were all scattered throughout the regions of Judea and Samaria, except the apostles." (Ac 8:1) So thereafter, through these scattered ones and the work of the evangelists, congregations were being started all through the Roman Empire. In fact, we find Peter using the same words as James, "the

Dispersion in Pontus, Galatia, Cappadocia, Asia, and Bithynia." (1 Pet. 1:1) Therefore, there were Jews living in dispersed nations at the times of James writing. Whatever the case, James letter is writing to Christians that were going through trials of many various kinds.

Literary Form

James is written as an epistle since it is written to a specific group of scattered Christians. Throughout the letter of James, he provides these first-century believers with practical wisdom for their life and functions as the Proverbs of the New Testament. James writes as one who was very familiar with the Hebrew wisdom literature as he discusses such things as wisdom, wealth, and the usage of the tongue. James uses very clear, concise and direct statements to his readers that make it very understandable even for the modern reader. The use of the Greek language as used by James shows that he was familiar with the Greek culture and the language. Many modern scholars believe that the book of James is of the literary[3] Koine in regards to the level of the Greek (common, conversational, literary). In addition, James also writes in a way that that shows he is very familiar with the words of Christ in particular the Sermon on the Mount.

James' letter does not seem to focus on one particular topic but rather he deals with a variety of specific issues to the first-century believers. James deals with the everyday realities that the first-century believers would have been dealing with in their Christian life. James at times is very direct and to the point, other times he asks rhetorical questions, and often uses illustrations from Palestinian landscape and climate to make his points. More than likely, this letter was written with the intent to be read publicly or at least among the believers.

Theme

James throughout his letter seems to move rapidly to cover a variety of topics pertaining to these early Christians. James letter is not a large theological letter like Paul's letter to the Romans. Rather James is very pinpointed and precise, jumping from one subject matter to another. James is very direct in dealing with the issues that were pertaining to these first century Christians, and is concerned that they remain steadfast in the

---

[3] Literary Koine is scholarly writing, i.e., professional writing.

midst of their trials. James throughout his letter covers several different topics that would affect his audience.

Introduction (1:1)

Expectation of trials (1:2-4)

What to do when trials come (1:5-8)

Position of the man in trials (1:9-12)

Position of the man in trials (1:9-12)

Truth of temptation (1:13-15)

God the giver of good gifts (1:16-18)

Essential attitudes and behaviors (1:19-25)

True religion (1:26-27)

Warning against favoritism (2:1-13)

Faith without works is dead (2:14-20)

Faith justified by works (2:21-26)

Warning to teachers (3:1)

The uncontrolled tongue (3:1-12)

Proper understanding of wisdom (3:13-18)

Source of quarrels and conflicts (4:1-10)

Warning against oath taking (4:11-12)

Improper planning and boasting (4:13-17)

Judgment on the rich (5:1-6)

Call for patient endurance (5:7-11)

Reality of swearing (5:12)

Responsibility of the sick and elders (5:13-18)

Restoration of the strayed brother (5:19-20)

Purpose

The fact that James refers to the Jewish Law would at first glance, seem to indicate that the audience of whom he was writing to was

Jewish. James seems to write to those familiar with the Old Testament. James used Old Testament examples such as Abraham, Job, and Elijah, persons with which his audience would have been familiar. However, the ones James was primarily writing to are outside of Palestine (1:2; 2:1, 7; 5:7), and it has been almost 30 years since the death, resurrection and ascension of Jesus Christ. In other words, many Gentiles have come into the Christian congregation, especially outside of Palestine. Because of regular reading from the Hebrew Old Testament, likely by way of the Septuagint, the Gentile Christians would have been aware of every Old Testament aspect in the book of James. When he said, "Was not Abraham our father" (2:21), it was similar to the way Paul expressed it at Galatians 3:28-29. There Paul was making the point that: one **need not be** a fleshly Jew, to be Abraham's descendants.

Additionally, James does not mention much of the life, death, or resurrection of Christ in his letter. Therefore, his readers must have understood and have been familiar with Christ and no explanation seems to have been necessary, as to the deity of Christ. Rather James gives his readers principles and ethical standards to abide by in their relationship with Christ, in light of the trials that they were facing.

Canonicity and Authenticity

The letter of James is included in three very prominent manuscripts, the Vaticanus,[4] the Sinaiticus[5] and the Codex Alexandrinus[6] of the 4th and 5th centuries C.E. In addition, it was found in the Syriac Peshitta, as well as at least ten ancient catalogs before the Council of Carthage in 397 C.E. The early Church Fathers quoted from it, such as Origen (184-254 C.E.), Eusebius (260-340 C.E.), Cyril of Jerusalem (313-386 C.E.), Gregory Nazianzus (329-390 C.E.), Chrysostom (347-407 C.E.), and Jerome (340-420). In addition, some of the early Apologists and Apostolic Fathers used James in their writings, such as Clement of Rome (d. about 99 C.E.),

---

[4] The Codex Vaticanus is one of the oldest and most valuable extant manuscripts of the Greek Bible (Gregory number: B/03).

[5] The Sinaiticus or the "Sinai Bible" is one of the four great uncial codices, an ancient, handwritten copy of the Greek Bible.

[6] Codex Alexandrinus is a 5th-century manuscript of the Greek Bible, containing the majority of the Septuagint and the New Testament. It is one of the four Great uncial [i.e., written in all caps] codices.

Ignatius[7] of Antioch (35-107 C.E.), Polycarp[8] (69-155 C.E.) and Justin Martyr (100-165 C.E.).

Place and Date of Writing

The first-century Jewish historian records that James, Jesus' half-brother, was martyred by being stoned to death, with the High Priest Ananus (Ananias), a Sadducee, being responsible. This took place after the death of the Roman governor Festus, about 62 C.E., yet before his successor, Albinus, took office. Josephus writes,

> (197) And now Caesar, upon hearing the death of Festus, sent Albinus into Judea, as procurator; but the king deprived Joseph of the high priesthood, and bestowed the succession to that dignity on the son of Ananus, who was also himself called Ananus. (198) Now the report goes, that this elder Ananus proved a most fortunate man; for he had five sons, who had all performed the office of a high priest to God, and he had himself enjoyed that dignity a long time formerly, which had never happened to any other of our high priests: (199) but this younger Ananus, who, as we have told you already, took the high priesthood, was a bold man in his temper, and very insolent; he was also of the sect of the Sadducees,[9] who are very rigid in judging offenders, above all the rest of the Jews, as we have already observed; (200) when, therefore, Ananus was of this disposition, he thought he had now a proper opportunity [to exercise his authority]. Festus was now dead, and Albinus was but upon the road; so he assembled the Sanhedrin of judges, and brought before them the brother of Jesus, who was called Christ, whose name was James, and some others, [or, some of his companions]; and when he had formed an

---

[7] Ignatius was a student of the apostle John.

[8] Polycarp was a student of the apostle John. Irenaeus relates that Polycarp "was not only instructed by apostles, and had intercourse with many who had seen Christ, but was also appointed for Asia by apostles, in the church that is in Smyrna an overseer."--*A Critical History of Christian Literature and Doctrine* by James Donaldson (p. 155, 2009)

[9] It hence evidently appears that Sadducees might be high priests in the days of Josephus, and that these Sadducees were usually very severe and inexorable judges, while the Pharisees were much milder, and more merciful, as appears by Reland's instances in his note on this place, and on Josephus's *Life* 34, and those taken from the New Testament, from Josephus himself, and from the rabbis; nor do we meet with any Sadducees later than this high priest in all Josephus.

accusation against them as breakers of the law, he delivered them to be stoned.[10]

This brings us to the question of, just when did James pen his letter? Well, he addressed the letter from Jerusalem "to the twelve tribes in the Dispersion." (Jam. 1:1, ESV) The dispersion took place around 50 C.E. We must consider that Christianity did not get its start until the ascension of Jesus Christ in 33 C.E., and it would have taken time to spread out to the dispersion that James speaks of, which came about by the work of Paul and others. Not only would this scattering out, and growth need to take place, but then the time to develop the problems that James speaks of in his letter. The letter shows that Christianity has progressed to the point of no longer being in small groups, but rather in congregations, with elders (overseers) taking the lead among them. Enough time has passed that these congregations have grown complacent and were just going through the motions, an outward appearance of religious worship. (Jam. 2:1-4; 4:1-3; 5:14; 1:26, 27) Therefore, James likely wrote his letter just before his death, say between 60-62 C.E.

---

[10] *Jewish Antiquities*, XX, 197-200 (ix, 1); *Webster's New Biographical Dictionary*, 1983, page 350.

domain of darkness and transferred us to the kingdom of his beloved Son.' (Col. 1:13) In another letter, Paul says, "Christ is the head of the congregation, his body, and is himself its Savior." (Eph. 5:22-24) As a result, all Christians are a slave of the Father and his appointed Son, Jesus Christ. Therefore, James rightly begins his letter recognizing his accountability to Jesus Christ, and as a slave, he is required to carry out the will of the Father.--Matthew 7:21-23

To the twelve tribes in the Dispersion: (1:1c)

The **twelve tribes in the dispersion** that James mentions are not the actual 12 tribes of Israel. We note in verse 2 James says, "Consider it all joy, my brothers," and the tribes of Jewish Israel were not James' brother, 'who were holding their faith in their glorious Lord Jesus Christ, as natural Israel rejected Jesus Christ vehemently. (Jam. 1:2; 2:1, 5) During the last days of Jesus' ministry, he explicitly stated what was to happen to natural Israel. Jesus said, "I tell you, the kingdom of God will be taken away from you and given to a people producing its fruits." (Matt. 21:43) A short time later, he said,

Matthew 23:37-39 English Standard Version (ESV)

Lament over Jerusalem

[37] "O Jerusalem, Jerusalem, the city that kills the prophets and stones those who are sent to it! How often would I have gathered your children together as a hen gathers her brood under her wings, and you were not willing! [38] See, your house is left to you desolate. [39] For I tell you, you will not see me again, until you say, 'Blessed is he who comes in the name of the Lord.'"

In looking at verse 37 of Matthew 23, we see that Jesus' words are not those of a harsh judge, who is looking readily to punish the Jewish people for their 1,500 years of rebelling and sinning horrendously against the Father. Rather, he has tried to be patient with them throughout his last three and half year ministry. When Jesus began his ministry, all Jesus wanted was nothing more than what his Father wanted, i.e., repentance for centuries of willful sinning, so that they could avoid the judgment that was coming. Well, over five hundred natural Israel responded to Jesus' words, with thousands upon thousands more listening to the apostle Paul and other evangelists. They escaped the judgment that came upon Jerusalem in 70 C.E. (Lu 21:20-22) In verse 38, Jesus indicated that very soon God was not going to accept the worship of the Israelites, at the typical temple in Jerusalem. (Matt 24:1-2) In verse 39, Jesus is saying, they will never see him with eyes of faith unless they accept him and his Father.

In other words, natural Israel lost its favored position as God's chosen people, and this was to be given to another. Who? This new nation proved to be a spiritual Israel, which the apostle Paul referred to as "the Israel of God." It would be made up of Jews who accepted Jesus Christ and non-Jews. Entry into this "Israel of God" was not dependent on the natural descent, but rather on one coming to "know you the only true God, and Jesus Christ whom you have sent." (John 17:3), In other words, it was a matter of 'trusting in Jesus Christ.' (John 3:16) Nevertheless, natural Israel was made up of 12 tribes, so James was merely drawing on the number 12, which carries the connotation of completeness. If a natural Jew or a non-Jew were to become a part of this spiritual Israel, the Israel of God, they would have to acknowledge, "Circumcision is a matter of the heart, by the Spirit, not by the letter." (Rom. 2:29) He must further understand "it depends on faith, in order that the promise may rest on grace and be guaranteed to all ..." (Rom. 4:16) There are many verses, which qualify what it means to be a part of this Israel of God. See also, Romans 4:17; 9:6-8; Galatians 3:7, 29; 4:21-31; Philippians 3:3

These spiritual Israelites were dispersed throughout the Roman Empire. Shortly after Pentecost 33 C.E., there were arrests, threats, and beatings. (Ac 4:1-3, 21; 5:17, 18) At that time, Stephen was seized and stoned to death. " (Ac 7:52-60) The murder of Stephen was only the beginning, as Saul of Tarsus was to bring great persecution on the Christians in the Jerusalem area, which led to the dispersing of Christians throughout the then known world. (Ac 8:1-4; 9:1, 2) However, this really failed, as it was not long before Christian congregations were found everywhere, by the evangelism of none other than the very persecutor turned Christian, namely, the apostle Paul (formerly known as Saul). In fact, about 62-64 C.E., Peter writes, "To those who are elect exiles of the Dispersion in Pontus, Galatia, Cappadocia, Asia, and Bithynia."--1 Peter 1:1

Greetings (1:1d)

The word **greeting is** unique to James, as Paul does not use it in any of his letters. The word for greeting here in the Greek, *chairo*, means, "to rejoice." This was a greeting by which James was expressing to his readers joy and happiness that comes through obeying the commands of the scriptures. Ones in the marketplace or village gave this familiar greeting. We might also note that the letter on circumcision suggested by James also contained this salutation. (Acts 15:23) Therefore, this only adds more credence to James being the author of this letter bearing his name.

Endurance Brings Happiness

James 1:2-4 Updated American Standard Version (UASV)

² Consider it all joy, my brothers,[15] when you encounter various trials, ³ knowing that the testing of your faith produces endurance. ⁴ And let endurance have its perfect work, so that you may be perfect and complete, lacking in nothing.

Consider it all joy (1:2a)

James starts his letter by asking that these believers **consider** the trials that they were currently going through. James wanted his readers to think about why their trial, any trial that took place in their lives, so that his readers would have the proper perspective of the trial before they can actually know how to handle them when they come. Once they had the proper perspective of their trials, they could consider it **all joy**. The word for joy is *chara*, which means to have "joy or delight (Vine, 1996, pg. 335)." The joy is not in the fact that one is going through the trial, but rather in what that trial will be able to produce in their lives. James wants his readers to realize that if they can understand that God is the one who allowed imperfection to come into humanity for a particular reason then they can consider any trial with a response of joy, i.e., an opportunity for them to show an evident demonstration of their faith. Do not believe that God placed these trials here to grow their faith, but rather, because the trials (difficult times) are here because of human imperfection, here was their opportunity to grow from difficult times.

my brothers (1:2b)

In the Scriptures, '**brothers**' often refer to both men and women, and is simply a convention of writing. James here is not referring to his physical family but rather to his spiritual family. Jesus says the same things in Matthew 12:50 "For whoever does the will of my Father who is in heaven, he is my brother and sister and mother."

---

[15] Both *brothers and sisters*

The Apostle Paul was very fond of using the word brother in his letters to the churches as well. The fact that James calls them brothers signifies that he is in a spiritual relationship with them through Jesus Christ, and they are bound together in the unity of Christ and part of a spiritual family. James uses the word brother in his letter 14 times and is writing with sincerity of heart to his spiritual family.

when you encounter various trials (1:2c)

James makes an affirmative statement when he writes **when you encounter various trials**. This does not mean that these believers might face trials but rather that they currently were in the midst of trials. The word that James uses here for trials is the word *peirasmos*, which means, "testing for proof or putting to the test (Vine, 1996, pg. 622)." This word is often used in the scriptures to refer to testing or temptation, and the context upon which it is used tells which one it is. James makes mention of some of the trials that these believers were going through in that some were facing poverty (James 2:15) and oppression from the rich (James 5:1-5.). James says the trials were various which signifies that the trials these believers were facing came in many different forms.

We will find nowhere in all of the scripture where the believers in the Lord were spared from having any difficult, even extremely difficult times in life, so many of the holy ones faced difficulties. The Apostle Paul tells us that by faith Abraham, when he was tested, as good as offered up Isaac. The Israelites rejected Moses, who had specifically been sent by God, so Moses had to endure dealing with Pharaoh. Joseph had to face the trials of being blamed for a rape of which he did not do and then be put into prison unfairly for almost thirteen years. Nehemiah and Ezra suffered the agony of the moral decay around them, and their enemies constantly tried to destroy their work and instill fear in the people. Daniel was placed in the lion's den and his three friends Shadrach, Meshach, and Abednego all had to face the fire of a great furnace for their remaining faithful. Isaiah had to deal with the fact that though he would preach his heart out that nobody would listen to his message. Jeremiah was put into stocks, jailed, tar pits and was rejected by his family because he preached the wrath of God to his people. Then there was the mighty prophet Ezekiel who when he confronted Ahab with the truth was sought to be killed and known as the "troubler of Israel."

In the New Testament, we read about John the Baptist, who was put in prison and eventually beheaded for confronting King Herod. Peter was put in prison for preaching the gospel and eventually killed on a cross for his faith. John was exiled to the island of Patmos for the word of God. Then of course, the Apostle Paul was kicked out of many of the towns he went to for preaching the word of God. Paul makes mentions of his trials in 2 Corinthians 11:24-29); (2 Corinthians 4:8-10

knowing that the testing of your faith produces endurance (1:3a)

The word used here for testing is the Greek word *dokimion*, which means, "putting to proof." (Mounce, 2006, Greek GK #1510) Now known from the papyri examples of *dokimios* as an adjective in the same sense (good gold, standard gold) as *dokimos* proved or tested (James 1:12).' (Robertson 1933, 1997, Jam. 1:3) When a merchant proofs Gold, he is establishing whether it is genuine. In other words, when we face a trial or difficult time, and faithfully come through on the other side, our faith has been proofed or tested as being genuine. James was making it clear that God was allowing these trials, which were simply the result of imperfection entering into humanity, because of the rebellion in Eden. When these believers experienced trials (difficult times), their faith became one that was 'put to the proof.' It became a 'proved' or 'tested' faith that had survived a difficult time, with their approved relationship with God intact. When the believer's faith was proofed, tested, by trials, it was developed so that it was strengthened, enabling them to possess the quality of endurance. This was no mere living through a difficulty, but rather fortitude, resolution, strength, staying power, steadfastness, and integrity when tempted to take the easy way out of the affliction by abandoning the faith.

We see this happening in the life of Job when God allowed Satan to take Job's livestock, servants, family, and his health. In all this, Job remained steadfast and never lost his faith in God, and evidenced his faith. James wants his readers to understand that though God is not the cause of trials he is allowing the trials in their lives to proof the genuineness of their faith, which leads to endurance. James states that God could produce endurance in the believer's life by allowing the trials.

And let endurance have its perfect work, so that you may be perfect, complete, lacking in noting. (1:4)

James here states as to why a believer can rejoice in his trials when he writes **let endurance have its perfect work, so that you may be perfect**. James uses the word perfect more than any other New

Testament writer does. The perfection that James is talking about is not a moral perfection but rather has to do with wholeness or completeness in the believer's spiritual walk with Christ. The trials can help produce the desired outcome that God has for the believer and be more complete in God. It is for this reason that God, although not the cause of the trials, would allow them to come about. James also adds that the trials be permitted by God to make one more **complete**. The trials make the believer complete in the fact that they serve to develop Godly character in the life of the one who is enduring them, producing greater holiness in the life of the believer, so that they are **lacking in nothing** and being content with and resting in God.

James 1:5-8 Updated American Standard Version (UASV)

5 But if any of you lacks wisdom, let him ask of God, who gives to all generously and without reproaching,[16] and it will be given to him. **6** But let him ask in faith, without any doubting, for the one who doubts is like a wave of the sea that is driven and tossed by the wind. **7** For let not that man suppose that he will receive anything from the Lord; **8** he is a double-minded[17] man, unstable in all his ways.

But if any of you lacks wisdom let him ask of God, (1:5a)

If there were any believers that were having difficulty understanding their trials James tells them what they are to do. James says **if any of you lacks wisdom let him ask of God.** When James refers here to wisdom he is not talking about a mere intellectual wisdom. It is a wisdom, which comes from God and having a reverential fear of displeasing him, which is the beginning of wisdom. (Proverbs 1:7) The proper understanding therefore of Godly wisdom is that one then puts the wisdom in practical use In everyday life. Solomon wrote in (Proverbs 2:6) "For the Lord gives wisdom, from his mouth come knowledge and understanding." When James says **any of you** in this passage he is referencing specifically to the believers that God was allowing to go through trials. He is not talking to just anyone in general that they can ask for wisdom, but in context those Christians that were enduring the trails.

James tells these believers if they lacked the wisdom to understand the trials then go to the one who could give them the discernment and wisdom in regards to the trial. God was sovereign over the trials in

---

[16] Without *criticizing*

[17] Or *indecisive*, i.e., wavering in mind

allowing the trial to happen, and then he would be the only one to go to for us to properly understand as to the nature of the trial. The Greek word that James uses for ask is the word *aiteo* which means to "beg or request." (Vine, 1996, pg. 40) The believers were to request of God that they understand their trials for some insight and guidance to see how allowing the trial was a part of God's plan and how it applied to their life.

We see from scripture an example of God answering those in their trial with Solomon who asked God to help him to be able to lead the nation he had become leader of (1 Kings 3:9). David, a man familiar with trials, wrote in (Psalms 55:22) "Cast your burden upon the Lord, and he will sustain you, He will never allow the righteous to be forsaken." Peter also wrote in (I Peter 5:6-7) "Therefore humble yourselves under the mighty hand of God, that He may exalt you at the proper time, casting all your anxiety on Him, because He cares for you."

who gives to all generously without finding reproaching and it will be given to him (1:5b)

Here James states an important, significant, and weighty promise that will happen to the believers that called upon God in the midst of the trial for wisdom. The promise he says is that God will give wisdom to those who seek the Lord for it. James assures that promise by stating that God **gives to all generously without finding reproach**. James makes it clear that not only will God give wisdom to those that ask but also he will do so with generosity. In other words, God desires to give believers wisdom and understanding to discern properly the trials they were enduring. The word that James uses here for reproach is the Greek word *oneidezo* which means to "defame, reproach, or disgrace (Vine, 1996, pg. 526)." It did not matter the nature of situation or the background these believers may have come from, if they called upon God for wisdom **it will be given to him**. We should not expect what Abraham David, Solomon, Elijah or Nehemiah received. Our main wisdom for how to deal with trials is not going to come miraculously, but rather through the Word of God. If we do not take in that lifesaving knowledge, how can we make wise decisions, as it is the very knowledge of God?

But let him must ask in faith, without any doubting for the one who doubts is like a wave of the sea that is driven and tossed by the wind. (1:6a)

There is an approach to praying for wisdom that must be applied when coming to God in asking for wisdom and that is the believer **must ask in faith without any doubting.** The Greek word used here for faith is the word *pistis* and it means to be "confident of, fully assured or persuaded of (Vine, 1996, pg. 222)." James is telling these believers that when they come to God to ask for this wisdom they must be fully confident and convinced that God does hear. Faith gives sight to that which can't be seen and be believed upon. James also indicates that one not only has faith but without any doubting as well. If these believers doubted God in what they were asking for, they would be negating the very thing the prayer is predicated upon and that is faith. These believers were to pray in faith that God would give them the wisdom to understand their trial and help them to be able to endure.

James here gives an object lesson to show what it looks like when one claims to ask with belief and yet doubts at the same time. James states **the one who doubts is like a wave of the sea.** A wave of the sea is helpless in the fact that is directed in many different directions upon the sea and has not stability, due to the wind. A wave may start far off in the distance and then be lead to the shore in the next moment. The waves are helpless against the wind because the waves have nothing to stabilize them except to be helplessly **driven and tossed by the wind.** James is telling these believers that if they do not have faith in prayers for wisdom that they are asking God in helping him to understand their trials, then trials end up controlling the person's life and taking them where they do not want to go. The prayer for wisdom gives the believers the understanding to remain steady amongst the trials.

For let not that man suppose that he will receive anything from the Lord; he is a double-minded man; unstable in all his ways. (1:7-8)

James here presents two realities for those believers that were not praying in faith that God could hear their prayers for wisdom and would answer. Certainly, when one prays, while he has a doubtful heart, he should not **suppose that he will receive anything from the Lord.** This one does not expect in his heart that he is going to receive divine help. He allows his doubts to impede him from placing his complete trust in the Father, failing to be guided in the way in which he should go. He does not have the genuine faith that is required by God, because "without faith it is impossible to please him, for whoever would draw near to God must believe that he is and that is the rewarder of those seeking him." – Hebrews 11:6

James also presents a second reality and that is the reason God will not answer the believer who doubts when he prays, and that is because he is **double minded**. The Greek word used for double-minded is *dipsuchos*, and it literally means "two souled (Vine, 1996, pg. 181)." James is the only New Testament writer to use this word. James clarifies his point by stating the reason God does not answer a double-minded man, and that reason is that he is **unstable in all his ways**. An unstable person that is two souled is often unable to be trusted, because of the constant changing of their minds. A two souled person is one who often has divided loyalties: in one moment, they desire God and in the next moment, they engage in the acts of the flesh, and never decide between the two.

James 1:9-12 Updated American Standard Version (UASV)

9 But Let the lowly brother boast[18] in his exaltation, **10** and the rich man should boast in his humiliation, because like flowering grass he will pass away. **11** For the sun rises with a scorching wind and withers the grass; its flower falls, and its beauty perishes; so too will the rich man fade away in the midst of his pursuits.

12 Blessed is the man[19] who endures under trial; for when he has been approved, he will receive the crown of life which the Lord[20] has promised to those who love him.

But let the lowly brother boast in his exaltation, (1:9)

Most Christians in the first-century up unto our day, come from a humble background. (1 Cor. 1:26) Most were poor prior to their finding and accepting Jesus Christ. (Jam. 2:5) The world tends to view such poor ones in a bad light, spurning them, feeling contempt for them. However, after they have come to know (in an experiential way) the Father, and the one he sent forth, Jesus Christ, they are exalted, elevated to a dignified standing with Jesus Christ.—John 17:3

---

[18] Or *rejoice*

[19] Literally "the man," but here is referring to a man or woman

[20] i.e., God (the Father)

In addition, there were some in the congregation, who were rich prior to their finding and accepting Jesus Christ. However, they became poor through some form of persecution. (Heb. 10:32-34) While one might suspect that this would cause doubts, it enabled them to appreciate the precious relationship they had with Jesus Christ and the hope of eternal life that lay ahead. In a Christian congregation, unlike the world, poor Christians are on equal ground as to position and wealth (i.e., they are rich in Christ), suffering no shortcomings whatsoever. They have the same opportunity to possess the same amount of spiritual riches as anyone else.[21]

and the rich man should boast in his humiliation, because like flowering grass he will pass away. (1:10)

When a wealthy person comes to an accurate or full knowledge of the truth, he will come to the realization that the wealth he had trust in, is fleeting. He will then clearly understand "the deceitfulness of wealth." (Matt. 13:22) Now, this rich person must humble himself, as he is shown from the Word of God that he and his riches need to be placed in the right perspective. In other words, it is not the riches that are wicked, but rather the love of riches. In addition, he must see that spending excessive time in the pursuit of further wealth is a waste. It will cause him to miss family time, personal Bible study time, preparing for Christian meetings, attending and participating in Christian meetings. Moreover, chasing after wealth will cut into the time he could spend sharing the good news with others. Namely, it will affect his spirituality. (1 Tim. 6:9-10) If he ponders the Scriptures, he will see that the spiritual blessings outweigh any material wealth that could be accumulated in multiple lifetimes. See Philippians 3:8.

Rather than an elevated belief in oneself, which is often a direct result of riches, the apostle Paul encouraged just the opposite. He wrote, "Do nothing from selfishness or empty conceit, but in humility consider others as more important than yourselves. Everyone should look out not only for his own interests, but also for the interests of others. Have this mind in yourselves which was also in Christ Jesus." (Phil. 2:3-8) The rich one must also consider that the world sees the wealthy man in an elevated position to everyone else. However, once he becomes a Christian, a disciple of Jesus Christ, this may very well change, as the

---

[21] 2 Cor. 6:10; 8:9; Gal. 3:28, 29; 1 Pet. 4:10, 11; Rev. 2:9; see comments on James 2:1-9.

world will begin to hate him due to his relationship with Jesus. (John 15:17-19; See also John 7:47-52; 12:42-43) Now, the rich man, who has become a disciple of Christ, possessing spiritual riches, he can rejoice in his humiliation. In the end it must be remembered, the splendor of wealth is temporary, as the rich one will eventually grow old and die. Riches cannot add a single hour to his life. Psalm 49:6-9; Matthew 6:27.

For the sun rises with a scorching wind, and withers the grass; and its flower falls, and its beauty perishes; (1:11a)

James adds further illustration to expound his position writing the **sun rises with a scorching wind and withers the grass.** James uses a concept that the Jewish believers would have been familiar with in the Palestinian landscape. The flowers in Palestine were abundant and beautiful, yet when the scorching wind from the sun would hit them, they withered and **flower falls**, and **beauty perishes** in just a short amount of time. James uses this illustration to make the point to the uselessness of putting one's hope in riches, because of their insecurity. The riches may seem to be a security to the man who has them and they may look good but who knows when the scorching heat of life death, disease, destruction comes and the riches are destroyed. (Compare Ps. 49:6-9; Matt. 6:27.) The rich man has no more control over his riches and what may happen to them, than does the flower that is scorched by the hot sun. As quickly as the man may have received his riches they could be taken away. Solomon wrote, "Do not weary yourself to gain wealth, Cease from your consideration *of it*. When you set your eyes on it, it is gone. For wealth certainly makes itself wings like an eagle that flies toward the heavens"—Proverbs 23:4-5

so too will the rich man fade away in the midst of his pursuits. (1:11b)

Just as the flower arises and is destroyed *so* also the **rich man will fade away in the midst of his pursuits**. The point that James is trying to get across is that just as the flower is here one day and gone the next so riches are so uncertain because you may have it one day and then gone the next. Once an individual takes his last breath, all that he worked so hard to gain here in riches will be lost and done away with. Solomon wrote, "As he had come naked from his mother's womb, so will he return as he came. He will take nothing from the fruit of his labor that he can carry in his hand." (Eccl. 6:15) Solomon also wrote, "Riches do not profit in the day of wrath, but righteousness delivers from death."—Proverbs 11:4

James is stressing the fact that a man does not have to wait until the time of his death for his riches to fade away, but they do so even in the midst of his pursuit of them. The trials that come to the rich, can serve as a great reminder of how uncertain one's riches really are and they cannot save him. The trials of the man with riches serve to remind him of the fact life does not depend on the abundance of his possessions.

Blessed is the man who endures under trial; (1:12a)

James here continues with his progression of the person who is undergoing the difficult trials in stating **blessed is the man who endures under trial**. James calls these believers that endure the trial blessed. The word for blessed is not some joy that the world could offer to man, but rather it was a joy that only God could give to man. It is the highest good possible that only God is able to give man by his own spirit. It is an inward peace and comfort of the soul that is not determined by outward circumstances but is a continuous inner joy through all situations of life. This is the same word that Jesus used to describe the beatitudes in (Matthew 5:3-12).The word for **endures** is *hupomone* that means to "*remain under*." (Vine, 1996, pg. 200) The blessedness that James talks about only comes to the one who remains firm in his faith in the midst of the trial. James simply confirms what Jesus said in Matthew 5:11-12.

Alternatively, those Christians who are wealthy can find joy in their wealth beyond the pleasures that it can provide, by using some of it to support the interests of Christianity and to spread the Gospel. (1 Tim. 6:17-19) Moreover, they can use some of his wealth to help their needy brothers and sisters within the Christian congregation. – Acts 4:32-37; James 1:27

Jesus also illustrated this point by the parable of the rich fool who rejoiced in his riches: [16] And he told them a parable, saying, "The land of a rich man produced plentifully, [17] and he thought to himself, 'What shall I do, for I have nowhere to store my crops?' [18] And he said, 'I will do this: I will tear down my barns and build larger ones, and there I will store all my grain and my goods. [19] And I will say to my soul, "Soul, you have ample goods laid up for many years; relax, eat, drink, be merry."' [20] But God said to him, 'Fool! This night your soul is required of you, and the things you have prepared, whose will they be?' [21] So is the one who lays up treasure for himself and is not rich toward God. (Luke 12:16-21)

for when he has been approved, he will receive the crown of life (1:12b)

The approval or acceptance comes from the fact that one's faith has been tested and **has been approved** by God because of the way that he has persevered through it. James gives further motivation and encouragement for his readers in the fact that they are not only blessed in what they are going through if they persevere, but that in the end they **will receive the crown of life.** The crown of life is not a mere physical crown to wear but rather a spiritual reward of getting to abide in the presence of God for all eternity. God himself will give this crown in eternity for those who have remained faithful to him until the end. (Matt 24:13)This crown will be for those who have fought the battle against Satan, sin, and trials and have through Christ come out victorious. These victors did not gain their crown through fame, success, accolades, but rather they gained their crown from what they suffered and overcame. The apostle Paul makes this clear at Hebrews 11:37-40. It should be explicitly stated that these ones did not earn eternal life by their *endurance* of trials, but rather they were *privileged* as with a "crown" by the gift of heavenly life. We **cannot** earn eternal life but it is a free undeserved gift from our heavenly Father through our faith in Jesus Christ. (Rom. 6:23) Christians who *maintain* their integrity through trial after trial have made an evident demonstration that their faith is genuine. The quality of their faith has survived the difficulties of this imperfect world, and has been found complete.

which the Lord has promised to those who love him (1:12c)

James makes it clear about the crown of life **the Lord has promised to those who love him.** This would have been a great source of encouragement for those believers as they are going through their trials. We can see from the scriptures that when God promises something it is as good as done. In Genesis God promised to never flood the entire earth again and he never has since. God promised Abraham that he would have a son that would produce many nations and he allowed Sarah to have Isaac. Numerous times in the Old Testament God spoke through the prophets promising to send the Messiah into the world. That promise was fulfilled in the New Testament with Jesus Christ. God makes this promise to those that love him because he is in a relationship with them and is their Father. God is always faithful to his promises and for those who endure trials they will indeed receive the crown of life.

James 1:13-15 Updated American Standard Version (UASV)

[13] Let no one say when he is tempted, "I am being tempted by God," for God cannot be tempted[22] with evil,[23] and he himself tempts no one. [14] But each one is tempted when he is carried away and enticed by his own desire.[24] [15] Then the desire when it has conceived gives birth to sin, and sin when it is fully grown brings forth death.

Romans 5:12 English Standard Version (ESV)

[12] Therefore, just as **sin came into the world** through one man, and death through sin, and so death spread to all men because all sinned

In addition, God had already inform us that we are mentally bent toward evil, that man's mind is evil from his very youth.

Genesis 6:5 The American Translation (AT)

[5] When the LORD saw that the wickedness of man on the earth was great, and that the **whole bent of his thinking was never anything but evil**, the LORD regretted that he had ever made man on the earth.

Genesis 8:21 The American Translation (AT)

[21] I will never again curse the soil, though the **bent of man's mind** may be **evil from his very youth**; nor ever again will I ever again destroy all life creature as I have just done.

Jeremiah informs us that,

Jeremiah 17:9 English Standard Version (ESV)

[9] The **heart is deceitful** above all things,
and **desperately sick**;
who can understand it?

The apostle Paul writes,

Romans 7:21-24 English Standard Version (ESV)

[21] So I find it to be a law that when I want to do right, evil lies close at hand. [22] For I delight in **the law of God**, in my inner being, [23] but I see in my members another law waging war against **the law of my mind** and making me captive to the **law of sin** that dwells in my

---

[22] Lit untempted

[23] That is *evil persons*, or *evil things*

[24] Or own *lust*

members. [24] Wretched man that I am! Who will deliver me from this body of death?

Edward D. Andrews' comments on Paul's words, "Notice in the above that Paul references "the law of [his] mind." For a person who has a strong faith, that **law of his mind** is ruled by a phenomenon that he delights in, namely **"the law of God.**" Certainly, we see that **"the law of sin"** is waging a war against the law of the mind. Nevertheless, the Christian can conquer 'the law of sin' with the help of God. Paul goes on to say in verse 25, "Thanks be to God through Jesus Christ our Lord! So then, I myself serve the law of God with my mind, but with my flesh I serve the law of sin.'" (Andrews 2014, 55)

Thus, the imperfect human, in his human weaknesses has the following stacked up against him, (1) he is missing the mark of perfection, (2) the whole bent of his mind leans toward evil, (3) his inner self is deceitful and sick, (4) which he cannot understand, and (5) the law of sin dwells in his members. Therefore, it is easy to see that if he dwells on, entertains, or cultivates wrong thoughts, as opposed to immediately dismissing them, it will lead to sin. However, Andrews' comments on how not all is lost.

> However, not all is lost, because Paul also tells us that we can 'be renewed in the spirit of our minds.' (Eph. 4:23) We can 'put off the old person with its practices and have put on the new self. We will then be renewed in knowledge according to the image of our Creator.' We will be transformed by the renewing of our mind, so that you may discern what is the good, pleasing, and perfect will of God.'—Colossians 3:9-10; Romans 12:2 (Andrews 2014, 8)

Let no one say when he is tempted, "I am being tempted by God." for God cannot be tempted with evil, and He himself tempts no one. (1:13)

Let no one say when he is tempted, [25] **"I am being tempted by God."** If any Christian were under any kind of affliction or hardship, he

---

[25] Edward D. Andrews writes, "God does **not** tempt us, but he does allow us to go through temptations. As we know from Abraham, God can test us, but never tempt us with sin. God allows us to face the trials that the natural course of life takes within this imperfect age. He allows us to face the trials of our own free will decisions. Simply being steadfast to a Christian life that is counterintuitive to the wicked world that we live in can be a trial that

would be wrong to attribute this to God, as though God were trying to tempt him into sinning. If he lets some aspect of the trial turn into a temptation for him (e.g., if he goes from a refusal to give in to giving in or bending under pressure because of some selfish gain, or because he is looking for a way to evade facing and enduring the trial), it is not God who deserves the blame. We need to understand that God will strengthen us to endure the trials of this imperfect word, only if we continue unwavering in our own heart. (Phil. 4:13) God will never carry out any action that would lead his servant to sin. While God permitted sin and imperfection to come into the world after the rebellion of Satan, Adam and Eve, it was not to test or tempt humanity into sin, but rather to teach us the object lesson that we were not designed to walk on our own. We were designed to be under God's sovereign rulership, which Adam rejected. The world under Satan's rulership caters to the fallen flesh, not to God.

God is holy and pure, so he **cannot be tempted with evil**. It is impossible for God to be tempted by evil of any kind or by any objectionable situation, or by some condition that would motivate him to commit wrong. It is impossible to make something that is contrary to God's standards and values attractive to the point that it would be trying him.

God **himself tempts no one**, just as he himself cannot be tempted into sin. God does not place alluring things before his creatures, to embolden them to transgress against him. He is not seeking to test their weaknesses or their steadfastness. He does not place things before us that we must have for survival, and the situation requires us to violate his standards to achieve it. However, God has allowed the trials of an imperfect world of humanity to continue, as he has "morally sufficient reasons for permitting the evil and suffering in the world." (William Lane Craig) God offers us nothing but good for our improvement, never for our impairment. The ruler of this imperfect world, Satan the Devil, has no qualms about using trials as a means of tempting us to violate God's Word. This is not to say that God will not allow some trial that he could have prevented for the sake of disciple (i.e., correction), making his servants more complete. – Hebrews 12:7, and 11

But each one is tempted when he is carried away and enticed by his own desire. (1:14)

God has allowed."– (Andrews, FOR AS I THINK IN MY HEART—SO I AM: Combining Biblical Counseling with Cognitive Behavioral Therapy 2013, 92)

James states **but each one is tempted**, which signifies that temptation is on an individual basis. The temptation is not another individual's problem but is an individual choice that one gives into or rejects. James also writes one is tempted when he is **carried away and enticed by his desire**, which exposes that the problem of temptation lies not with God, but rather it is in oneself. James says that temptation is always directed at the desire of one's heart. Therefore, God is not the one who is causing the temptation but the temptation comes through the enticement of one's lust within his heart.

The word James uses here for **enticed** is *deleazo*, which means to "*lure as bait*." (Vine 1996, 203) James tells us in the passage that the underlying motivation for all temptation is selfish desire, that all temptations springs from man's **desire** to satisfy his own flesh and personal forbidden desires. This means the temptation that Satan offers to people always deals with that which is pleasurable to man, and appeals to his desires. This is not to say that human desires in and of itself are wrong. Moreover, human pleasure is not wrong in and of itself. Satan has corrupted the desires of the flesh, which were perfectly natural prior to the sin of Adam. For example, there was a natural desire for a physical relationship between man and woman. After the fall, Paul tells us that it has become a common practice "For their women [to] exchange natural relations for those that are contrary to nature," i.e., homosexuality. (Rom. 1:26) Once the lust is manifested in the heart then the more it lingers there without being dealt with then it will begin to carry away the individual with the enticement of what that fulfilled lust can bring.

Then the desire when it has conceived gives birth to sin, and sin when it is fully grown brings forth death. (1:15)

Temptation always begins with an enticement towards one's lust or an unwarranted desire. If not casted down, one then is carried away by the bait of the enticement. Then soon after, one will take the bait, give into the temptation, and satisfy the lust of his flesh. It is for this reason that James writes **then the desire when it has conceived gives birth to sin**. James continues with the progression stating **sin when it is fully-grown brings forth death**. Once the desire is conceived or once the individual gives acts upon that temptation by giving into its evil desire, it gives birth to sin that can lead to death.

James is telling these believers that once sin is conceived and begins to take root in the heart, if it is not dealt with, it will become fully grown within the heart to attain what their hearts desire. James makes it very clear that once we give into the temptation of that lust, it only gives birth to sin. What was meant to produce pleasure and satisfaction only caused chaos and devastation. James warns these believers that the only result to fulfilling their lust brought about death. This death could for some have led to physical death depending upon the lust they were giving into. James has a deeper meaning in the fact that it was causing spiritual death to these believers when they gave into sin.

Again we can see from Adam and Eve that when they ate of the fruit they did so out of their desire and pleasure for power and control that stemmed from their lust. When they ate of the fruit, the promise of fulfillment only resulted in death. When Adam and Eve ate of the fruit, they faced spiritual death, in the fact that their sin had separated them from God. In turn because of the curse, they would also suffer physical death due to their sin. James is warning these believers of the great danger of temptation and of the consequences if they were to give into their lust. James wants his readers to understand that for the one who persisted in his temptation and living in that manner, then in the end he would face eternal death separated from God. Paul wrote in Romans 7:20-21, "For when you were slaves of sin, you were free in regard to righteousness. Therefore what benefit were you then deriving from the things of which you are now ashamed? For the outcome of those things is death."

Every Good Gift is from Above

James 1:16-18 Updated American Standard Version (UASV)

¹⁶ Do not be deceived, my beloved brothers. ¹⁷ Every good gift and every perfect gift is from above, coming down from the Father of lights with whom there is no variation or shifting shadow.[26] ¹⁸ Of his own will he brought us forth by the word of truth, that we should be a kind of firstfruits of his creatures.

Do not be deceived my beloved brothers. Every good gift and every perfect gift is from above, (1:16-17a)

James did not want his fellow brothers and sisters to **be deceived** into the belief that God was their cause of trials. Such an idea would distort the character and person of the Almighty God, as it would make

---

[26] Or "with whom there is not a variation or *the turning of the shadow*."

him the author of evil, meaning that he willfully brought sin into the world. James' Christian brothers cannot make the claim that any temptation is more than they can bear, as Paul writes, "No temptation has overtaken you that are not common to man. God is faithful, and he will not let you be tempted beyond your ability, but with the temptation he will also provide the way of escape, that you may be able to endure it." (1 Cor. 10:13) It would be harmful, damaging to the Christian, if he believed that God was behind his difficult times and such a view could contribute to his possibly, wrongly, taking offense against God.

As was true of James himself, his brothers were imperfect and missed the mark of perfection every day of their lives. So there was no good reason for James to take some superior position. Rather he sees them as his spiritual brothers, to whom he refers to as "beloved," for he has affection for them. He now wishes to get their attention as he transitions to the important point he is about to make.

James describes these gifts as being good which God gives. Greek is the word *agathos* and it means "*profitable or useful.* (Vine, 1996, pg. 273) What gifts is James specifically talking about when he calls the gifts good and perfect? In the Bible, several gifts are specifically mentioned as coming directly from God. For instance, Jesus said in Matthew 5:45 'God gives the gifts of the sun and rain on the wicked and the good.' Paul mentioned in Ephesians 4:11-12 that God gives spiritual gifts to those in the church to help build up the body. Jesus mentioned in his parable in Luke 11:10-13 that God gives the Holy Spirit to those that ask of him. However, God gives many other good gifts such as food, clothing, freedom, joy, love, and many more. These gifts are good and perfect because they reflect the source from which they come. Only perfect gifts come from him. "He himself gives to all mankind life and breath and all things." (Acts 17:25) God's giving is always clean, wholesome and supports the well-being and contentment of mankind; (Acts 14:17) He supplies us all things "richly provides us with everything to enjoy." (1 Tim. 6:17) In addition, God's gifts are far-reaching, faultless, sound and unblemished. There is nothing deficient or missing in them.

coming down from the Father of lights, with whom there is no variation or shifting shadow. (1:17b)

James writes that the gifts are **coming down from the father of lights**, which is the only time in the Bible where the term lights are used in connection with God. By James calling God the **Father of lights**, he is referring to the fact that God is the author of all creation (e.g., the sun, the moon and the stars). He speaks of himself as the one "who gives the sun for light by day and the fixed order of the moon and the stars for light by night, who stirs up the sea so that its waves roar; Jehovah of hosts is his name." (Jer. 31:35, UASV) Nevertheless, he is not just the creator of the sun, the moon and the stars; he is also the basis of spiritual illumination. The apostle Paul writes: "For God, who said, 'Let light shine out of darkness,' has shone in our hearts to give the light of the knowledge of the glory of God in the face of Jesus Christ." (2 Cor. 4:6) Therefore, God is not only good and perfect because he gives good gifts, but he is also the Creator of the lights and his sovereignty rules over all the stars, planets, and solar system.

In the sun's rising and setting, it casts shadows of varying measurement and concentration. Contingent on the location of the earth in its rotation and its orbit, significant variation happens in the way that the sun is glowing, producing heat and light, to be dispersed over the surface. With this in mind, James writes that with God there **is no variation or shifting shadow**. James here is pointing out the fact that God does not change like the planets that are continually rotating causing different seasons. Rather God is always consistent with his nature, and he has never changed from the beginning of time and never will until the end of time. The writer of Hebrews says in Hebrews 13:8, "Jesus Christ is the same yesterday and today and forever." James is wanting his readers to understand that if God was the one who was tempting them, then why does he give good and perfect gifts and the very light which they need for daily existence on this earth. If God were the one doing the tempting all the time then surely God would not be so kind and gracious to his creation, but rather an evil tyrant.

Of his own will he brought us forth by the word of truth, that we should be a kind of firstfruits of his creatures. (1:18)

It is **his own will**, working toward his purposes, one of which that he brings forth spiritual sons. Looking back at what he has already written, one of his greatest gifts to mankind was that we "have been born again, not from perishable seed but imperishable, through the living and enduring word of God." (1 Pet. 1:13) We can contrast this with the fact that "sin came into the world through one man, and death through sin, and so death spread to all men because all sinned." (Rom. 5:12) God did not cause Satan, Adam, or Eve to sin, nor does he cause us to sin. God's born again sons are brought about by the Holy Spirit, by way of the Word of God. The Holy Spirit transforms a person, empowering him through the Word of God, to put on the "new person" required of true Christians: "So, as those who have been chosen of God, holy and beloved, put on a heart of compassion, kindness, humility, gentleness and patience." (Col. 3:12) This is the good news of the kingdom. The apostle Paul says of this: "In him [Christ] you also, when you heard the word of truth, the gospel of your salvation, and believed in him, were sealed with the promised Holy Spirit, who is the guarantee of our inheritance until we acquire possession of it, to the praise of his glory." (Eph. 1:13-14) So James again proves his point of God not being a tempter in the fact that if God was nothing but a tempter, then why would he give humanity his written Word that mankind could have the knowledge of salvation.

It was God's purpose for the first-century Christian congregation to bring about those, who were born again by Holy Spirit. They were to be **a kind of firstfruits of his creatures**. In other words, they were taken out of mankind at that time as **firstfruits** to God. Under the Mosaic Law, God received the firstfruits of everything. (Ex. 22:29-30; 23:19) In fact, "Israel was holy to the Lord, the firstfruits of his harvest." (Jer. 2:3) We see, from the Apostle John's words that these ones and others up unto our day were 'made a kingdom and priests to our God, and they shall reign over the earth.'[27] (Rev. 5:10) James could have also been thinking of the "Feast of Passover was to begin on the fourteenth day of the first month and was followed the next day by the Feast of Unleavened Bread (23:4–6)." "The next festive event in the Israelite calendar was the Feast of Firstfruits, which began the day after the Sabbath in the week of Unleavened Bread. On this day the Israelite presented a sheaf of the first grain of barley (23:9–11). The presentation of the first sheaf was representative of the entire crop, acknowledging that the yield came from the hand of God." (Rooker 2000, 286-7) The barley firstfruits was on Nisan 16 in 33 C.E., which landed on the day of Jesus' resurrection, with a sheaf of the first grain of barley on Pentecost day, the occurrence of the outpouring of the Holy Spirit. (Lev. 23:4-11, 15-17) If this were the case, Jesus Christ would be the "firstfruits that Paul spoke of, saying, "in fact Christ has been raised from the dead, the **firstfruits** of those who have fallen asleep." (1 Cor. 15:20, 23) Then, in a more general sense, Christians are **a kind of firstfruits of his creatures** who are important in God's new created order. The apostle John tells us "It is these who have not defiled themselves with women, for they are virgins. It is these who follow the Lamb wherever he goes. These have been redeemed from mankind as **firstfruits** for God and the Lamb." – Revelation 14:4.

---

[27] http://www.christianpublishers.org/resurrection-hope-where

Hearing and Doing the Word

James 1:19-25 Updated American Standard Version (UASV)

[19] Know this, my beloved brothers: let every man be quick to hear, slow to speak, slow to anger; [20] for the anger of man does not achieve the righteousness of God. [21] Therefore, putting aside all filthiness and abundance of wickedness, and receive with meekness the implanted word, which is able to save your souls.[28] [22] But be doers of the word, and not hearers only, deceiving yourselves. [23] For if anyone is a hearer of the word and not a doer, he is like a man who looks intently at his natural face[29] in a mirror.[24] for he looks at himself and goes away, and immediately forgets what sort of man he was. [25] But he that looks into the perfect law, the law of liberty, and abides by it, being no hearer who forgets but a doer of a work, he will be blessed in his doing.

Know this, my beloved brothers (1:19a)

James says **know this**, which is a reference to the fact that these Christians are "a kind of firstfruits of his creatures." 'Knowing this' is suggestive of action not so much an awareness, which they had. Remember, Jesus said to his disciples that "If you know these things, blessed are you if you do them." (John 13:17) A Christian in a righteous standing with God will act on what he knows to be true about God. The apostle John tells us, "No one who abides in him [God] keeps on sinning; no one who keeps on sinning has either seen him or known him." (1 John 3:6) As he has done previously, he calls them **"my beloved brothers,"** (1) to draw their attention to an important point (2), and to let them know that this applies to him as well as them. In essence, James is saying, you know that God has made you a kind of firstfruits by the word of truth, meaning that you should feel privileged, by evidencing your new Christian personality, living up to being a disciple of Christ.

let every man be quick to hear (1:19a)

Just as 'knowing' in the above was suggestive of an action, so too, "hearing" is suggesting obedience. (John 8:37, 38, 47) In other words, 'to hear is to obey.' Jesus said, "He who has ears to hear, let him hear." (Matt. 11:15) We should not fail to hear aright. It takes more than hearing

---

[28] Or is able to save you

[29] Lit the face of his birth

the audio sound of what is being said, so as to hear with understanding. We are challenged to pay close attention to what the speaker has said and to ask ourselves what he meant by the words that he used. The apostle Paul wrote, "So faith comes from hearing, and hearing through the word of Christ." (Rom. 10:17) What did Paul mean? He meant that by taking in the Word of God, our faith and sureness grows in God, as we see the outworking of his promises. If we are not obeying the Word of God, then, apparently, we have not truly heard the Word of God. We want to move beyond being hearers to being doers as well. All self-importance, willfulness, preconception and personal opinion should be set aside as we humbly hear the Word of God. We should long for the Word of God, seeking it and being eager to obey.[30]

slow to speak (1:19b)

Slow to speak, means that we should ponder what we are going to say. (Prov. 15:28; 16:23) This certainly does not mean that we can never speak. We are to proclaim the Word of God, as we are to contend for the faith and defend the Word of God and to speak the Word without fear. (Matt. 24:14; 28:19-20; 1 Pet 3:15; Jude 1:3, 22-23; Phil. 1:14; 1 Thess. 5:14; Eph. 5:15-16) However, we should not use the Bible as a tool to help others until we have incorporated the Word of God in our lives first. Then we can more clearly see how we might use it to benefit another. (Rom. 2:17-24) Paul speaks to Timothy about those "desiring to be teachers of the law, without understanding either what they are saying or the things about which they make confident assertions." (1 Tim 1:7) We do not want to use God's Word to offer advice counsel, comfort, or even to console until we have first used the Word of God effectively in our lives. The reason for this is simple, the Bible is a book for all those things and more. However, it can be misused in the hands of anyone, who does not have a correct understanding of what it means and has not truly experienced its ability to transform by way of application.

slow to anger; (1:19c)

Injustices surround us in this wicked world, filled with imperfect people, who lean toward sin and are mentally bent toward evil. Yet, James counsels us to work in harmony with Scripture and prayer to keep our anger under control. Because this is in context with our being obedient to the "word" of God, clearly any analysis of the Word of God

---

[30] See Matthew 11:15; 13:43; Mark 4:9; 4:23; Luke 14:35; Revelation 2:7, 11; 3:6, and 13.

must be treated with the correct mindset and heart condition. If we are upset to the point of being angry, he will likely be blinded to the value that lies in the Word of God. (Prov. 19:3) He will not see the light while in a provoked state of mind, let alone be able to apply the counsel in his life in a balanced manner. If another has made us angry by saying something inappropriate or mistreating us in some unjust way, we need to slow down, to avoid responding to them in kind, i.e., some vicious, hostile, spiteful comeback, which will only serve to escalate the anger and the void between us and them. There are times to be angry with righteous indignation, but after that Paul warns us, "Be angry and do not sin; do not let the sun go down on your anger." (Eph. 4:26) This is why we combat the irrational thinking, which contributes to anger, with slowing down and rationalizing the situation before we respond.

for the anger of man does not achieve the righteousness of God (1:20)

No one displaying a wrathful disposition can ever have a righteous standing before God. Wrathful ones will not see the wisdom of obedience to the Scriptures. When angry, we tend to make irrational decisions that will generally not be for the good of anyone, even creating long-lasting ripples within relationships. It could even be as simple as our destroying property in a fit of rage, irrationally not caring about the cost. However, once we are calm, the realization that those seconds of rage have cost us hundreds of dollars if not thousands, maybe even an irreplaceable family heirloom, can be very depressing. Our wrath also makes the righteousness of God difficult to accept by unbelievers who see our fits of rage, as opposed to seeing the qualities of God. If we are always angry, how are we projecting the image of God in giving a witness by our behavior? Can we imagine our stumbling someone out of seeking God because they question God based on our personality? Yes, a wrathful attitude from one who claims to be a Christian blocks the righteousness of God. It will cause the unbeliever to turn away from hearing the Word of God. Solomon writes, "Whoever is slow to anger has great understanding, but he who has a hasty temper exalts folly." – Proverbs 14:29

Therefore, putting aside all filthiness and abundance of wickedness (1:21a)

Here in these passages after James has told these believers the attitudes that they were to have when they come to the Word, he now tells them the behaviors which they must put away in order to be able to accept the word of truth. James tells his audience that they are to be **putting aside all filthiness and abundance of wickedness**. Putting aside carries with it the idea of taking off filthy and dirty clothes and casting them to the side. In other words, they were to take off the old and put it out of the way to be done away with. Keep in mind, while not addressed here, it is important to replace the old with something new. If we do not fill a void, it will return to an unusual extent. If we remove unrighteous anger from our lives, it must be replaced with understanding, compassion, empathy, kindness, and things like these.

For this reason, it is important to note that James is making the point that it is a personal act of the will to do away with these things, and not God's responsibility. The first thing that James tells his readers is that they are to put aside its filthiness. The word for filthiness is *rhuparia* and means "dirty or filthy." (Vine, 1996, pg. 237) Things such as fornication, lust, adultery, immorality, and things like these would be included in the filthiness and wickedness that James is talking about. Also in the context of this verse, James could be specifically referring to anger of which he just stated does not bring about the righteous life that God desires. The reason James tells them to put aside the filth is because as long as a person lives in filth it will keep him away from the Word of truth because imperfect humans are naturally drawn to sin. If one is coming to the Word with the wrong attitudes or the wrong behaviors, then he is nullifying that which he is reading or hearing in the Word of truth.

and receive with meekness the implanted word, which is able to save your souls. (1:21b)

After this, James describes the attitude we are to have when coming to the Word, and the behavior changes we must make, he now describes the manner with which we come to the Word of God. We are to **receive with meekness the implanted word, which is able to save your souls**. Meekness is to have a teachable and willing spirit to be ready to submit to the commands that come with the Word of God. It is a condition of the spirit and heart, which means being willing to yield to the commands coming from the word of truth.

Meekness would be the key for these believers to be able to receive, understand, and apply the Word of God into their lives. James states that the Word was already implanted if they would just become humble enough to receive it. James was talking to believers who were living with the indwelling presence of the Holy Spirit. With the inward law being already written upon their heart and the Holy Spirit dwelling within, these believers knew the Word God because it was already implanted. Edward D. Andrews writes about the indwelling of the Holy Spirit,

> The Holy Spirit, through the spirit inspired, inerrant Word of God is the motivating factor for our taking off the old person and putting on the new person. (Eph. 4:20-24; Col. 3:8-9) It is also the tool used by God so that we can "be transformed by the renewal of your mind, so that you may approve what is the good and well-pleasing and perfect will of God." (Rom 12:2; See 8:9)

> Just how do we **renew our mind**? This is done by taking in an accurate knowledge of Biblical truth, which enables us to meet God's current standards of righteousness. (Titus 1:1) This Bible knowledge, if applied, will enable us to move our mind in a different direction by filling the void after having removed our former sinful practices, and with the principles of God's Word, principles that guide our actions, and especially ones that guide moral behavior.

> The Biblical truths that lay in between Genesis 1:1 and Revelation 22:21 will transform our way of thinking, which will in return affect our mood and actions and our inner person. It will be as the apostle Paul said to the Ephesians, We need to "put off your old self, which belongs to your former manner of life and is corrupt through deceitful desires, and to be renewed in the spirit of your minds, and to put on the new self, created after the likeness of God in true righteousness and holiness. . . ." (Ephesians 4:22-24) This force that contributes to our acting or behaving in a certain way for our best interest is internal.[31]

James here is telling his readers the reason they are to accept this Word of God in humility and why they needed to come to it with proper attitude and behavior, i.e., it contained the words of eternal life, it contains the words which places them on the path of salvation. Peter in writing of the power of the word of truth wrote,

1 Peter 1:23 English Standard Version (ESV)

[23] since you have been born again, not of perishable seed but of imperishable, through the living and abiding word of God;

---

[31] http://www.christianpublishers.org/holy-spirit-indwelling

In the Word of God, these believers learned of the salvation that came through Christ alone. It was the message that they, being wicked sinners at heart, can be saved through the redeeming power of Jesus Christ. This was not just some ordinary book but the very book that leads to salvation and eternal life. It has practical benefits even now, as it will guide us through our everyday lives and then preserve us for all eternity.

The apostle Paul wrote to the Christians in Rome,

Romans 1:16 English Standard Version (ESV)

¹⁶ For I am not ashamed of the gospel, for it is the power of God for salvation to everyone who believes, to the Jew first and also to the Greek.

Paul also said to the Christians in Corinth,

1 Corinthians 1:18 English Standard Version (ESV)

¹⁸ For the word of the cross is folly to those who are perishing, but to us who are being saved it is the power of God.

But be doers of the word, (1:22a)

James is telling his readers to **be doers of the word** as obedience to the Word is not optional, it is required, if one is to walk faithfully with God. Jesus pointed out: "Not everyone who says to me, 'Lord, Lord,' will enter the kingdom of heaven, but the one who does the will of my Father who is in heaven." (Matt. 7:21, 24-27) He also said, "Blessed rather are those who hear the word of God and keep it!" (Luke 11:28) The Greek verb (*ginesthe*) is an imperative in the present tense, "be you becoming," which carries the force of an exhortation for a continuous action. James is not suggesting they *become* doers, but that they *be* doers, i.e., make sure that they are continuously doers. The expression *doer of the word is* a Hebrew idiom that literally means 'makers of word.' It could mean a writer or speaker, but more likely carries the meaning of one who lives by the word, one who obeys the word, who practices the word.

and not hearers only, (1:22b)

It does not make one a Christian because they listen dutifully as one is sharing the Word of God. While it is great if a Christian attends Christian services and reads the Scriptures daily, but there is more to being a Christian. Literally hearing the Word, even understanding the Word, is not enough. In the early first-century, Jews and Christians had similar services, wherein a lecturer would read from the Scriptures regularly while also explaining what had been read. However, this alone does not lead to faith. If one is to be the type of hearer that James is speaking of here, he would have genuine faith, meaning that his faith in what he heard would result in works. (Rom. 10:17; Jam. 2:20) In other words, a Christian, who was a hearer only, would be one who lacked faith.

deceiving yourselves (1:22c)

Over 41,000 different Christian denominations today are filled with dutiful persons who regularly attend Christian services, regularly read their Bibles, and involve themselves in the social actions of the congregation. In this, they all believe that they are fulfilling their Christian obligations. However, many of these people's lives are no different from the atheist that is a good person, living by the laws, paying his taxes, and doing good to others. We are **deceiving ourselves** if our entire *life* is not inundated in our worship of God. We may not be aware of or maybe we even block out the fact that obeying the Word of God is an unnegotiable requirement. What we may not realize is that this **deceiving ourselves** is like a roadblock on our path to salvation and harder to set aside than ignorance or skepticism itself. God expects exclusive devotion from his worshipers, which encompasses every aspect of the Christian life. (1 Cor. 10:31) If our worship is merely an outward display, a going through the motions, we are falling short. We were given the great commission of proclaiming and teaching God's Word, as well as making disciples. If we are not regularly engaged in such work in our own communities, we are missing the most important act of obedience.

For if anyone is a hearer of the word and not a doer, he is like a man who looks intently at his natural face in a mirror. (1:23)

When looking into a mirror, man has his image reflected back at himself, where he can see all of his flaws and faults. The purpose of looking into the mirror is so he can see if anything is out of place, so he can make any needed corrections. Can we imagine looking into a mirror, seeing a big stain on our shirt, our hair is completely disheveled, or that we have something on our face, but we ignore them and head off to work?

The image he sees in the mirror is sent to the mind, where it is evaluated, reasoned on, considered. For this reason, by looking at the Word of God, by hearing the Word of God, we are able to see our true selves. We can see all of our imperfections, character flaws, and human weaknesses. We can also see any wrongdoings, misdeeds, even thinking that is out of harmony with the Word of God.

We must keep in mind this analogy is a negative one that is looking at a person who looks **intently at his natural face in the mirror**, sees the things that need to be corrected, but walks away ignoring them. The same is true with the Word of God. He looks into the Word, listens to the needed corrections as he reads, ignores them, and chooses to remain inactive, and fails to respond.

For he looks at himself and goes away, and immediately forgets what sort of man he was. (1:24)

When a person looks into a mirror, he is good at quickly seeing what is out of place as to his appearance. Maybe he has been unable to sleep, so he sees the yellow skin and puffy eyes and dark circles under the eyes. Maybe he sees that he has more gray hair coming in from increased age. When he looks intently into a mirror, he is aware of the things that should give him pause as to how he is living his life. Sleepless nights can cause high blood pressure, heart attacks, strokes, memory loss, diabetes, and lower libidos, and less interest in sex. Does it seem logical to ignore the physical signs of lacking sleep? Should we not consider how we could turn things around? Nevertheless, the man in James' analogy quickly forgets, once he has turned away from the mirror. It is a case of, 'out of sight, out of mind,' as he may want to forget some unwelcome features. Yes, once he has walked away from the mirror he allows the anxieties of the day to crowd out his appearance, forgetting what he may have needed to correct. (See 2 Pet. 1:9) However, the man that is a doer reacts quite differently as he looks into the perfect law.

But he that looks into the perfect law, (1:25a)

James now gives a comparison to the man who not only hears the Word but also actually applies that Word to his life. James says the man who applies the word is he that looks into the perfect law, the law of liberty. The Greek word used for "looks" is the word *parakupto*, which means to "bend inside, lean over, or stoop down to look into." (Vine 1996, Volume 2, Page 378) The sense here is of one seeking to get a better look of something by leaning forward, peering at it. (See John 20:5, 11; 1 Peter 1:12) "The same verb—translated as bent over—pictures the apostle John staring into Jesus' empty tomb (John 20:5). John's look led to an obedient faith (John 20:8)." (Lea 1999, 267) One who is wanting to obey the law of Christ does just that, as he peers into the perfect law to inspect, examine and study it, with a heart motivated toward obedience. He is able to visualize himself as it relates to being a biblical father, husband, son, or to herself as a biblical mother, wife or daughter. The law is perfect in the sense that it is complete, everything we in our imperfect state need to walk with God, to have and maintain a righteous standing before the Father and the Son. It is a pathway to salvation through the grace of God. – Proverbs 30:5-6; Psalm 119:105, 140.

the law of liberty, (1:25b)

Jesus said to the Jews who had believed him, "If you abide in my word, you are truly my disciples, and you will know the truth, and the truth will set you free." (John 8:31-32) The Word of God frees his people from slavery to sin and death, putting them on the path of life. (Rom. 7:5-6, 9; 8:2, 4; 2 Cor. 3:6-9) This "law of liberty" is a reference not to the Mosaic Law, but to the new covenant, in which the Father declared, "I will put my law within them, and I will write it on their hearts. And I will be their God, and they shall be my people." (Jer. 31:33) Christians are under the principles behind the Mosaic Law, but not under some lengthy code of rules and regulations but rather the inspired, inerrant Word of God, which enables them to know the will of the Father. (Matt. 7:21-23; 1 John 2:15-17; Gal. 5:1, 13-14) In other words, they have a developed fine-tuned Christian conscience, which leads them in the way that they should go, not because of some fearful dread of displeasing some all-powerful being. The Christian's worship is out of love and is principally positive, not negative. – Matthew 22:37-40; see James 2:12

and abides by it, (1:25c)

James also says that the doer of the word does not just obey it occasionally but **abides in it**. The word for abide is *parameno* which means "to remain by or near" *para*, "beside," hence, "to continue or persevere in anything." (Vine 1996, Volume 2, Page 127) He is abiding in these things in the fact he is daily striving to live these truths out in a manner that is pleasing to his master who gave him these commands. This is moving beyond a mere examination of it. This one is different than the man who had looked into the mirror, being dissatisfied with what he saw, but nonetheless walking away forgetting or even losing interest in what he saw. The Christian perseveres and continues to pore over the perfect law with the mindset of keeping his life in harmony with it. (Ps. 119:9, 16, 97) We need to be immersed and engaged fully with the Word of God, as it guides us through this imperfect age.

being no hearer who forgets but a doer of a work, he will be blessed in his doing. (1:25d)

The Christian who has moved over from being a forgetful hearer into the world of being a doer, is one who has a biblical mindset. This biblical mindset leads him to every decision he makes, no matter how great or small. Before, he had been one who may have sat listening respectfully but then failed to act on the insights he gained from the Word of God. Now, he takes everything that he hears from the Word to heart (his inner person), the seat of motivation, and puts it to work in his daily life. He now has an inner joy that he had never previously known. The Word of God proves to be beneficial in ways he had never imagined. (Ps. 19:7-11; see 1 Tim. 4:8.) He draws real comfort from the fact that he has a righteous standing before God, and that God finds him pleasing.

Clean and Pure Worship

James 1:26-27 Updated American Standard Version (UASV)

²⁶ If anyone thinks himself to be religious, and yet does not bridle his tongue but deceives his *own* heart, this man's religion is worthless. ²⁷ Pure and undefiled religion in the sight of *our* God and Father is this: to visit orphans and widows in their distress, *and* to keep oneself unstained by the world.

If any man thinks he is religious (1:26a)

A man may think that he is religious, i.e., (1) belief in the faith, (2) belief in the teachings of the faith, and (3) living by those teachings in one's daily life. He may believe that he is a devout person, completely dedicated to God. He may be attending Christian meetings, or he may be doing some religious works, which on the surface makes him come across as a truly committed worshiper. However, there may be something in his conduct, some flaw, which would cast doubt on the validity of his truly being a religious man. If he is truly, a religious man his entire life will be in harmony with the Word of God. His Christian conscience, mind of Christ, and inner person should be led by the Holy Spirit inspired Word of God, not a mere observance to some formalities or ritualistic practices. We need to understand that it is how God perceives us, not how we perceive ourselves. – 1 Corinthians 4:4

and does not bridle his tongue (1:26b)

James brings to his readers attention one of the most difficult tasks of the imperfect human, the failure to control the tongue, i.e., what one says, namely bad things. It is of such serious concern that James spends almost all of chapter 2 on this one issue. Not controlling one's speech would include malicious gossip, slanderous talk, badmouthing, impulsive and reckless statements, flattery, using their tongues to deceive, and the like. While he may put on great airs or an appearance of being religious, his tongue (speech) convicts him of being one who pretends.

(1) He pretends to have belief in the faith,

(2) to have belief in the teachings of the faith,

(3) and to be living by those teachings in his daily life, but actually behaves otherwise when outside of the churches view.

In James' day, the Pharisees were a self-righteous lot, who used their many words to flatter, to lie, to deceive, and to seek their own glory, while speaking ill of the common Jew as though he were less than human. – Mark 12:38-40; John 7:47-48; compare Romans 3:10-18.

but deceives his heart, (1:26c)

When one begins to think more of himself than he ought, he is surely hip deep in self-deception. Our relationship with the Father and the Son necessitates that we have control over our entire body, which includes the tongue. Paul told the Corinthian congregation that they needed to bring "every thought into captivity to the obedience of Christ." (2 Cor. 10:5) Therefore, if any is living a life that seems to be religious on the surface, yet has not gotten control over the tongue that causes pain to others and to self, this is deception in the heart, i.e., inner person. Even if one has many Christian gifts that stand out, such as being a good speaker, having a warm and charismatic personality, and is generous but falls short in his speech, this is deception. This one has not realized what all is involved in truly being a religious person. (1 Cor. 13:1-3) We cannot practice any sin, and at the same time consider ourselves a genuine Christian. The apostle John makes it clear that Jesus' ransom sacrifice covers the committing of a sin not the practice of sinning, i.e., living in sin. – 1 John 2:1; 3:6, 9-10.

this person's religion is worthless. (1:26d)

First, we should understand that James is not speaking about the religious organization, but rather the type of worship that this person carries out. This one has a major flaw in his walk with God, his Christian conduct, and so he is not pleasing in the eyes of God who would view his worship (religion) as worthless. This is a case of a formalistic worship, not a true worship of God, as he has infected his relationship with his self-deception by way of his failing to control his tongue. It is worthless to the point that all he is doing is wearing out the floors of the church as he ritualistically enters and leaves each service. His worship is tainted and polluted and, therefore, pointless or useless.

Pure and undefiled religion before our God and Father is this: to visit orphans and widows in their affliction, (1:27a)

The word that James uses here for "pure" is the Greek word *katharos* and it means "*clean or unmixed.*" (Vine, 1996, pg. 498) This is the kind of purity that is not mixed with anything nor tainted with anything but clear and clean. It would be like looking at a glass of water from an area that has unclean water, if one swirls the glass, he can see little particles floating around in the bottom, unlike bottled water that is pure and clean. Jesus said at Matthew 5:8, "Blessed are the pure (*katharos*) in heart, for they shall see God." James and Jesus are saying the same thing. In the Bible, "pure" can specify what is clean in a physical sense. However, the word in other contexts can apply to what is uncontaminated, i.e., **not** adulterated, stained or dirty, or corrupted, in a moral and religious sense. Jesus said in Luke 10:27, "You shall love the Lord your God with all your heart and with all your soul and with all your strength and with all your mind, and your neighbor as yourself."

The Greek word for undefiled is *amiantos* and it means "undefiled, free from contamination." (Vine, 1996, pg. 650) The word carries with it the idea that there is nothing within the inner person of a Christian, which defiles or stains him. Therefore, James is saying that the first criterion is to see if one's worship is pure and undefiled, is in the way that they use their tongue. Then, the second criterion has to do **not** just with the tongue, but also with our actions toward people. Keep in mind, James is not giving an exhaustive list here of what pure worship should be. In other words, there are more requirements than simply taking care of widows and orphans and keeping oneself unstained by the world. When listing things, no one ever gives an exhaustive list. It is usually three or four examples and the inference is *things like these*. The point is pure worship is more than mere formalism, such as following some basic rules, or of attending meetings regularly. Rather, pure worship is that worship, which gets down to the inner person, and encompasses his entire life, and which includes his love of God and neighbor. – 1 John 3:18.

James then gives what God would consider to be pure and undefiled worship is **to visit orphans and widows in their affliction.** James here is showing that true worship is more than just living by some basic Bible rules and going to Christian meetings but it involves actions. James mentions two specific groups of people who would have been very significant in his day. He specifically mentions the orphans and the widows who should be of special interest for those who claim to have pure worship. It is the actions of Christians, who are willing to help those like orphans and widows, who are truly right in God's eye because their actions show forth their true belief. It would have been the orphans and the widows, who would have been the most rejected, and most unlikely to survive the conditions in which they found themselves.

James specifically mentions that these people were to be visited in their times of distress. The word in Greek used here for distress is *thlipsis* and it means "pressure or a pressing together." (Vine, 1996, pg. 17) James is not saying they were to be helped when they had no more troubles but rather it was *in the midst of* their troubles. They were to be helped as they were going through the pressures of life that were coming against them. This could include clothing, feeding, and giving them shelter, and show the love of Christ to them. James echoes what John wrote in I John 3:16-18 "We know love by this, that He laid down His life for us; and we ought to lay down our lives for the brethren. But whoever has the world's goods, and sees his brother in need and closes his heart against him, how does the love of God abide in him? Little children, let us not love with word or with tongue, but in deed and truth." Several Scriptures point to the fact that God has a great concern for the orphans and widows.[32]

and to keep oneself unstained by the world. (1:27b)

This is the third and final criterion, which James presents to Christians to see if their worship is true. The first criterion dealt with their speech, the second dealt with their actions, and now this third test deals with their

---

[32] See Deuteronomy 10:18; 14:28–29; 16:11; 24:17; 26:12; Jeremiah 22:3; Zechariah 7:8–10; Malachi 3:5; cf. Acts 6:1; 1 Timothy 5:16

integrity before God, in the fact that they were **to keep oneself unstained by the world**. The word "unstained" means "spotless" or "without spot." James is saying that the one who is truly religious, pure in worship, will keep himself from being spotted and tainted by the evil and the wickedness of this world. To be stained by the world would be to allow the sinfulness of the world to engage in the evil desires of the flesh. To be stained by the world is to engage in the wicked practices that it has to offer. The word "world" here is a reference to humankind that are alienated from God, who are "lying in the power of the evil one (i.e., Satan)." (1 John 5:19) A Christian should stand out from those using Satan's world fully. (John 17:14) Are we truly separate from the violence and corruption of the world, which would also include our entertainment? Have we adopted any of its attitudes, speech or conduct that would not be in harmony with the will of God? (Matt 7:21-23) Paul warns Timothy,

2 Timothy 2:20-22 English Standard Version (ESV)

²⁰ Now in a great house there are not only vessels of gold and silver but also of wood and clay, some for honorable use, some for dishonorable.²¹ Therefore, if anyone cleanses himself from what is dishonorable, he will be a vessel for honorable use, set apart as holy, useful to the master of the house, ready for every good work.

²² So flee youthful passions and pursue righteousness, faith, love, and peace, along with those who call on the Lord from a pure heart.

It is important to note that James says, "keep oneself" from being stained by the world, which signifies that sinning or being polluted by the world is always a personal act of the will. It is the personal responsibility to actively resist the evil desires of the flesh that the world has to offer. Paul said to the Christians in Rome,

Romans 12:1-2 English Standard Version (ESV)

¹ I appeal to you therefore, brothers, by the mercies of God, to present your bodies as a living sacrifice, holy and acceptable to God, which is your spiritual worship.² Do not be conformed to this world, but be transformed by the renewal of your mind, that by testing you may discern what is the will of God, what is good and acceptable and perfect.

The sacrifice that Christians regularly make would be beyond anything that unchristian people would normally consider. Yes, Christians evidence that gratefulness by a life of self-sacrifice. It is toward this that we have made our minds over.

Review Question

(1) **[vs 1]** Which of the four men mentioned in the Greek New Testament named James was the author of this letter?

(2) **[vs 1]** Who are the "twelve tribes" to whom James writes?

(3) **[vs 2]** Why should we consider it all joy when we encounter various trials?

(4) **[vs 2]** What type of trial may we have to face?

(5) **[vs 3]** How does the testing of our faith produce endurance?

(6) **[vs 4]** How does endurance have its perfect work, and how may we be perfect and complete, lacking in nothing?

(7) **[vs 5]** What is wisdom? What kind of wisdom should we be asking for and where can it be found?

(8) **[vs 6]** What does it mean to ask in faith? What kind of condition is the one who doubts in?

(9) **[vs 7]** Why should no one suppose that he would receive anything from the Lord if he doubts?

(10) **[vs 8]** What does it mean to be a double-minded man?

(11) **[vs 9]** How is the poor person who becomes a Christian exalted?

(12) **[vs 10]** How does the rich man boast in his humiliation?

(13) **[vs 11]** How is it that the rich man will fade away in the midst of his pursuits?

(14) **[vs 12]** What does James mean here by the term "trial"?

(15) **[vs 13]** Why can we rightfully say that God cannot be tempted with evil?

(16) **[vs 14]** What is it when a person is undergoing a trial that cause him to sin?

(17) **[vs 15]** What brings a person to the point of sinning?

(18) **[vs 16]** How might a Christian while in the midst of a trial be deceived?

(19) **[vs 17]** How do we know that we can always completely rely on God?

(20) **[vs 18]** What is the word of truth? How are Christians firstfruits of his creatures?

(21) **[vs 19]** What is involved in being quick to hear, slow to speak, and slow to anger?

(22) **[vs 20]** How is it that the anger of man does not achieve the righteousness of God?

(23) **[vs 21]** Why must we put aside all filthiness and abundance of wickedness? How is the implanted word able to save our souls?

(24) **[vs 22]** What does it mean to be doers of the word, and not hearers only, and how would we be deceiving ourselves?

(25) **[vs 23]** What does James mean when he speaks of a man who looks intently at his natural face in a mirror?

(26) **[vs 24]** What does a man who looks at himself and goes away, and immediately forgets what sort of man he was mean?

(27) **[vs 25]** What is the perfect law, the law of liberty?

(28) **[vs 26]** How can one's form of worship become worthless?

(29) **[vs 27]** Pure and undefiled religion before our God and Father is what?

JAMES CHAPTER 2 The Sin of Favoritism

The Sin of Favoritism

James 2:1 Updated American Standard Version (UASV)

¹My brothers, do not hold your faith in our glorious Lord Jesus Christ with an attitude of personal favoritism.

My brothers, (2:1a)

Even though James was offering some strong correction concerning some very unchristian arrogance, he still referred to his readers as, "**my brothers.**" This evidences that he did not feel that their thinking and actions meant they had fallen away, but that they just had stumbled in their reasoning. Nevertheless, James does not parse words when it comes to those who claim to call themselves Christian, but their conduct belies that claim, as they lack brotherly love.

do not hold your faith (2:1b)

The foundation of any true Christian is an active faith in Jesus Christ. Thus, the readers of James' letter had side stepped or stumbled in that faith, as they ignored the life and times of Jesus Christ's three and half year ministry. They set aside his example of being impartial, as well as his great love for those who were receptive to his message, and his sadness over those that had ignored him.

in our glorious Lord Jesus Christ (2:1c)

The Greek word (hēmōn doxēs), which is rendered "**our glorious,**" is in apposition[33] to Jesus Christ. In other words, Jesus Christ is the one who all Christians should praise. Jesus was "taken up **in glory,**" and one day 'the Son of Man will come **in his glory,** and all the angels with him, and then he will sit on his **glorious throne.**" (Matt. 24:30; 25:31) James is making the point that Christian's faith in their glorious Lord Jesus Christ is not accomplished by giving glory and honor to the wealthy and the powerful, victimizing the poor with disdain as though they were not

---

[33] Grammar: **relationship between noun phrases:** the relationship between two usually consecutive nouns or noun phrases that refer to the same person or thing and have the same relationship to other sentence elements. In the sentence "My son, an actor, lives with me," the phrase "My son, an actor" is an example of apposition.

there. This would actually put them at odds with Jesus Christ, the one who truly matters in the equation. It is one's "faith in our glorious Lord Jesus Christ," which truly matters, not in the wealth and power that one possesses.

with an attitude of personal favoritism. (2:1d)

Favoritism is so dangerous, as it gives a false representation of who God is. Christians, according to Matthew 5:16 are to be a light unto this world regardless of status or ethnicity or any other reason. Favoritism can be dangerous also in the fact that it defines the worth of an individual based on the externals of a person rather than on the internal heart and soul of the individual.

Favoritism most often places the emphasis on the possessions, intellect, or station in life. At its core, bias is selfish because one only seeks to give attention to an individual based on what he thinks that individual can do for him. Favoritism often excludes the ones that God wants and includes the ones that God despises. In turn, favoritism does not place the value of a person in the reality of his heart or in the fact that he was made in the image of God. Instead, it sets the value of an individual based on one's assumption of how that person to whom they show special attention can benefit him. Many of James' readers should have known from the Mosaic Law that God forbade favoritism. In Leviticus 19:15, Moses writes, "You shall do no injustice in judgment; you shall not be partial to the poor nor defer to the great, but you are to judge your neighbor fairly."

We can look at the life of Christ and see that he did not play favorites with people. We see Jesus one moment with a high standing synagogue official (John 5), and then the next moment he is ministering to lepers (Matthew 8:3) who can do him no good. After that, we see him spending time with adulterers (John 8), which were despised. In addition, we see Jesus in one instance spending time with the religious elite Pharisees (Luke 18), then offering his love and attention to little children. (Matthew 19) Jesus does not see himself as being better than anyone else is, even though he was/is the Son of God. In fact, his core apostles were lowly fishermen. (Luke 5) Jesus never based someone's value on what he felt they could do for him. He placed the value of people in the fact that they were created in the image of his Father.

Further evidence from Scripture that God does not show favoritism is recorded in Deuteronomy 10:17-18. It reads, "For the Lord your God is the God of gods and the Lord of lords, the great, the mighty, and the awesome God who does not show partiality nor take a bribe. He executes justice for the orphan and the widow, and shows His love for the alien by giving him food and clothing." Peter in talking of the Gentiles said in Acts 10:34-35, "I most certainly understand *now* that God is not one to show partiality, but in every nation the man who fears Him and does what is right is welcome to Him." In addition, the apostle Paul said in Romans 2:11, "For there is no partiality with God."

James 2:2-13 Updated American Standard Version (UASV)

² For if a man comes into your assembly with a gold ring and dressed in fine clothes, and there also comes in a poor man in filthy clothes, ³ and you look with favor upon the one who is wearing the fine clothes, and say, "You sit here in a good place," and you say to the poor man, "You stand over there, or sit down by my footstool," ⁴ have you not then made distinctions among yourselves and become judges with evil thoughts? ⁵ Listen, my beloved brothers: did not God choose the poor of this world to be rich in faith and heirs of the kingdom which He promised to those who love him? ⁶ But you have dishonored the poor man. Are not the rich the ones who oppress you, and the ones who drag you into court? ⁷ Do they not blaspheme the honorable name by which you have been called? ⁸ If you really fulfill the royal law according to the Scripture, "You shall love your neighbor as yourself,"[34] you are doing well. ⁹ But if you show favoritism, you commit sin and are convicted by the law as transgressors. ¹⁰ For whoever keeps the whole law and yet stumbles in one point, he has become guilty of all. ¹¹ For he who said, "Do not commit adultery,"[35] also said, "Do not murder."[36] If you do not commit adultery but do murder, you have become a transgressor of the law. ¹² So speak and so act as men who are to be judged by the law of liberty. ¹³ For judgment is without mercy to him who has shown no mercy. Mercy triumphs over judgment.

For if a man comes into your assembly with a gold ring and dressed in fine clothes, and there also comes in a poor man in filthy clothes, (2:2)

---

[34] Quote from Lev. 19:18

[35] Quote from Ex. 20:14; Deut. 5:18

[36] Quote from Ex. 20:13; Deut. 5:17

The potential of any given Christian meeting is that an unbelieving rich man with gold rings and fine clothes could decide to attend, as well as a poor man in filthy clothes. This rich, well-dressed man would likely have been one of power and status within the community as well.

If the poor unbeliever were to start regularly attending the Christian meeting in his filthy clothes, the congregation should come together to aid this one with something clean and proper to wear. (Compare 1 Tim. 2:9-10; Rom. 12:13) Regardless of his little means, he should be welcomed no differently than the rich man, as there is no place for impartiality within God's house. In reference to the poor one, Richardson writes, "Throughout Scripture these poor are often said to fall into desperate conditions because of the injustices committed against them by wealthy and powerful oppressors.[37] Painfully, the congregation becomes a party to the oppression of the poor. The poor man is demeaned and devalued. His treatment readies him for dissociation through disgrace. 'The poor you always have with you' (Matt 26:11), which was the Lord's way of telling his disciples that they would always be ministering to the poor, has been twisted around to mean that they are a hopeless case and that they should be helped only when it's convenient. Of course, helping the poor is never convenient." (Richardson 1997, 112)

and you look with favor upon the one who is wearing the fine clothes, and say "You sit here in a good place," and you say to the poor man, "You stand over there, or sit down by my footstool," (2:3)

James highlights the fact that these believers decided that he was worthy of special attention. James says these believers **look with favor upon the one who is wearing the fine clothes**. The believers determined the rich man rather than the poor man to be worthy of their attention due to his external appearance. They even give the rich man special privileges in the fact that they tell him **you sit here in a good place**. In the synagogue in the first century, the best seats were those at the end of the room where everyone could see them and that faced Jerusalem. The seat was also next to the platform where the speaker would give his exposition of Scripture. This was a seat of honor for a special guest or speaker coming into town, and all knew that the one who sat there was a person of honor. Favoritism is always easily spotted in the fact that favors, time, and focus are given to a particular person. Here in

---

[37] Cf. Pss 9:18; 10:1–18; 35:10; 37:14; 40:16–17; 109:16; Isa 3:14–15; 10:1–2; Amos 4:1; 8:4; also Matt 26:11.

this passage the ones who were favorites were getting the good seats of the synagogue simply because of their wealth.

While the rich man was being treated with special honors, James presents the contrast with how the poor are treated. They are quick to notice the rich man, give him all the attention, and yet barely even recognize the poor man who came into the assembly. They treat the poor man as if he was less than human, saying; **you stand over there, or sit down by my footstool**. Based on the externals of the poor man as having **no** wealth or anything valuable, they deemed him not worthy of their time or their attention. Sadly, "the situation is clear enough: Christians in positions of some authority in the community (the verb "show special attention" is in the plural) are fawning over the rich and treating the poor with disdain and contempt." (Moo 2000, 104)

have you not then made distinctions among yourselves and become judges of evil thoughts? (2:4)

James asks **have you not then made distinctions among yourselves**? The problem with judging is that it is never based on the internal nature of the heart but is always based on the external appearance an individual and James says they **become judges with evil thoughts.** Therefore, when people judge, assumptions about another are based on the external's they perceive of that individual. They are discriminating among themselves as to who is worthy and who is not, based on one's appearance. The standard by which they decide the truth about an individual is based on their personal assumption. God looks at the heart to make a decision about the status of a person. (1 Sam. 16:7) When a mere man judges based on assumptions, it is based on externals. Whether the difference is with respect to wealth, social status, political status, education, profession, race or language, there is no reason for favoritism.

Listen, my beloved brothers: did not God choose the poor of this world to be rich in faith (2:5a)

James is calling these believers to take special heed and pay close attention to what he is about to say in writing when he says, **Listen, my beloved brothers.** He is going to use a play on words to get his point across about this poor man. In this context, when he describes the man as being poor, he is saying that this one is poor because of what he does not have. It is the poor, who have nothing materially, who are usually rich spiritually, as they have circumstances, which move them to listen receptively to the Good News.

James asks these believers to consider the reality that **God chooses the poor of this world to be rich in faith.** The poor due to their status in life are more often prone, to want to seek after a God who does care for them. Because of their being poor, they are humble and receptive to the good news. One major purpose for Christ coming was for people who are poor in spirit to realize their sin and need for repentance. The poor man is more aware of his need for help and struggles with sin while the rich are often blinded by their wealth. Therefore, James says that the first reason that these believers should stop showing favoritism to the poor man is because they were the very ones that God chose.

This does not mean that all that are poor are going to receive eternal life just because they are poor. In addition, it is not saying that we cannot be rich and receive eternal life. Rather James is trying to get his readers to understand that so often due to the status of one's life, i.e., living in poverty; they are more willing to listen to the message of Christ. The faith that the poor man has cannot be bought with the expensive clothes of the rich man and his jewelry. The faith of the poor man can only be attained by that which has already been done in Christ. The man who has faith in Christ is rich because not only does he have fullness of life within this imperfect age of Satan's rule, but also he will have eternal life when Jesus returns. Paul tells those in Corinth that often God chooses the things that this world so often considers worthless. – 1 Corinthians 1:26-29.

and heirs of the kingdom which He promised to those who love Him? But you have dishonored the poor man. (2:5b-6a)

James says the poor that he has chosen are **heirs of the kingdom promised to those who love him.** The Greek word *kleronomos*, rendered heir, means, "*obtain a lot.*" (Vine 1996, 300) An heir is like a son who would receive his father's property or possessions because of his blood relation to his father. Whether one is rich or poor to repent unto Christ means that you come into a relationship with God through Jesus Christ. As a result, one becomes an heir unto God and a child of God. Paul wrote,

Galatians 4:3-7 New American Standard Bible (NASB)

³ So also we, while we were children, were held in bondage under the elemental things of the world. ⁴ But when the fullness of the time

came, God sent forth His Son, born of a woman, born under the Law, [5] so that He might redeem those who were under the Law, that we might receive the adoption as sons. [6] Because you are sons, God has sent forth the Spirit of His Son into our hearts, crying, "Abba! Father!" [7] Therefore you are no longer a slave, but a son; and if a son, then an heir through God.

It is only those, who are in a relationship with Christ that become heirs to God's kingdom. A child of God gains their father's property, which is an eternal relationship with the Son and his Father. For this reason, God is saying that the poor man who is rich in faith and rejected by most is just as much a part of God's family and Kingdom as anyone else. This would also include the rich with the right heart attitude. The interesting thing that James makes clear here is that the very people that God would honor were the very ones who were being dishonored. James states that by these believers showing favoritism to the rich and excluding the poor, they **have dishonored the poor man**. They were dishonoring the poor man by saying that based upon his external appearances he was not worthy enough to worship God in the synagogue. As a result, they were making it difficult for the poor man to worship by giving him the worst seat in the assembly, as well as giving him the disheartening feeling that he deserved that place.

Are not the rich the ones who oppress you and the ones who drag you into court? Do they not blaspheme the honorable name by which you have been called? (2:6b-7)

In the days of James, there was a significant issue with the rich taking individuals to court. Their financial resources allowed them to do so whenever they liked. It is interesting how these rich people to whom they were showing favoritism, were the very ones taking them to court. For this reason, James asks a rhetorical question, **are not the rich the ones who oppress you and the ones who drag you into court**? If the Christians were thinking that by showing favoritism to the rich man that they were going to gain something from him, they were wrong. If the rich took them to court to oppress them, then what would make them think that the rich would give them anything by showing favoritism? James also says that the rich are the very ones who **blaspheme the honorable name by which you have been called**. These rich were speaking against the name of Christ whom these Christians were worshipping in their assemblies.

If you really fulfill the royal law according to the scripture, "You shall love your neighbor as yourself," you are doing well. (2:8)

This law is called the "royal law." Although the definite article is absent, this in no way obscures the meaning of the term as being the law of God or of Christ (cf. 4:11). This is the chief command that entails all of God's other commands (cf. Lev 19:18, quoted by Jesus in Matt 22:39; Rom 13:8; Gal 5:14). A vast literature throughout the history of theology reflects on this love command. For example, Justin[38] associates it with the ascribing of the people of God as a "kingdom of priests." (Ex. 19:6; 1 Pet 2:9)[39] (Richardson 1997, 120) Jesus said,

Matthew 22:37-40 English Standard Version (ESV)

[37] And he said to him, "You shall love the Lord your God with all your heart and with all your soul and with all your mind.[38] This is the great and first commandment.[39] And a second is like it: You shall love your neighbor as yourself. [40] On these two commandments depend all the Law and the Prophets."

On this, the apostle Paul wrote, "For the whole law is fulfilled in one word: 'You shall love your neighbor as yourself.'" (Gal. 5:14) He also wrote, "Love does no wrong to a neighbor; for this reason love is the fulfilling of the law." (Rom. 13:10) The apostle John wrote, "If anyone says, 'I love God,' and hates his brother, he is a liar; for he who does not love his brother whom he has seen cannot love God whom he has not seen." (1 John 4:20) This "royal law" was clearly stated in Leviticus 19:18, "You shall not take vengeance or bear a grudge against the sons of your own people, but you shall love your neighbor as yourself: I am the Lord."

James says to his readers that if they were to live by the "royal law according to scripture;" then, "you are doing well." James is penning his letter from the mindset of his readers, as though he were thinking what they were thinking and he covers one subject after another, which had and has a tremendous impact on the readers then and now. (See James 1:13, 26; 2:14; 3:13; 4:13) If these ones were trying to rationalize that their favoritism of the rich was merely their showing 'love of neighbor,' they missed the mark. Their love of God and neighbor was to be

---

[38] Apol. I.12; Cl. Al. Strom. 6.164; 7.73

[39] cf. F. E. Vokes, "The Ten Commandments in the New Testament and in First Century Judaism," SE 5 (1968): 145–54.

according to Scripture, and Scripture does not suggest that they express their love by their being hospitable to the rich, yet showing disdain for the poor. Thus, from the beginning, love of neighbor was applicable to all regardless of one's means or station in life. This will be made all too clear below in verses 10-11.

If any in the congregation felt that James' comments on the rich were over the top, he is setting them straight here, as Scripture is the final authority on all matters. The rich are among those that are to receive love of neighbor but not as though they should be loved in some favored, privileged, exceptional way, as the "royal law" makes clear. Jesus helped his disciples to appreciate that we not only love those who are friendly toward us, but also even our enemies. We need to be impartial and practical in our love of others, just as was true of Jesus himself. (Matt. 5:43-48) If the congregation that James wrote to was carrying out the "royal law" in harmony with what Scripture meant, not what they felt it meant, they 'were doing well.' James was saying that Christians are obligated to show loving kindness to anyone, anytime. Both rich and poor were to be treated equally, as both are neighbors in the eyes of God.

But if you show favoritism, you commit sin and are convicted by the law as transgressors. (2:9)

While these brothers were no longer under the Mosaic Law, this "royal Law" was carried over by Jesus' statements, as well as Paul's, being now a part of the law of Christ. In fact, the whole of the Old Testament is encompassed in this law. The principles of the law did not allow for any injustice, whether one was rich or poor. (Lev. 19:15) For this reason, a Christian does well if he shows loving kindness to a rich man, as long as he would have done the same if the person had been poor. Impartiality is sinning. If one is truly obedient to the "royal law," he will love all of his neighbors. If he fails to do so, he is a sinner in the eyes of God. The primary meaning of *hamartia* (sin) is missing the mark of perfection. In other words, an impartial person is missing the mark of dealing with someone fairly, lovingly, and justly. This very sin or missing the mark of partiality is condemned in Leviticus 19:15 and Deuteronomy 1:17 and 16:19.

It is God's standard to be impartial in expressions of love. This means the one playing favorites, while claiming to walk rightly with God as to the "royal law" has stepped over the line, transgressing against God. Like the original readers of Jame's letter, Christians today need to have an evident demonstration that they are genuine Christians, setting aside all partiality toward any class of people.

For whoever keeps the whole law and yet stumbles in one point, he has become guilty of all. For he who said, "Do not commit adultery," also said, "Do not murder." If you do not commit adultery but do murder, you have become a transgressor of the law. (2:10-11)

Here James continues the point of not showing favoritism by stating **for whoever keeps the whole law and yet stumbles in one point; he has become guilty of all.** When one breaks the commands of God, it does not matter how big or small the sin is, it is wrong in God's sight.[40] James is saying that even if one broke even the least of God's commandments it was as if he broke the greatest of the commandments. James emphasizes the two laws that most deem the worst of all the laws to be broken in stating **for he who said do not commit adultery also said do not murder**. James appeals to the Ten Commandments to make his point. James emphasizes the seventh commandment found in (Exodus 20:14) which says "Do not commit adultery." James also uses the sixth commandment found in (Exodus 20:13) which says, "Do not commit murder." James is making the case that "to resist one requirement of the Law is to resist God, the authority beneath its requirements." (Lea 1999, 285)

---

[40] The Bible is quite clear that some sins are more serious than others are. Certainly, stealing is not as bad as murder. While sin is sin, it is also shown in Scripture to be of a comparative gravity of wrongdoing. In other words, serious sin is qualified as "gross," "exceedingly grave," "great sin," and the like. If God just viewed any sin as being exactly equal in all ways, he would not need to qualify serious sins out of the 1083 times sin is addressed. Moreover, if sin is sin were absolute, there would not have been different penalties for the sin. If an Israelite was caught stealing an Ox, he would be required to return what he stole, plus extra. If he murdered, he would have received the death penalty, but if it were unintentional, he would have received manslaughter, being required to live out his life in a city of refuge.

It is true, to some degree, sin is sin, and any sin could justly make the guilty one worthy of sin's "wages" (i.e., death). Scriptures show that God views humankind's wrongdoing as varying degrees of seriousness. Thus, the men of Sodom were "were extremely wicked sinners (LEB)," and their 'sin was exceedingly grave." (Gen 13:13; 18:20; compare 2 Tim 3:6-7, NASB) The Israelites' making of a golden calf was also called "a great sin." (Ex 32:30-31, ESV) In addition, Jeroboam's calf worship similarly caused those of the northern kingdom "to sin with a great sin." (2 Ki 17:16, 21, LEB) Judah's sin became "like Sodom," making the kingdom of Judah abhorrent in God's eyes, as they "sinned grievously."—Isaiah 1:4, 10; 3:9; Lamentations. 1:8; 4:6.

James wants the people to understand that in the same way when they show favoritism then they are breaking the law of God. Though they may never have committed adultery or ever have committed murder, they still broke the command to love your neighbor as yourself. As a result, the person who practices the sin of favoritism is just as guilty before God as a murderer and adulterer. The man who plays favorites is in violation of God's law just the same as the murderer and adulterer and is no different from any other sinner. For this reason, if one breaks God's law by showing favoritism, then he is just as guilty of breaking all the other commandments.

So speak and so act as men who are to be judged by the law of liberty. (2:12)

James tells his readers that they need to **speak and act like men who are to be judged by the law of liberty**. We are told to speak and act, because it is with our words and our actions, that favoritism is shown. James wants his readers to understand that the very law of God, which they were breaking, was the very same law that was going to judge them when God judges them. These needed to understand, comprehend, and accept responsibility for their impartiality before they would ever make the needed changes to their Christian self. They needed to speak and act as Christ would expect them to do; i.e., setting aside favoritism and replacing it with loving kindness for all. They would be judged by God's law of liberty. If God's law was meant to set individuals free, then these believers were not to judge by their laws that restricted people with favoritism.

For judgment is without mercy to him who has shown no mercy. Mercy triumphs over judgment. (2:13)

James awakens his readers to just how dangerous a judgmental attitude is, as he shows them the peril in which they are placing themselves by showing favoritism. (Rom. 2:6, 16; 14:12; Matt. 12:36) Reasonably and logically, how could these believers expect that God would show them mercy when they were guilty of withholding mercy on those who were 'poor in filthy clothing'? (Jam. 2:2) What a conflict that contradicts all reason, for here is James writing to a group of Christians encompassing the lowly ones, as well as those who were discriminating against such ones! Can we imagine the emotional turmoil of a poor believer who was visiting another congregation and was treated as if he were inconsequential? Wise King Solomon was inspired to write,

"Whoever closes his ear to the cry of the poor will himself call out and not be answered." Jesus gave a convincing illustration that made just this point in Matthew 18:23-35. Jesus explicitly said,

Matthew 7:1-2 English Standard Version (ESV)

[1] "Judge not, that you be not judged. [2] For with the judgment you pronounce you will be judged, and with the measure you use it will be measured to you."

"Blessed are the merciful, for they shall receive mercy." (Matt. 5:7) Imagine a young man, who went on robbing the elderly. Now picture him mercilessly beating them first before taking their money, when they never posed any threat to him. If we were in a human courtroom with a judge of perfect justice, we would see him never hand out mercy to a defendant who failed to show mercy to his victims. However, we must keep in mind although our analogy helps us see the point; James is not talking about someone breaking the Mosaic Law or the law of any land. James is speaking about judging by "the law of liberty." A born-again Christian should possess a mind and heart of mercy by the Spirit of God, by his faith life, and thus would naturally show mercy to others. Because of his showing others mercy, he will be shown mercy by God when he is judged. For this reason, this merciful Christian, he does not live his life in fear of how God is going to view him in the end. He knows that God is the epitome of mercy and it will be reciprocated. We have an excellent example of this in Scripture, where God had shown mercy to King David, who had been merciful in his past dealings with others. – 2 Samuel 12:13, 14; 22:24-27; Psalm 18:23-26

Faith Without Works is Dead

James 2:14-20 Updated American Standard Version (UASV)

[14] What use is it, my brothers, if someone says he has faith but he has no works? Can that faith save him? [15] If a brother or sister is without clothes and lacks daily food, [16] and one of you says to them, "Go in peace, be warmed and be filled," and yet you do not give them what is necessary for their body, what good is that? [17] Even so faith, if it has no works, is dead in itself. [18] But someone will say, "You have faith and I have works." Show me your faith apart from your works, and I will show you my faith by my works. [19] You believe that God is one. You do well; the demons also believe, and shudder. [20] But do you want to know, O foolish man, that faith without works is useless?

What use is it, my brothers, if someone says he has faith but he has no works? Can that faith save him? (2:14)

James uses the term **what use is it, my brothers,** to ask a rhetorical question to highlight or emphasize his point. James asks **if someone says he has faith, but he has no works, can that faith save him?** Faith is an assurance and confidence in what is believed in based on the knowledge of that particular object. Faith is not blindly hoping for something or someone, but rather knowing and trusting with complete certainty. Rather faith is based on knowledge of something that can be known. It is putting faith **into** something or someone. The Christian faith it is not blind at all since it is in an all-powerful and holy God. Instead, Christianity is built upon the knowledge of God who is the creator of the universe and all of humanity itself.

The major issue here is in the fact that one is merely claiming to have faith. They are giving nothing more than a verbal affirmation to a belief that consists only of the framework of their mind, but has not yet affected the nature of their will and produced proper actions. James makes it clear that faith is not just some head knowledge alone, but true faith is manifested in the fact that it produces appropriate actions consistent with what one claims to profess. James here asks the question for his audience to ponder and think about to come to their conclusion as he states **can such faith save him**?

Faith does not just begin and end at a mere profession of Christ. Good works in one's life then must evidence it. These works are not done as a way to earn salvation, but rather out of gratitude of a heart that has been changed by the power of Christ that made one a new creation in Christ. Good works are to be done out of the overflow of the heart that has been redeemed by the power of God through Christ. The answer to James question, as he will explain in the following verses, is faith without works is not true saving faith.

If a brother or sister is without clothes and lacks daily food, and one of you says to them, "Go in peace, be warmed and be filled," and yet do not give them what is necessary for their body, what good is that? (2:15-16)

James has just got through asking the question as to whether or not faith that has no works is a saving faith or not. James now is going to give an example to answer his question as to whether saving faith is one that produces no good works. James gives them a hypothetical situation of **a**

brother or sister is without clothes and lacks daily food. It is clear that the individual is without clothing and daily food, in other words, the individual did not have the essentials of life. The Jews would have known from the Old Testament about the importance and the necessity of showing hospitality. It was written in Leviticus 19:9-10, "Now when you reap the harvest of your land, you shall not reap to the very corners of your field, nor shall you gather the gleanings of your harvest. Nor shall you glean your vineyard, nor shall you gather the fallen fruit of your vineyard; you shall leave them for the needy and for the stranger. I am the Lord your God." James does not describe how this brother or sister got into the condition in which they found themselves but merely gives the reality of the condition.

James unfolds the progression of the situation and says **one of you says to them, go in peace**. Now the problem with what is happening here is that the Christians who were saying **go in peace, be warmed, and filled**, were content with just lip service. The problem is that what they were saying to the individual needed to be supported by actions. True faith would not just have said go in peace, because how could this person honestly go in peace when they were daily worrying about how to keep warm and be fed. There would have been daily anxiety and fear of not knowing where the next meal would come from or how to keep warm. Real faith not only expresses kind wishes to the individual in need, but takes action to see those needs come true.

These believers saying be warmed were telling the individual to do something that they were unable to do on their own. This individual they were telling to keep warm would benefit nothing from their merely good wishes. Real faith would not just make good wishes to keep warm but seek the resources to help the individual to keep warm. The whole point in the person coming to these believers was to try to get warm, and mere lip service does nothing without being accompanied by actions that would have enabled the individual to be warm and fed.

One more time we see that simple words are meaningless in this situation, for how can one be filled, if he has no means by which to be filled. You will note that the word "be" is used twice in this passage when James says be warmed and be filled. The emphasis on the word is put on the one coming to them to be fed and clothed. This was suggesting that it was in power of the one who was hungry and needed clothes to be able to do these things. However, they cannot in their current situation because they have no means by which to do so. Here again, real saving faith in this context would seek to get the individual the food that they needed or try to get them filled in some way.

It is for this reason that James says **and yet do not give them what is necessary for their body, what good is that**? James has given his readers a compelling example. Kind words and best wishes ring hollow when they are not supplemented by physical aid when he is capable to help materially. In fact, this is ridiculously inadequate and does nothing but generate more heartache and pain for the one suffering. (See Proverbs 3:27-28) The result is, one with this so-called faith who does nothing to bring any kind of relief to those in need, nor at least moves others to demonstrate their faith, is worthless. Anyone, who says, "go in peace," while offering nothing to this destitute one, leaving the helping to others, would be known as one who has no love or kindness about him. In addition, this faithless one would bring reproach on God and Christianity. Those from outside of Christianity looking in, would ask themselves, "Who would want to be a part of such a religion?"

Even so faith, if it has no works, is dead in itself. (2:17)

James is now connecting his example of what he has just said on how it relates to faith. It is pointless to say peace and keep warm and well fed when one takes no action to help alleviate the situation. The fact that one does not act in accordance with his words, therefore, proves his words to be dead and false. To just claim to have faith but **has no works, is dead in itself**. The word that James uses for dead is *nekros* that means "*inactive, inoperative.*" (Vine 1996, 148) This believer's mere lip service to faith without the outward expression of faith through works is inactive. James is making it clear that without works, his faith is dormant and dead and, therefore, proves that he truly does not have faith. Jesus himself said that many would be judged for the supposed claim of faith without works on judgment day with the parable of the sheep and the goats. – Matthew 25:31-46.

But someone will say, "You have faith and I have works. Show me your faith apart from your works, and I will show you my faith by my works. " (2:18a)

James now is going to deal with a statement that he foresees being raised because he said faith without works is dead. James makes the statement, **will say you have faith, and I have works**. Some may claim that they do not need any faith to do good works. This was the issue with the Pharisees of Jesus' day: it was all about knowing the law of God and interpreting it, but they never applied it to their lives. In fact, Jesus said to them in John 5:39-40, "You search the scriptures because you think that in them you have eternal life; and it is these that witness of me, and you are unwilling to come to me, that you may have life."

James twice uses the word show, signifying the fact that the only way true faith is authenticated is by works. James says **show me your faith apart from your works**, in other words, faith without works is impossible because faith is only known through works. Faith is not divided separately between works and faith, but rather they are inseparably linked together. James asks the reader here to show them faith without works because he knows that it is impossible to do. Anybody could claim that he believes in God and yet have a wicked and evil heart and still be able to affirm verbally that he loves God. That is as far as it goes with just a verbal affirmation that produces no evidence of faith being true although they can deceive themselves into thinking they do have faith. It is for this reason that James says **I will show you my faith by my works** because works are the only way to evidence the authentication of faith. Good works cannot save you; one does good works because it is an evident demonstration of who he is, a truly born-again Christian, with a genuine faith.

You believe that God is one. You do well; the demons also believe, and shudder. (2:19)

James here exposes the reality that having no works is, in fact, a pseudo-faith. James is going to compare the so-called believer, who allegedly has faith as he is without works to nothing more than the faith of a demon. This would have been a strike at the heart of those, who would have been reading his letter, comparing their faith without works to that of a demon. James says **you believe that God is one.** James then tells these believers if they believe that God is one, then the **do well**. However, James is going to make it clear that just merely to believe that God is one is not enough if good works do not accompany it because **demons also believe and shudder.**

Demons are Satan's fallen angels who serve as his agents against humanity to seduce, tempt, and destroy mankind. James tells his audience how the demons are just like them concerning their belief in God in the fact that the demons just like them, believe that God is one. Every Jew in the days of James would have had the word of Moses as recorded in Deuteronomy 6:4-5 embedded in their hearts. This passage was referred to as the Grand Shema and would have been quoted on a daily basis through prayer and petitions by all Jews living in the days of James. It reads in Deuteronomy 6:4-6 "Hear, O Israel! Jehovah, our God, is one Jehovah! You shall love Jehovah your God with all your heart, with all your soul, and with all your might. These words, which I am commanding you today, shall be on your heart." This was perhaps the essence of all the spiritual life of every Jew to love God, who had chosen them as his people. He was to be praised and honored in this way because he was the one and only true God, the Creator of heaven and earth and all humanity.

James states that the demons also believe that God is one and is no different from any believer that claims the same thing. However, what the demons lack is actionable evidence that there is something beyond their belief, i.e. a genuine faith. We know from several other parts of scriptures that the demons know and believe in God. In fact, they knew that Jesus Christ himself was the Son of the highest God. The demons clearly evidence their understanding of who Jesus is in the Gospels. – Mark 5:6-7; Mark 1:23-24; Luke 4:40-41.

It is interesting to note that here in his passage James uses the word shudder, which is the only time that this word is used in the entire New Testament. James is making it clear that not only do the demons believe in God, but also it causes a great disturbance and fear among them because they know his power and authority that he has over them. The problem with the demons is that their belief in God consists of just an awareness of his existence and his great power, never drawing close to him. They shudder out of fear because of the authority that they know God has over them, but that is as far as it goes for them. Even though they know God's great power, they continue to serve Satan.

But do you want to know, O foolish man, that faith without works is useless? (2:20)

The man spoken of here in verse 20 of chapter 2 applies to any Christian, male or female. This man has not taken in "the knowledge of God" by way of his Word. (Jam. 1:18, 21) Both his mind and heart are empty because no genuine faith exists there. The demons even fared better than this man did because the "faith" or belief that they possess at least generated the emotion of fear, which caused them to shudder, tremble uncontrollably at the thought of God's great power and authority. However, those demons and Christians such as this man, lack genuine faith that would move them toward salvation, it was categorically having no action, i.e., unproductive.

James 2:21-26 Updated American Standard Version (UASV)

21 Was not Abraham our father justified by works when he offered up Isaac his son on the altar? **22** You see that faith was working together with his works, and by the works the faith was perfected;[41] **23** and the Scripture was fulfilled that says, "Abraham believed God, and it was counted to him as righteousness,"[42] and he was called a friend of God. **24** You see that a man is justified by works and not by faith alone. **25** And in the same way was not also Rahab the prostitute justified by works when she received the messengers and sent them out by another way? **26** For as the body apart from the spirit[43] is dead, so also faith apart from works is dead.

Was not Abraham our father (2:21a)

James here now does something very significant to argue his point about faith and works by stating **was not Abraham, our father**. James makes his argument from the Old Testament scriptures using Abraham, who the Jews considered the father of their nation and perhaps the most respected man in all Old Testament history. The Jews took pride in their ancestry and could trace their lineage back to Abraham as the Father of the Jewish nation, which is why James says "Abraham, our father." The Jewish nation of Israel was God's chosen people, and that nation stemmed from the seed of Abraham, which God promised would happen.

The Jews highly esteemed their ethnicity and the father of their nation because they were God's chosen that came through the lineage of Abraham. For this reason, the Jews looked at Abraham as the most prominent figure in their history, since he was the father of their nation. It is because of this that James would select Abraham to make his point that faith and works must exist together for it to be true saving faith. James purposely used one of the most significant men in Jewish history to make his point. This way, the Jewish audience he was writing to would be more apt to listen and take heed to what he was saying.

---

[41] Or *completed*

[42] Quoted from Gen. 15:6

[43] Or *breath*

justified by works when he offered up Isaac his son on the altar? (2:21b)

Here James says that Abraham our father was **justified by works**. However, Paul wrote, "For by works of the law no human being will be justified." (Rom 3:20) How is it that these two were not contradicting one another? In Romans 4:2-3 Paul writes, "For if Abraham was justified by works, he has something to boast about, but not before God. For what does the Scripture say? 'Abraham believed God, and it was counted to him as righteousness.'" Paul is here quoting that same exact verse from Genesis 15:6 that James refers to in verse 23 of chapter 2. This verse that both are using was about Abraham's faith some 35 years before he ever attempted to offer up his son Isaac. This is the same event that James is referring to here in verse 21 of chapter 22. Thus, how are these two inspired New Testament authors in harmony?

If we look at the context of Genesis 15:1-6, we find that Abraham was declared righteous because of his trust in God's promise to make his offspring number like the stars of the heaven, even though Sarah was decades past being able to have a child. Therefore, how is it that James can say that Abraham was justified by works? Abraham's actions confirmed what God already knew was true of him. By Abraham's action, he proved, confirmed, demonstrated, beyond question that his faith in God for decades had been and was still real, i.e. genuine. Abraham evidenced that he had a living faith, not a dead one. It was not Abraham's works in and of themselves that made Abraham righteous, but rather his works were a result of his genuine faith, which God confirmed by declaring him righteous by way of this pronouncement or verdict.[44]

You see that faith was working together with his works, and by the works the faith was perfected; (2:22)

James is calling his believers attention to Abraham's faith stating **you see that faith was working together with his works.** Abraham's faith was authenticated not because he believed intellectually but was authenticated in the fact that he was willing to follow through with the

---

[44] Was God tempting or testing Abraham? Andrews writes, "God does **not** tempt us, but he does allow us to go through temptations. As we know from Abraham, God can test us, but never tempt us with sin ... The Greek word (*Peirazo*) can be rendered either as 'tempted' or 'tested,' and it is the context that determines which word should be chosen. In the case of Satan with Jesus in the wilderness, it should be rendered 'tempt.' However, in reference to God, in some very limited cases in history, he has put some to the test, i.e., Abraham, even his Son."–Hebrews 2:18.

act of sacrificing his son. It for this reason that James says **by the works the faith was perfected**. God told Abraham to sacrifice his son, and yet it was the very son, which God promised would bring him his descendants. Therefore, if Abraham was to offer up his son then how could he bring about descendants if he was dead?

Abraham would not have been sure how this would happen either, but he truly trusted God enough to follow through with the act of killing his son. Abraham believed that God would somehow allow descendants to come despite whether or not he sacrificed his son, and he was willing to trust God at all costs. Abraham's act of attempting to offer up his son authenticated his faith in God, which was evidenced by his actions of obedience. The word for perfection means complete or finished. Abraham's faith was complete in the fact that works, which made his trust in God complete by his actions of obedience, accompanied his faith. [45]

and the scripture was fulfilled that says, "Abraham believed God, and it was counted to him as righteousness," and he was called a friend of God. You see that a man is justified by works and not by faith alone. (2:23-24)

James says, **and the scripture was fulfilled that says Abraham believed God and it was counted to him as righteousness.** Here James is referring to Genesis 15:6 about Abraham. In Genesis 15:4, God had told Abraham that he would provide an heir and many descendants from his seed. Then in Genesis 15:5, to confirm his promise, God asked Abraham to go out and count the stars. In the same way, the stars were too numerous to count so would Abraham's descendants be through the promised child. Despite being old and against all odds, it says in Genesis 15:6, "Then he believed in the Lord, and He reckoned it to him as righteousness." Abraham had not seen his son and the child was not even conceived in the womb at this point. However, Abraham still believed God would carry out his promises. Since Abraham believed, what God said was firm and trustworthy, he was willing to kill his son, and as a

---

[45] An analogous situation might be a wealthy father testing his daughter's fiancé. The father offers the fiancé $50,000 to leave his daughter. This test will tell the father whether the poor fiancé is in love with his daughter, or after the father's money. Keep in mind, God never intended for Abraham to offer his son up, as he foreknew what Abraham would do in such a situation decades before even. Let us adapt apologist William Lane Craig's words to this situation. 'God had morally sufficient reasons for permitting the test, which he placed on Abraham.'

67

result be declared righteous in God's sight. The word righteousness here, as stated before, carries with it the idea of being right, moral, and just.

Abraham not only believed in God but was also willing to put that into practice by killing his son; he was declared right in God's sight. God declared him right in the fact that Abraham acted upon his faith through his actions. As a result, he was also called **a friend of God**, which is the only time in the Bible where someone is called a friend of God. Abraham was first called a friend of God in Jehoshaphat's prayer in 2 Chronicles 20:7, "Did you not, O our God, drive out the inhabitants of this land before thy people Israel and give it to the descendants of Abraham thy friend forever?" Isaiah also makes mention of Abraham as a friend of God in Isaiah 41:8, "But you Israel, My servant, Jacob whom I have chosen, descendant of Abraham my friend."

Abraham's belief and actions were working together in a real, genuine faith and Abraham became a friend of God. James reaffirms the argument that he has been making by saying you see. James wants his readers to have a focused view of what he has been talking about in regards to faith and action. He has just offered Abraham as his example that faith is justified when accompanied by works. As a result, these Jews would have a hard time arguing against their forefather. Faith and works must go together, they are inseparably linked, and we cannot have one without the other. For this reason, as James says **a man is justified by works and not by faith alone**.

And in the same way was not also Rahab the prostitute justified by works when she received the messengers and sent them out by another way? (2:25)

In the same manner that Abraham's faith was evidenced by his actions, **was not also Rahab the prostitute justified by works**. The story of Rahab is found in the Old Testament book of Joshua chapter 2, shortly after Moses died, and Joshua took over in leading the nation of Israel. It would be Joshua, who would guide the nation of Israel into the promised land of Canaan. However, to get there many obstacles would be in their way and that through the power of God they would have to overcome. One of these major obstacles would be conquering the city of Jericho.

The problem is that Jericho had very thick and high walls that surrounded their city, and it was nearly impossible to penetrate. Joshua summoned two men who were to go and spy out the city and come to report to Joshua what they had seen and learned. When the spies got into the city, they went to the home of a prostitute whose name was Rahab. The king of the town somehow caught wind that the spies had come into town and were at Rahab's home, and he sent to have them killed. Rahab knew that the king wanted to kill the spies and so decided to hide them on the roof of her home under stalks of flax. The king's officials arrived at the house, but Rahab told them that the spies had already left. The king's officials went off trying to find the direction of the men to kill them.

When the king's officials had left, Rahab asked a favor of the spies found in Joshua 2:8-14, "Now therefore, please swear to me by the Lord, since I have dealt kindly with you, that you also will deal kindly with my father's household, and give me a pledge of truth, and spare my father and my mother and my brothers and my sisters, with all who belong to them, and deliver our lives from death." Therefore, the men said to her, "Our life for yours if you do not tell this business of ours; and it shall come about when the Lord gives us the land that we will deal kindly and faithfully with you."

The spies told Rahab that they would indeed spare her life if she tied a scarlet cord in her window. The scarlet cord was what Rahab used to let the spies down out of the city to spare their lives. Rahab could have just told the spies to get out of her house and never have let them in. Because she feared God and believed in the God of the spies, she took the risk of letting the men stay in her home. Rahab's belief in God was authenticated in that **she received the messengers and sent them out by another way**. It would be a direct result of the action of Rahab saving the spies that would help in giving Joshua the victory over the city of Jericho.

For the body apart from the spirit is dead, so also faith apart from works is dead. (2:26)

When a person (a soul) dies (beyond clinical death), there is no longer any animating force or "spirit" within any single cell out of the body's one hundred trillion cells. Many of us have seen the animation video in science classes at school, where the cell is shown to be like a microscopic factory with an enormous amount of work taking place. Therefore, no work is taking place within the lifeless body, as all of the cells that were animated by the spirit are dead. The body is not good for anything. This is the similarity that James is trying to draw as a faith that lacks works is just as lifeless, producing no results and of no use as a corpse. The literal eye cannot see faith; however, works is an evident demonstration that faith can be seen. When one has is not moved to good works, it is all too clear that this one has no real faith. Alternatively, any Christian that is motivated to good works possesses a genuine faith.

Review Question

(1) **[vs 1]** How is it that James could call his readers "brothers" when they were exhibiting some incorrect attitudes?

(2) **[vs 1]** Why is it a noteworthy sin to show favoritism?

(3) **[vs 2]** Who was the man that James was speaking of here?

(4) **[vs 2]** Who was the poor man?

(5) **[vs 3]** How was the congregation treating this poor man?

(6) **[vs 4]** What serious failings did James' readers have in their faith?

(7) **[vs 5]** Does God select people simply because they are poor?

(8) **[vs 6]** Are we to assume from verse 6 that the poor never oppose Christians?

(9) **[vs 7]** What is blasphemy and how were the rich oppressors blaspheming the honorable name by which they had been called?

(10) **[vs 8]** Why is it that we can say the law at Leviticus 19:18 is the "royal law"?

(11) **[vs 9]** How does the "royal law" admonish the person showing favoritism as a transgressor?

(12) **[vs 10]** How is it that if one keeps the whole law and yet stumbles in one point, he has become guilty of all?

(13) **[vs 11]** Why might James have chosen to cite the laws on adultery and murder here?

(14) **[vs 12]** Does the law of liberty give us the freedom to act according to our own desires, i.e., absolute freedom?

(15) **[vs 13]** How does mercy triumph over judgment?

(16) **[vs 14]** Do the faith/works that Paul was talking about contradict the faith/works that James discusses? How did Jesus touch on faith and works?

(17) **[vs 15-16]** What point is James making here in verses 15-16?

(18) **[vs 17]** Why is faith, if it has no works, dead in itself?

(19) **[vs 18]** How can we know that a person has genuine faith?

(20) **[vs 19]** Why do the demons believe and shudder over belief in God and how should that impact us?

(21) **[vs 20]** Why are we foolish if we **do not** believe that faith without works is useless?

(22) **[vs 21]** What does Paul say about Abraham being declared righteous?

(23) **[vs 22]** How was faith working together with Abraham's works? How did the works of Abraham perfect his faith?

(24) **[vs 23]** How do we know that Abraham had faith in God all along? How did Abraham become God's friend?

(25) **[vs 24]** Why is it that a man is justified by works and not by faith alone?

(26) **[vs 25]** How does the account about Rahab add to the conversation of faith and works?

(27) **[vs 26]** Why is a dead body a good analogy of faith without works? How do the works of Christians evidence that they have a genuine faith?

JAMES CHAPTER 3 Controlling the Tongue

Taming the Tongue

James 3:1 Updated American Standard Version (UASV)

¹Not many of you should become teachers, my brothers, knowing that we shall receive heavier judgment.

Not many of you should become teachers, my brothers, knowing that we shall receive heavier judgment. (3:1)

The Scriptures show that within the first-century congregation, Christians possessed different abilities, callings, and services. Some became capable teachers, serving remarkably in that capacity. (See Rom. 12:3-8; 1 Cor. 12:4-11, 29) Right after Pentecost 33 C.E., the twelve apostles were the teachers, who got Christianity underway in the beginning, bringing thousands into the Way. (Acts 2:42; 6:2-4) Paul tells us that after Jesus' ascension "he gave gifts to men." (Eph. 4:8) Jesus gave them the apostles, the prophets (Gr., *prophetes* primarily means explainer of God's Word and secondary foreteller of events),[46] the evangelists, the shepherds, and teachers. (Eph. 4:11-16) At Acts 13:1, we read, "there were in the church at Antioch prophets (explained God's Word and foretold events) and teachers (gave instruction in the Scriptures and in Christian living)." Because all overseers were teachers within the congregation, clearly these "teachers" were especially proficient and active in this service to God. (See Ac 15:35; 1 Tim. 4:13-16) The apostle Paul appointed three responsibilities: "preacher and apostle and teacher." – 2 Timothy 1:11; 1 Timothy 2:7.

What we will be learning from James below is that teachers carry a heavier responsibility, as they are imperfect and prone to stumble in word. Herein lies the danger, as some sincerely sought to be teachers but was not qualified to teach. When a congregation receives an unqualified teacher, it can dramatically affect the spirituality of the congregation. Then, there were those, who sought to be a teacher because of self-importance and a desire for success. They pushed their way into the

---

[46] After the completion of the entire Bible in 98 C.E., and the death of the last apostle, John, in 100 C.E., there was no longer a prophet in the *sense* of foretelling events, because the Bible was and is complete, all we need to get to the second coming of Christ. A prophet thereafter was and is an explainer of God's Word.

position of overseer because they were attempting to achieve power and importance as teachers. Paul writes,

1 Timothy 6:3-4 English Standard Version (ESV)

³ If anyone teaches a different doctrine and does not agree with the sound words of our Lord Jesus Christ and the teaching that accords with godliness, ⁴ he is puffed up with conceit and understands nothing. He has an unhealthy craving for controversy and for quarrels about words, which produce envy, dissension, slander, evil suspicions,

This seeking power and position would be very attractive to "the twelve tribes in the Dispersion." These were Jewish people scattered throughout Gentile lands, to which James wrote. (Jam. 1:1) In that ancient world, the Jewish people held teachers in high esteem, like that of a high governmental official would have been held. Within Judaism, the title "Rabbi," which meant "teacher" was a highly respected and even feared position. (John 1:38; John 3:2) The Jewish Rabbis sought fame, adoration and preferential treatment, for which Jesus resoundingly condemned them. (Matt. 23:6-7) For this reason, Jesus cautioned his disciples against wrongly motivated desire for preeminence. In fact, he warned them, "you are not to be called rabbi, for you have one teacher, and you are all brothers ... Neither be called instructors, for you have one instructor, the Christ. The greatest among you shall be your servant. Whoever exalts himself will be humbled, and whoever humbles himself will be exalted." – Matthew 23:8-12; compare Luke 22:25226.

The reason for James' counsel can be seen through the advice Paul gave to Timothy, who was assigned to appointing overseers. Paul warned him about false teachers,

1 Timothy 1:3-4 English Standard Version (ESV)

³ As I urged you when I was going to Macedonia, remain at Ephesus so that you may charge certain persons not to teach any different doctrine, ⁴ nor to devote themselves to myths and endless genealogies, which promote speculations rather than the stewardship from God that is by faith.

Paul went on to say,

1 Timothy 1:5-7 English Standard Version (ESV)

⁵ The aim of our charge is love that issues from a pure heart and a good conscience and a sincere faith. ⁶ Certain persons, by swerving from these, have wandered away into vain discussion, ⁷ desiring to be teachers

of the law, without understanding either what they are saying or the things about which they make confident assertions.

The "teachers of the law" that Paul spoke of were extremely rigid, unbending, and apparently impressed those who listened to them, by way of their belief in their own abilities and doggedness. However, if scrutinized by an accurate knowledge of God's Word (Ac 17:11; Col. 1:9-10), these teachers were nothing but pretenders with their deception, i.e., false teachers. – Acts 15:1; 2 Corinthians 11:5, 12, 13; 2 Timothy 4:1-4.

Because of this heavy responsibility, therefore, anyone who desire to be overseer or deacon within the congregation, he should pause to contemplate his motives, while he also takes an honest look at his qualifications. (Rom. 12:3, 16) He needs to possess more than mere head knowledge, even though knowledge is a crucial part. Also, mere charismatic ability in communication does not alone make a good teacher, but rather spiritual maturity and a love of God and neighbor are the most important factors. (Matt. 22:37-40; 1 Cor. 13:1-2, 4; 14:6, 26) One major indicator that this is his calling is not that he notices that he has a knack as a teacher, speaker, communicator, but others without prompting continue to tell him such things. – 2 Corinthians 10:12, 18; compare Proverbs 25:27; 27:2.

James 3:2-4 Updated American Standard Version (UASV)

[21]For we all stumble[47] in many ways. If anyone does not stumble in what he says,[48] he is a perfect man, able also to bridle his whole body. [3] Now if we put bits into the mouths of horses so that they obey us, we also guide their whole bodies. [4] Look at the ships also, though they are so great and are driven by strong winds, are still directed by a very small rudder wherever the inclination of the pilot wills.

For we all stumble in many ways. If anyone does not stumble in what he says, he is a perfect man, able also to bridle his whole body. (3:2)

James does not exclude himself from the rest of the Christian congregation, as all are prone to stumble while walking with God. James presents an obvious truth in that **we all stumble in many ways**. The fact we all stumble in many ways is confirmed in Romans 2:23, "for all

---

[47] Or "make mistakes."

[48] Lit., "word"

have sinned and fall short of the glory of God." Because of human imperfection, weakness and leanings toward bad, all, including *teachers*, fall short or miss the mark of perfection. (Rom. 7:19-23; 1 John 1:8) In all likelihood, aside from thinking, what we say is the most frequent way we fall short, and the one way that will damage our relationship with God and our fellow humans. It is for this reason that teachers in the congregation and all Christians should be very cautious about the biblical truths that they share. Kurt A. Richardson makes this remark,

> The standard for teachers disallows their failing in the matter of speech, and yet human nature is prone to violation of God's standards. James added this confession for a dual effect: knowing that James himself stumbled in many ways puts the admonition to pursue perfection into perspective; because believers stumble in many ways, their teachers need to be particularly circumspect about their conduct, above all in the way they speak. (Richardson 1997, 148)

Even the best imperfect Christian teacher, the apostle Paul did not fail to stumble in word. (Ac 15:37-41) This should wake us up to the reality of the damage that we are capable of, even if we are quite competent and qualified. Stumbling in word will cause damage within the congregation. If the teacher has erred greatly, this will mean more severe the damage to his fellow brothers and sisters.

James informs his readers that only a perfect man can keep his words under complete control, never erring. If he can prevent himself from uttering wrong understandings, outlooks, feelings, and desires, then such a man has complete, perfect control over himself. At present, all of humankind is imperfect, so any who would claim they can go without erring in speech is a liar, "for we all stumble in many ways," including with our words. The only man, who had complete, perfect control over himself, was Jesus Christ. (Heb. 7:26) However, we do not want to take on a fatalist attitude, saying, 'well, we cannot get the tongue under control, and God is every forgiving, so why worry about it.' No, Christians cannot have complete control, but they can strive to get as close to the goal as possible. Over time, they will make continued improvements as they grow spiritually.

We know that even having significant control is never going to be accomplished in our own strength, and as an evangelist of the good news, the option of remaining silent is on the table. We must apply the Spirit inspired Word of God in an accurate and balanced manner. We must have our minds molded by "whatever is true, whatever is honorable, whatever is just, whatever is pure, whatever is lovely, whatever is commendable, if there is any excellence, if there is anything worthy of praise, think about these things." (Phil. 4:8) Richard L., Pratt Jr. writes, "As Paul traveled the world proclaiming the gospel of Christ, he encountered pretentious disbelief supported by clever arguments and powerful personalities. But through the "weakness" of preaching Christ, Paul went about taking **captive every thought to make it obedient to Christ**." (Pratt Jr 2000, 2 Cor. 10:5, 417) Jesus said, "The good person out of the good treasure of his heart produces good, and the evil person out of his evil treasure produces evil, for out of the abundance of the heart his mouth speaks." – Luke 6:45.

There is little doubt in an entire human life that it will be his tongue, which will cause him the most grief. If that man could bridle his tongue, he would also be able to control his whole body.

Now if we put bits into the mouths of horses so that they obey us, we also guide their whole bodies. (3:3)

Here James offers his readers an example or comparison that helps to clarify or explain that the gift to control the tongue is connected to the ability to achieve with difficulty, control of the entire body. With a set of leather straps fitted to a horse's head, incorporating the bit in the mouth of the horse, and the reins, even a young child can control these powerful animals. Even a higher spirited horse can be controlled with a bridle. In fact, within the English language, we have the idiom of "reining someone or something in," which means, "any means of guiding, controlling, or restraining somebody or something." Of course, with such a powerful creature, it requires a firm grip on the reins that are attached to the bridle. In the same way, Christians can control their body, even with our leanings toward sin, if they can control the tongue. Within the boundaries of imperfection this will require an accurate understanding of God's Word, being applied in a balanced manner within our lives.

Look at the ships also, though they are so great and are driven by strong winds, are still directed by a very small rudder wherever the inclination of the pilot wills. (3:4)

Look at the ships also; here James uses the second example to further explain his connecting the tongue with its need to be **controlled.** James illustrates by using another massive object, a ship. Ships in the days of James could be enormous, well over 100ft long. The ship that Paul would have taken in Acts 27:37 was big enough that it could have seated nearly 300 passengers. The fact that these vessels were big and powerful meant that it would also take a powerful wind to carry them along in the sea.

This example helps to emphasize the same point, but with something even greater in size. A ship is massive when we consider its steering mechanism, the rudder. Just was the case within the Mosaic Law, having a matter be established with two witnesses, James develops his point with two illustrations. One can control his entire body if he could perfectly control his tongue. (2 Cor. 13:1; Deut. 17:6) A ship of even the most tremendous size is at the mercy of high winds and waves while at sea. Nevertheless, it is the tiny rudder under the control of a man, which will determine whether the ship stays on course. Thus, this same rudder, within the stable grip of the human hands, exercises control over the colossal ship. Even though mighty forces of sea and wind affect the ship, the somewhat small rudder will counterbalance these tremendous forces.

James 3:5-6 Updated American Standard Version (UASV)

5 So also the tongue is a small member, yet it boasts of great things. See how great a forest is set ablaze by such a small fire! **6** And the tongue is a fire, the world of iniquity;[49] the tongue is set among our members as that which defiles the entire body, and sets on fire the course of our life,[50] and is set on fire by Gehenna.[51]

So also the tongue is a small member, yet it boasts of great things. (3:5a)

After giving two examples of powerful objects that can be controlled by small objects, James brings it back around now to show how the horse and the ship can be compared to the tongue. When James talks about the horse and the ships, he starts by talking about their power and then mentions how they are controlled by something small like a bit and a rudder. By James writing **so also the tongue is a small member,** he

---

[49] Or "unrighteousness"

[50] Lit., "the wheel of birth (existence, origin)."

[51] geenna 12x pr. the valley of Hinnom, south of Jerusalem, once celebrated for the horrid worship of Moloch, and afterwards polluted with every species of filth, as well as the carcasses of animals, and dead bodies of malefactors; to consume which, in order to avert the pestilence which such a mass of corruption would occasion, constant fires were kept burning – MCEDONTW

begins with how small it is first and then deals with the power of the tongue secondly. He argues from the lesser to the greater when dealing with the tongue. James says the tongue is a small organ of the body, and though the tongue is small it can be most powerful when it is used.

We must make clear that the tongue is a gift from God and can be used aright to accomplish great things, like the great commission of proclaiming God's Word, teaching, and making disciples. (Matt 28:19-20) "Death and life are in the power of the tongue, and those who love it will eat its fruits." (Prov. 18:21) In other words, the tongue has the power to help or heal. If we are to safeguard our life, the tongue must be kept under control. "With patience a ruler may be persuaded, and a soft tongue will break a bone." (Prov. 25:15) Endurance, tolerance, persistence and mildness, though not easy to show when living in an unjust world, can soften even the most hardest of hearts, who is in opposition to us, like the strong construction of bones. However, when the tongue is not kept under control, it can do much damage, to oneself and to others. (Prov. 10:14; 17:4, 20; 21:6) James highlights that of all the ways the tongue can be used, it prominently loves more than others to **boasts of great things**. How often prides shows through by the words that one speaks of their great boasting. By nature, the heart of man is proud and expresses itself through the tongue and its boastful claims.

See how great a forest is set ablaze by such a small fire! (3:5b)

James continues with his description of the tongue and tells his audience to **see how great a forest is set ablaze by such a small fire**. Often when there are uncontrolled wildfires, they are often started by just a little spark or small fire that was not contained. In the same way, James says the tongue though it is small can cause great devastation with the words that come out of it. It is through the tongue that children are destroyed by parent's hurtful words and relationships broken because hateful things are spoken and can cause great destruction in the lives of others, and in one's own personal life.

And the tongue is a fire, the world of iniquity; the tongue is set among our members as that which defiles the entire body, and sets on fire the course of our life, and is set on fire by Gehenna. (3:6)

James now makes a comparison of a forest being set aflame by a small fire stating **the tongue is a fire**. James adds that **the world of iniquity among our members as that, which defiles the entire body, is** quicker than any other part of the body. The tongue can actually set one's life on fire in the way that it is used and that it can destroy families, marriages, children, and friendships. The tongue can destroy everything and everyone around if, not controlled. James also describes the tongue as being full of iniquity, and it can bring about a lot of sin and havoc into one's life and the life of others. The tongue is full of evil through gossip, slander, lies, and manipulations. Solomon wrote in Proverbs 16:27 "A worthless man digs up evil, while his words are like scorching fire." He also wrote in Proverbs 26:20-21 "For lack of wood the fire goes out, and where there is no whisperer, contention quiets down. *Like* charcoal to hot embers and wood to fire, so is a contentious man to kindle strife."

In the original Greek, the expression "the course of our life" is, literally, "the wheel of birth."[52] The unbridled tongue can set afire the entire course of our lives, making the cycle of life a brutal circle, even to the point of ending in destruction as if by fire. (Eccl. 10:12, 13) It can also affect our neighbor as Proverbs 11:9 informs us, "With his mouth the godless man would destroy his neighbor, but by knowledge the righteous are delivered." If one uses his tongue wrongly throughout the course of his life, he gives off destructiveness and may do much harm to those who encounter him. (Prov. 16:28; 6:12) In some cases, one person with an uncontrollable tongue has defiled an entire Christian congregation, or even an entire denomination. (Heb. 12:15; Gal. 5:9; compare Ecclesiastes 9:18) What about Gehenna, how are we to understand it? Christian Publishing House writes,

> Gehenna Hebrew Ge' Hinnom, literally, valley of Hinnom appears 12 times in the Greek New Testament books, and many translators render it by the word "hell." Most translations have chosen poorly not to use a transliteration, Gehenna or Geenna, as opposed to the English hell, ASV, AT, RSV, ESV, LEB, HCSB, and NASB. There is little doubt that the New Testament writers and Jesus used "Gehenna" to speak of the place of final punishment. What was Gehenna?
>
> According to the *Holman Illustrated Bible Dictionary* (p. 632), Gehenna or the Valley of Hinnom was "the valley south

---

[52] Or *the cycle of life*

of Jerusalem now called the Wadi er-Rababi (Josh. 15:8; 18:16; 2 Chron. 33:6; Jer. 32:35) became the place of child sacrifice to foreign gods. The Jews later used the valley for the dumping of refuse, the dead bodies of animals, and executed criminals."[53] We would disagree with the other comments by the Holman Illustrated Dictionary, "The continuing fires in the valley (to consume the refuse and dead bodies) apparently led the people to transfer the name to the place where the wicked dead suffer." This just is not the case.

In the Old Testament, the Israelites did burn sons in the fires as part of a sacrifice to false gods, but not for the purpose of punishment, or torture. By the time of the New Testament period, hundreds of years later, the only thing thrown in Gehenna was trash and the dead bodies of executed criminals. For what purpose were these thrown into Gehenna? It was used as an incinerator, a furnace for destroying things by burning them. Notice that any bodies thrown in Gehenna during the New Testament period were already dead. Thus, if anything, these people saw Gehenna as a place where they destroyed their trash and the bodies of dead criminals. Thus, if Jesus used this to illustrate as the place of the wicked, it would have represented destruction as the punishment.

Gehenna was a garbage dump that was used as an incinerator, to destroy whatever was thrown in, and only bodies of criminals were thrown in after they were already dead. In other words, the fire was used as a symbol, not of torment, but rather of being destroyed, complete destruction, namely annihilation by fire.

James 3:7-8 Updated American Standard Version (UASV)

⁷ For every kind[54] of beast and bird, of reptile and sea creature, can be tamed and has been tamed by mankind. ⁸ But no man can tame the tongue; it is a restless evil full of deadly poison.

For every kind of beast and bird, of reptile and sea creature, can be tamed and has been tamed by mankind. (3:7)

---

[53] http://biblia.com/books/hlmnillbbldict/Page.p_632

[54] Lit., "*nature*"

James makes a useful contrast, showing just how dangerous the tongue can be. James says **every kind of beast and bird, of reptile and sea creature, can be tamed**. The tiger is a powerful beast that is fierce, yet man can tame this savage beast. Elephants weigh more than a ton and can crush anything in its path and yet man can tame these large creatures. Falcons, hawks and even eagles in hunting can be trained. Parrots from the tropical forest can be taught by men to repeat every word that comes out of their mouths and cobras can be put into trances through the playing of a flute. Although there are many wild beasts and animals that can be tamed, that is not the central point that James is conveying. The reality that James is making in regards to these beasts and birds is that they have **been tamed by mankind**. However, man has something more dangerous than wild animals that he often cannot control and that is his tongue. The tongue can cause much more danger and destruction than any wild beast that man can tame.

But no man can tame the tongue; it is a restless evil full of deadly poison. (3:8)

Although man can tame all kinds of wild beasts that are fearful and dangerous, **no man can tame the tongue.** James describes the danger of the tongue in two distinct ways. James says that the tongue **is a restless evil**. Restless means that the evil that the tongue can bring out is an always-present continuing problem that must be kept in check, with us knowing that it is always poised to strike. Restlessness implies that something cannot remain still, but must always be doing something. This is what the uncontrolled tongue does in that it is always restless wanting to spread another lie, to gossip, or to slander. The tongue often seems never to have its fill of gossip, slander, malice, lies and accusations. It is a restless force that one must exert self-control over the body that nobody else can bring under control apart from the individual himself. James also describes the tongue as being **full of deadly poison**. Poison is meant to kill and cause harm to its victim. The tongue is full of poison in the fact that so often it is used as a means to destroy one's character, ego, hopes, and self-esteem. David wrote this of his enemies in Psalms 140:3 "They sharpen their tongues as a serpent; poison of a viper is under their lips."

James 3:9-12 Updated American Standard Version (UASV)

⁹ With it we bless our Lord[55] and Father, and with it we curse men who are made in the likeness of God. ¹⁰ from the same mouth come both blessing and cursing. My brothers, these things ought not to be so. ¹¹ Does a fountain send forth from the same opening both sweet water and bitter? ¹² Can a fig tree, my brothers, produce olives, or a vine produce figs? Neither can salt water produce fresh water.

With it we bless our Lord and Father, and with it we curse men who are made in the likeness of God. (3:9)

Every human that has ever lived owes his or her existence to God, the Almighty Creator. This is why we start our prayers with "Father." In fact, the Model prayer that Jesus gave us starts with, Our Father in heaven, "hallowed be your name." (Matt 6:9-13) and even the Son of God speaks of him as his Father. Jesus says, "The Father loves the Son and has given all things into his hand." (John 3:35) Therefore, Paul could say in his evangelism, to those who studied Greek philosophy, "[God] himself gives to all mankind life and breath and everything. And he made from one man every nation of mankind … 'In him we live and move and have our being' … 'For we are indeed his offspring.'"[56] (Acts 17:22, 25-29) However, in a spiritual sense, he was the father of faithful patriarchs (Abraham, Isaac, Jacob), followed by the nation of Israel, and finally is now the father only of the true Christian congregation. The true Christian congregation seeks to imitate their heavenly Father and his Son, by being a part of the world, but not using it to the full, while developing their qualities.[57]

The counsel that James is giving to the first-century Christian congregation and every true Christian since is especially applicable to how he treats his brothers and sisters within the congregation. However, the implications that fall within the pattern of meaning is, this counsel is not restricted to how Christians interact with one another, but also those outside of the congregation. – See Matthew 5:43-48.

"God created man in his own image, in the image of God he created him; male and female he created them." (Gen. 1:27) Of course, God is a

---

[55] Gr., *ton Kurion*

[56] The first part of verse 28 comes from *Cretica* by Epimenides, and the second part of the verse from *Hymn to Zeus*, written by the Cilician poet Aratus.– (Gangel 1998, 290)

[57] See James 1:27; John 1:11-13; 8:42-44; Ephesians 5:1; 1 John 3:10-12

spirit person, so this text is referring to God's qualities as a person, his moral standards, as laid out in the Bible. These qualities include love, wisdom, justice, patience, kindness, goodness, faithfulness, gentleness, self-control, and honesty, which set us apart from the animals. All humans are born with a weakened, imperfect conscience that was perfect when God gave it to Adam and Even. Even in this weakened state, it enables humans to reflect the qualities of their Creator. However, if it is ignored to no end, it will grow calloused and unfeeling, failing to work as originally designed. Even the most faithful and devout Christians "fall short of the glory of God." (Rom. 3:23) Nevertheless, if the Word of God, family, and the congregation cultivate the conscience, it can become quite strong even in this fallen condition. (See Romans 2:13-15; Acts 28:1-2.) Imperfection and human weakness are not a license for dealing harshly with anyone, especially our brothers and sisters of the faith. While those outside of the congregation are not in harmony with, but contrary to, God's personality, standards, ways, and will, no one is inferior to another even if they are in the world. Thus, they should not be viewed with disdain or treated hatefully and abusively because they are not a part of the Christian congregation. (See John 3:16; Rom. 5:7-8; Acts 10:28-29)[58] If we recall from our studies of the Gospels, the Pharisees were guilty of viewing anyone outside of themselves with disdain. In fact, they viewed their people as "accursed." – John 7:49; Luke 18:9-14.

If we look throughout the whole of Scripture, we can see that the tongue is supposed to be used for praising God, not for demeaning those created in his image. Because of imperfection and human weaknesses, man has praised God out of one side of his mouth all the while cursing those in the image of God. The Baker Encyclopedia of the Bible says a "curse" is an "invocation of evil or injury against one's enemies. As practiced in Bible times, cursing was the opposite of blessing and should not be confused with profanity in the modern sense." (Elwell 1988, Volume 1, Page 560) At times, some of God's servants were inspired to

---

[58] Some might ask, "what about those that are clearly enemies of God, like an apostate, an atheist who evangelize against God, and persons such as Muslims who behead Christians?" Jesus said, "You have heard that it was said, 'You shall love your neighbor and hate your enemy.' But I say to you, Love your enemies and pray for those who persecute you." (Matt. 5:43-44) This does not mean that we love the terrorists, who behead Christians, as we would love our family or a Christian member. Rather, it means that we talk to enemies of God graciously and respectfully, and if an opportunity to share biblical truths with them arises, we take advantage of it. If ever they repent and accept Christ, we forgive and forget as God would.–See Psalm 103:12; Isaiah 38:17; 55:7; Jeremiah 31:24; 50:20; Micah 7:19

call curses against others in Old Testament times.[59] There are some cases within the New Testament as well.[60] The apostles were endowed with the power to make such curses on behalf of God, but Christians were not given this authority. Christians were actually encouraged to follow in the example of the archangel Michael, "when the archangel Michael, contending with the devil ... he did not presume to pronounce a blasphemous judgment." (Jude 1:9) The counsel for Christians is "Love your enemies; do good to those who hate you, bless those who curse you, pray for those who abuse you." (Luke 6:27-28) In fact, Paul specifically wrote,

Romans 12:14, 17-21 English Standard Version (ESV)

[14] Bless those who persecute you; bless and do not curse them. [17] Repay no one evil for evil, but give thought to do what is honorable in the sight of all.[18] If possible, so far as it depends on you, live peaceably with all.[19] Beloved, never avenge yourselves, but leave it to the wrath of God, for it is written, "Vengeance is mine, I will repay, says the Lord."[20] To the contrary, "if your enemy is hungry, feed him; if he is thirsty, give him something to drink; for by so doing you will heap burning coals on his head." [21] Do not be overcome by evil, but overcome evil with good.

While the Holy Spirit, by way of the Word of God, guides Christians, they are not inspired as was true of the apostle and other servants used in Bible times. Therefore, they use their tongue to praise God and to evangelize but never to curse others. The apostle John wrote, "If anyone says, 'I love God,' and hates his brother, he is a liar; for he who does not love his brother whom he has seen cannot love God whom he has not seen." If an uninspired person were to speak poorly of someone, to pronounce a curse, an evil or injury on another, it would be an act of hatred not love. Therefore, if we are uninspired and pronounce a curse on another our worship of God is empty and useless.

Even if we find ourselves having, success in keeping control over our tongue, remember that it is like a trained viper, in that it only takes one good strike to bring death and destruction. For this reason, we must be constant, incessant, and vigilant in keeping guard over our tongue. The greatest abuse by the tongue comes by way of anger, this is why Paul warned, "Be angry and do not sin." (Eph. 4:26) In other words, have

---

[59] See Genesis 9:24-25; 2 Kings 2:23-24; Joshua 6:26; 1 Kings 16:34.

[60] See Acts 5:1-10; 13:6-11; Gal. 1:8, 9; 2 Peter 2:14; 2 John 9-11.

righteous indignation (anger) toward injustice, but do not be provoked into rage or wrath, or even aggressive anger.

From the same mouth come both blessing and cursing. My brothers, these things ought not to be so. (3:10)

Yes, two things nothing like each other can come from the same tongue, one a blessing the other a curse. The primary point of James is that the Christian should not be praising God and then cursing others who were in the likeness of God. The only curses that Christians should utter are those that have been recorded in his Word. Even then, we cannot direct those curses toward any person because there is but one judge, Jesus Christ. Even if Christians are alone with each other, they should not utter something evil toward another, or even in their own heart. Think of the hypocrisy of standing in a Christian service singing praises to God, then on the car ride home together, they say something evil, gossip, or revile, or slander someone. This will place the reviler in a bad standing with God, causing God to draw away from him.

When we think of cursing another, or calling down evil upon him, not to mention associated wrongs, such as badmouthing, hateful gossip, cruel criticism, and slander, would make known the presence of a depraved heart (inner person). As Jesus said, "How can you speak good, when you are evil? For out of the abundance of the heart the mouth speaks." (Matt. 12:34) If we are honest with ourselves, using the God-given gift of speech in such an unpredictable way is at odds with why God gave us the ability to speak in the first place. But also we would not only be at odds with this divine will of God to evangelize to everyone, to love our neighbor and to pray for our enemy, it would also be a blatant, glaring, grave absurdity.

Does a fountain send forth the same opening both sweet water and bitter? (3:11)

Clearly, the intended answer is, no. Water coming from a fountain can either be bitter or sweet, but could never be mixed or one then another. This would actually be conflicting with nature. In the same way, it would be contrary to God's intended purpose of the gift of speech to have both good and bad speech coming out of the same mouth. It is because of our sinful nature, our human weakness that this abnormal ability is even possible. God knows that he has given us the tools to gain a tremendous control over the tongue. For this reason, he also knows that he can rely on us in our imperfect condition to use our speech to carry out the proclaiming of biblical truths, the teaching of others, and the making of disciples. He has made allowances for those times that we do fall short. The sin-atoning sacrifice of Jesus Christ will cover Adamic sin (i.e., inherited imperfection, human weaknesses, the committing of a sin), not the practice of sin. Thus, let us self-examine ourselves, as we need to make sure that we have not fallen into harmful practices with our speech.

Can a fig tree, my brothers, produce olives, or a vine produce figs? Neither can salt water produce fresh water. (3:12)

And God said, "Let the earth sprout vegetation, plants yielding seed, and fruit trees bearing fruit in which is their seed, each **according to its kind**, on the earth." (Gen. 1:11-12) On this Kurt A. Richardson writes, "Grapevines produce grapes, not figs; and fig trees produce figs, not olives ... Back to the principle at hand, those who truly praise God do not curse their brothers. James did not refer to a thoroughly new constitution of the person but to true faith that does what is natural to it, both toward God and toward other human beings. Such faith praises and blesses." (Richardson 1997, 160) The point that James is conveying is that if grapevines produced figs or fig trees produced grapes, they would not be producing what God had purposed. Therefore, the misuse of the tongue is contrary to its naturally intended purpose. Another aspect of this could be that the fruitage that comes from a person's mouth will identify whether he is acting contrary to design or not. Jesus said,

Matthew 7:17-20 English Standard Version (ESV)

¹⁷ So, every healthy tree bears good fruit, but the diseased tree bears bad fruit. ¹⁸ A healthy tree cannot bear bad fruit, nor can a diseased tree bear good fruit. ¹⁹ Every tree that does not bear good fruit is cut down and thrown into the fire. ²⁰ Thus you will recognize them by their fruits.

The Wisdom from Above

James 3:13-18 Updated American Standard Version (UASV)

¹³ Who is wise and understanding among you? Let him show by his good behavior his works in meekness of wisdom. ¹⁴ But if you have bitter jealousy and selfish ambition in your hearts, do not boast and tell lies against the truth. ¹⁵ This wisdom is not that which comes down from

above, but is earthly, soulical,[61] demonic. [16] For where there is jealousy and selfish ambition, there *is* disorder and every evil practice. [17] But the wisdom from above is first pure, then peaceable, gentle, reasonable, full of mercy and good fruits, impartial, without hypocrisy. [18] And the fruit of righteousness is sown in peace by[62] those who make peace.

Who is wise and understanding among you? (3:13a)

James has just gotten through telling his Christian audience that their true nature shows by the way that they use their tongues, so now in the same manner he will address these Christians with the proper attitudes and actions that the Christian should have. He begins by asking another question, **who is wise and understanding among you?**

The question that James is asking is directed primarily to those who teach the congregation. Then, by way of implication, it can also apply to every Christian evangelist. Let us address the primary point, i.e., what James meant by the words he used. Those men taking the lead in the congregation as teachers need to inspect themselves by way of this question. If one is to be an effective teacher, it will require more than being a charismatic, moving, motivational type of person. Moreover, it also requires more than having a witty and crafty mind. It requires true wisdom and understanding. 'The fear of God is the beginning of wisdom, and the knowledge of the Holy One is insight.' (Prov. 9:10) This fear is a reverential fear of displeasing God because the teacher's love is so great for God and neighbor.

The teacher, who possesses understanding, will be able to see into life and the lives of those he serves, gaining a sense of it and being able to detect the relationships within their lives: God, congregation, family, friends, workmates, associates, and the like. The teacher's ability to understand fully enables him to grasp fully the significance of what lies before him. The teacher takes in solid food, which makes him mature, as he has his powers of discernment trained by constant practice to distinguish good from evil.' (Heb. 5:14) What he offers in his counsel to the congregation as a whole, as a Bible study group, in a private family, or in one on one session will accurately reflect the wisdom from above. His understanding of Scripture is accurate, giving his listeners what God said and meant by what he said, not what he thinks, feels, or believes he

---

[61] Or "*natural, animalistic, unspiritual*"

[62] Or "for"; or possibly "among"

said. In other words, he does not interject his personal beliefs into (eisegesis) the Scriptures, but rather takes the meaning out of (exegesis) the Scriptures.

Let him show by his good behavior his works in meekness of wisdom. (3:13b)

We can see a person's faith by his works because he who has faith cannot go without doing Christlike works. His works are "an evident demonstration of his faith." The same holds true of those who possess wisdom and understanding, as they will produce evidence of those qualities, by way of the things they say and in their day-to-day actions. Everyone can make sensible decisions and judgments based on personal knowledge and experience every once in a while, but the man or woman of true wisdom and understanding does this so often it stands out, because, generally speaking, "in all that he [or she] does, he prospers." (Psa. 1:1-3) We already know "the fear of Jehovah is the beginning of wisdom," which means that we reverentially fear displeasing God because of our great love for him and his creation. Therefore, "all those who practice it (i.e., fear of) have a good understanding." (Ps. 111:10) In other words, we apply God's Word with a full, accurate and balanced understanding. It is impossible to say that we are a good Christian teacher unless our wisdom and understanding is visually evident through our words and actions, recommending us to others.

One who is meek is mild, meaning he is showing mildness or quietness of wisdom, especially the man who is teaching the Christian congregation. In fact, Isaiah 30:20 tells us that God is "your teacher," and the Psalmist informs us "he leads the humble in what is right, and **teaches** the humble his way." (Psa. 25:9) Thus, God will only teach a meek one. A teacher must be mild, composed and peaceful, not unforgiving, loud and narrow-minded or haughty.

But if you have bitter jealousy and selfish ambition in your hearts, do not boast and tell lies against the truth. (3:14)

James asks his audience to take a personal inventory to see **if you have bitter jealousy and selfish ambition in your hearts**. James points to the heart because so often, the outside can conceal these attitudes and emotions of the flesh but have a raging evil on the inside. James uses the word bitter in connection with jealousy. This is the kind of jealousy, which is not just a mere one-time feeling, but rather a deep-seated emotion firmly rooted in the heart. James is asking these believers to take inventory of themselves to see if this type of jealousy was residing in their hearts. Though man may be able to hide the bitterness that he holds in his heart for others, God sees all things even the very motives of the heart and the bitterness that can reside there.

James is primarily applying the words in verse 14 to those who were overly confident in their abilities as a teacher of God's people. He is saying that these need to take an inventory of their hearts. Were they hiding **bitter jealousy**? One aspect of bitter jealousy is an excessive desire to exalt themselves and their personal view of things, as opposed to giving God the glory as they work on behalf of his people. They do not seek to build up the faith of others through an accurate knowledge of God's Word. Some of "the works of the flesh are enmity, strife, jealousy, fits of anger, rivalries, dissensions, divisions," for which Paul warns us 'not to envy one another.' (Gal. 5:19, 20, 26) These qualities might bubble forth in an excessively enthusiastic beliefs and dogged fanaticism for one's own views, as they interject their opinions into the Word of God, rather than taking what the author meant out of Scripture. Bible scholar F. J. A. Hort makes this insightful observation:

> The mere possession of truth is no security for true utterance of it: all utterance is so coloured by the moral and spiritual state of the speaker that truth issues as falsehood from his lips in proportion as he himself is not in a right state: the correct language which he utters may carry a message of falsehood and evil in virtue of the bitterness and self-seeking which accompanies his speaking. (Hort 1909, 83)

This wisdom is not that which comes down from above, but is earthly, soulical, demonic. (3:15)

Wisdom of bitter jealousy and selfish ambition does not come down from heaven (i.e., from above), as "every good gift and every perfect gift is from above, coming down from the Father." (Jam. 1:17) God tells us through the prophet Jeremiah, "Let not the wise man boast in his wisdom, let not the mighty man boast in his might, let not the rich man boast in his riches, but let him who boasts boast in this, that he understands and knows me, that I am Jehovah who exercises lovingkindness, justice and righteousness on earth, for I delight in these things." (Jer. 9:23-24) Some who profess to be teachers of God's Word, yet they are looking out for themselves alone (self-seeking), they are not servants of God.

Earthly (Gr., *epigeios*) means that this wisdom is not from the Father in heaven, but rather from imperfect humanity, who is alienated from God. As Paul said, "Has not God made foolish the wisdom of the world?" (1 Corinthians 1:20) Such earthly wisdom may be the result of great learning, sharpness, skill and logical reasoning that appears on the outward to be reasonable and may be difficult to counter. However, let us keep in mind what Paul said,

1 Corinthians 2:1-5 English Standard Version (ESV)

¹ And I, when I came to you, brothers, did not come proclaiming to you the testimony of God with lofty speech or wisdom. ² For I decided to know nothing among you except Jesus Christ and him crucified.³ And I was with you in weakness and in fear and much trembling,⁴ and my speech and my message were not in plausible words of wisdom, but in demonstration of the Spirit and of power, ⁵ so that your faith might not rest in the wisdom of men but in the power of God.⁶³

Soulical (Gr., *psychikos*, lit. "of the soul") means that this wisdom is not spiritual. This wisdom belongs to the natural person, not the spiritual person. Wisdom derived from bitter jealousy and selfish ambition is not from one who is being guided in his life by God's Spirit-inspired Word. "It is these who cause divisions, worldly people, devoid of the Spirit." (Jude 1:9) Therefore, in being denoted as "animal," or soulical, this wisdom comes from fleshly feelings, cravings and leanings.

Demonic (Gr., *daimoniodes*) signifies "proceeding from, or resembling, a demon, demoniacal" (Vine 1996, Volume 2, Page 158) In other words, this wisdom does not just come from humans that are a lower lifeform, but is directly from their being mentally bent toward evil, inundated and catered to by Satan's rule over the earth, which is in opposition to God. So this wisdom comes from their "father the devil, and [their] will is to do [their] father's desires." (John 8:44) Of course, Satan and the angels, who rebelled and rejected the sovereignty of God have wisdom and believe in God as they were created by him and have seen him,⁶⁴ truly knowing of his almighty power. However, the wisdom

---

⁶³ Warning: Many times religious leaders will downplay the importance of biblical knowledge, as though it were unnecessary. This just is not the case. Even though Paul said the above, he has the knowledge and the skill to debate, explain, reason and overcome argumentation from the leading Greek philosophers of his day.

⁶⁴ Yes, God created the spirit creature, who would rebel and become Satan (resister) the Devil (slanderer). However, God did not create this spirit creature evil or wicked, this is something that he become by entertaining wrong desires, until they became fertile, leading to the sin where he rebelled.

that they have is being guided by desires that are contrary to God's will and purposes, so it must be avoided. – 1 Corinthians 10:20–21; 1 Timothy 4:1.

For where there is jealousy and selfish ambition, there is disorder and every evil practice. (3:16)

James here presents the results of **jealousy and selfish ambition**. This is to say that the internal issues of the heart manifest themselves through disorder and evil practices. Anytime someone acts jealous or seeks his own selfish ambitious interests, it will always result in evil every time. Cain was bitterly jealous of his brother Abel, and that led him to murdering his own brother. (Gen. 4) King Saul was so full of jealousy against David because of how the people praised him, that he made it a life goal to kill David.

King Herod was so bent on his selfish ambition of the keeping the throne that his heart was filled with jealousy when he heard a new king had been born in Bethlehem. As a result, he sends out his soldiers to kill all the boys two years old and younger. The Pharisees hated Jesus and wanted him put to death on the cross. Christians would do good to heed the word of Paul in Philippians 2:3-4 "Do nothing from selfishness or empty conceit, but in humility[65] consider others as more important than yourselves. Everyone should look out not only for his own interests,[66] but also for the interests of others."

Jealousy and selfish ambition are two traits that lead to destructive behaviors. In their wake, we have volatility, self-doubt, disorder, conquest, removing any hope of happiness, confidence, harmony, and peace. Some evil practices might include offensiveness, disrespect, vulgarity, groundless suspicions, hurtful gossip, slander, verbal abuse, backbiting, hostilities, spite and malice, stubbornness, disloyalty, two-facedness, discord, fights, favoritism, even violence toward friends and family. In fact, the Scriptures are filled with examples of improper jealousy and the bad results. The first human death came about because Cain gave way to his improper jealousy. The Philistines envied the growing prosperity of Isaac so they persecuted him. Rachel was jealous of her sister Leah's fertility in childbearing. Jacob's sons were jealous of their younger brother Joseph because of the favor shown toward him. (Genesis 4:4-8;

---

[65] Lit lowly mindedness

[66] Lit not the (things) of themselves each (ones).

26:14; 30:1; 37:11) In contrast, 'love binds everything together in perfect harmony.' – Colossians 3:14.

1 Corinthians 13:4-7 Updated American Standard Version (UASV)

[4] Love is long suffering and kind; Love is not jealous, it does not brag; it is not puffed up,[67] [5] does not behave indecently;[68] is not seeking its own interests, is not provoked, does not keep a record of wrong, [6] does not rejoice over unrighteousness, but rejoices with the truth; [7] bears all things, believes all things, hopes all things, endures all things.

But the wisdom from above is first pure (3:17a)

The first quality of wisdom is purity, which is especially vital. A person must possess it if there is any hope of the others existing. The Christian *heart* has to be pure. All who have wisdom from above will be able to know the difference between right and wrong, rejecting evil outright. On three occasions, weakened by hunger and thirst, Jesus rejected Satan's misuse of Scripture. (Matt. 4:1-10) Joseph from the Old Testament did not even have the Mosaic Law to guide him, just the conscience that God gave him, and yet he still saw the evil proposition of Potiphar's wife. In fact, Joseph wisely exclaimed, "How then could I do this great evil and sin against God?" (Gen. 39:9, 12) All of God's teachers, those leading the congregation and those making disciples with their teaching, need this qualification overwhelmingly.

James began by saying that **the wisdom that is from above is first pure**. The word that James uses here for pure is *hagnos* which means *"free from defilement or uncontaminated"* (Vine 1996, 498). Jesus said something very similar in Matthew 5:8 "Blessed are the pure in heart, for they shall see God." This word expresses freedom from any defilement or impurity. James here states that heavenly wisdom starts with being pure towards God. If one's heart is not set on God and serving Jesus Christ with full devotion, then he will not possess the next seven qualities of heavenly wisdom.

If one's motives or intentions in following Christ are mixed with any selfish gain or selfish ambitions, then the relationship is not pure, but rather mixed with selfish intentions. This was the problem with the

---

[67] I.e., self-important or made proud

[68] Or *is not rude*

Pharisees, who wanted to follow all the rules of religion without having a personal relationship with God. As a result, their religion became nothing more than just a show for men to see and to gain approval for, and so their worship of God was mixed with their desire to be noticed by men. It is impossible for one to claim Christ as his Savior and yet practice the world's behaviors, attitudes, and actions. All of the other seven qualities, which James describes as being heavenly wisdom, will flow from purity.

then peaceable (3:17b)

Wisdom from above pursues **peace**. (Matt. 5:9; Gal. 5:22; Rom. 12:18; Eph. 6:15; Heb. 12:11, 14) Heavenly wisdom will make us a supporter or advocate of peace. Not only will we sidestep attacking or being confrontational but we will also be a peacemaker, meaning that we will search out ways to get along with those who have difficult personalities. We will not even allow thoughts in our mind that could disrupt peace. We will be a good example to others within the congregation of how to avoid aggression, and step in to find peace where there was none before. (Rom. 14:19; Heb. 12:14) Jesus said, "Blessed are the peacemakers, for they shall be called sons of God"–Matthew 5:9

gentle (3:17c)

Heavenly wisdom will also give us the quality of **gentleness**. The saying is, "A gentle answer turns away wrath, but a painful[69] word stirs up anger." (Pro. 15:1) The apostle Paul told Titus, "to speak evil of no man, not to be fighting, gentle, showing all mildness toward all men." (Titus 3:2) If we carry around wrath within us, there is no way that we will be able to carry out the will and purposes of God. Our greatest teacher and example, Jesus Christ, said, "Take my yoke upon you and learn from me, for I am gentle and lowly in heart, and you will find rest for your souls." (Matt. 11:29) Regardless of whether we are the one doing the teaching or are the one being taught, there is no room for harsh words or holding anger within us until it bursts forth.

reasonable (3:17d)

Heavenly wisdom will make us **reasonable**, ready to obey,[70] long-suffering, not fanatical in our worship. (Phil. 4:5; 1 Tim. 3:3; Titus 3:2) If we recall early in the book of Acts before Paul was converted, when he

---

[69] I.e. *harsh*

[70] Not if it violates God's Word.

went by his Hebrew name Saul, he was an overly zealous young Pharisee, who allowed his fanaticism to drive him to condone locking up and murdering Christians. This unreasonable spirit of radicalism was because of his earthly wisdom. (Acts 9:1-2; Gal. 1:13, 14) However, Saul would meet Jesus on the road to Damascus, where he would convert to Christianity, becoming one of the most reasonable men ever to live. He never insisted that it had to be his way or that it must be the letter of the law, rather he treated others, even enemies of Christ, with kindness, and understanding. We know Paul reasoned from the Scriptures, explaining and proving (Ac 17:2-3). Yes, he spoke boldly in the name of Jesus (Ac 9:27-28), following in the footsteps of Christ, as should we.

If we are to be God's teachers, we cannot be dogmatic. We must treat everyone according to his or her abilities as well as their situations. We would never expect more from a person than he can carry. We may be teaching an unbeliever and he accepts the truth after a few good conversations while another may take far longer based on his situations. Even after the apostles had spent over three years in ministry with Jesus, he said to them, "I still have many things to say to you, but you cannot bear them now."

When we first begin to teach a new one, he may come with decades of life experience and a worldview that is not biblical. He will have beliefs about the Bible, God, and Christianity that is unbiblical, and maybe even hatred toward God in some cases. He may have bad habits like smoking, drugs, abuse of alcohol, gambling, lying, and the like. He may have behaviors that are unscriptural like laziness, bluntness with his words, procrastination, no respect for authority, watching inappropriate movies, and so on.

However, over time, some more than others, will take off this old person and put on the new person. (Eph. 4:20-24; Col. 3:6-10) In time, they will acquire the mind of Christ, (1 Cor. 2:16) Yes, their mind will be renewed so they can know the will of God. (Rom. 12:2) Therefore, a good teacher will **not** make it about his rules and regulations, but will allow God's Word to guide and direct his steps. – 1 Corinthians 9:19-23.

full of mercy and good fruits (3:17e)

The wisdom from above is evidenced through our actions, which stems from mercy and compassion. As Jesus said, "Blessed are the merciful, for they shall receive mercy." (Matt. 5:7) Such a merciful man is one who cares for orphans and widows (Jam 1:27), as well as clothing the poor and feeding the hungry.[71] (Jam. 2:15-17) Mercy, the result of heavenly wisdom, moves us to come to the needs of those we can help. We are not to mechanically go about helping the less fortunate merely because they are such. We use the Word of God to apply knowledge, insight, and understanding, along with justice. We must consider many factors when we give aid to another. Why? What if we used our last resources to help one who is in need, but he is there because of his abusing drugs like crack cocaine or heroin, and we could have used that aid to help a mother, who is homeless with three children. We must look at the backgrounds of these, their current situation, and the pressures they are facing, if they are seeking to change their life or just seeking handouts because our mercy and compassion can be abused. Moreover, a person may need our assistance to get into some treatment place, not continue down the path of dependence.

We need to realize that we are of imperfect, sinful flesh as well. We also must realize that we live in an imperfect, wicked world; therefore, life can have us walking in the shoes of needing clothing, food, housing, and so forth. If we believe that because we are good Christians life cannot displace us from our comfort zone and believing that we are the exception to the rule because we are righteous and God will protect us, remember 9/11, 2001 and the Twin Towers of New York. There were Christians who died that day from the evilness of Satan's world. Christian wives or husbands sat at home that morning and watched those building crumble down on their loves ones.

The apostle Paul told the Ephesians, "For the fruit of the light is in all goodness and righteousness and truth." (5:9) We need to be compassionately concerned about human life, especially for our brothers and sisters in the faith. (See 1 Tim. 5:9-10.) Christian leaders and teachers of the congregation and all Christians responsible for teaching unbelievers have to be declared righteous in their walk with God; must also have goodness about them. The apostle Paul writes, "For one will scarcely die for **a <u>righteous</u> man**; though perhaps for **a <u>good</u> man** one would dare even to die." (Rom. 5:7) Paul seems to be suggesting that there is superiority to the **<u>good</u> man**. Goodness is an active, ongoing quality. God declares one as having a **<u>righteous</u>** standing before him if he lives according to an accurate understanding of the Scriptures (i.e., doing the will of the Father), is just in his dealings, impartial, honest and truthful,

---

[71] Of course, Christianity has one major priority before all else, which is the Great Commission of proclaiming biblical truths, teaching, and making disciples. We should never allow social ills of this world to sidetrack us from finding and saving souls.

not guilty of serious sin or not living in sin; hence, he is pure and upright in all of his ways. Notice that **a <u>righteous</u> man** is obedient to the rules, principles and laws of Scripture, which is excellent indeed, but **a good man** goes beyond obedience. The good man will seek out ways to do good for others, not just wait for it to come to his attention. He is driven by morally beneficial attention for others and the longing to assist and help them.

impartial (3:17g)

James has covered this quality quite extensively earlier in his letter, i.e., showing favoritism is a sin. (Jas. 2:1-9) The Christian possessing wisdom from above would not give special treatment to anyone based on his or her outward exterior, station, wealth or position in life, or his or her influence within the church. All Christians should endeavor to be impartial in his dealing with those inside and outside of the congregation.

without hypocrisy. (3:17h)

A Christian hypocrite is one who pretends to have a biblical worldview, beliefs, or love for God and neighbor but behaves contrary to God's Word. A person who possesses heavenly wisdom has no need to impress others with an outward display of one's life. Jesus regularly condemned hypocrisy by saying they had Godly wisdom but then failed to obey God when out of sight of human eyes. (Matt 6:2, 5, 16; 7:5; 15:7; Mark 12:15; Lu 12:56; 13:15) If one possesses wisdom from above, he will not be a hypocrite. He will want to live his life as he does in the congregation. The same holds true when he is outside of the congregation.

While in some sense sin is sin and all sin results in death, the Bible does express itself as recognizing that some are more egregious than others are. Hypocrisy is one of the most serious sins because it enables one to hide other sins, one of which is the grieving of the Holy Spirit. The Pharisees were condemned for this. (Matt. 23:23-28) Ananias and Sapphira were also guilty of hypocrisy. (Acts 5:1-10) James' words should be a warning for any seeking to be a Christian teacher. He needs to live by what he teaches. He knows God sees all, but there is the possibility of stumbling someone out of the faith based on his actions, for which he would be held accountable. The apostle Paul warns Timothy of this very danger of having hypocrisy in teaching. (1 Tim. 1:5-7) A hypocrite frequently is an exploiter, for he is typically directing events to obtain some integrity, position, prestige, benefit from others, or material gain. – See 1 Thessalonians 1:5.

And the fruit of righteousness is sown in peace for them that make peace. (3:18)

For those who **make peace**, it is more than acting peaceably, as he also endeavors to preserve and promote that peace. This peace is the opposite of jealousy and selfish ambition mentioned in verse 16. The one pursuing peace has a righteous standing before God. "Let us not become conceited, provoking one another, envying one another." (Gal. 5:25-26) While all Christians desire peace, this does not mean that we passively allow untruths to go by unchecked, or that we water down biblical truths to appease. All the same, the one making peace can respectfully share the biblical truth, but at the same time respectfully let others maintain their viewpoints. The primary concern for the teacher of the congregation is that the disciples within have a correct understanding of God's Word, protecting them from being influenced by false teachers. (Rom. 14:1-4, 10; Tit. 3:9-11) The teacher of the Christian congregation would follow the apostle Paul's counsel to young Timothy,

2 Timothy 2:23-26 English Standard Version (ESV)

[23] Have nothing to do with foolish, ignorant controversies; you know that they breed quarrels. [24] And the Lord's servant must not be quarrelsome but kind to everyone, able to teach, patiently enduring evil, [25] correcting his opponents with gentleness. God may perhaps grant them repentance leading to knowledge of the truth, [26] and they may come to their senses and escape from the snare of the devil, after being captured by him to do his will.

A teacher such as this will make peace. The recurrence of different forms of "peace" shows that this is the essential quality of wisdom. Heavenly wisdom continuously endeavors for oneness within God's congregation.

Review Question

(1) **[vs 1]** Why can we say that James was not discouraging ones from becoming teachers?

(2) **[vs 1]** What could be the result if an unqualified teacher were leading a church?

(3) **[vs 2]** Why can it be said that all humans stumble in many ways?

(4) **[vs 2]** Why can we say if no one stumbles in what he says, he is a perfect man?

(5) **[vs 3]** What does illustration mean?

(6) **[vs 4]** Why is this illustration even more powerful?

(7) **[vs 5]** Just how powerful is the tongue?

(8) **[vs 6]** How is it that the tongue can defile the entire body?

(9) **[vs 7]** What point is James making here?

(10) **[vs 8]** Just how difficult is it to tame the tongue? How much damage can an untamed tongue cause?

(11) **[vs 9]** What point is James making here?

(12) **[vs 10]** What polar opposites come from the same mouth? Explain.

(13) **[vs 11]** What point is James making here?

(14) **[vs 12]** What is James saying with this illustration?

(15) **[vs 13]** Who is truly wise? Why?

(16) **[vs 14]** What point is James making here?

(17) **[vs 15]** What is meant by earthly, soulical, and demonic?

(18) **[Vs 16]** How does jealousy and selfish ambition affect the church?

(19) **[vs 17]** Explain the qualities or characteristics listed here.

(20) **[vs 18]** How do we make peace?

JAMES CHAPTER 4 Warning Against Worldliness

Do Not Be a Friend of the World

James 4:1-3 Updated American Standard Version (UASV)

¹ What is the source of wars[72] and fights[73] among you? Are they not from this source, your pleasures that wage war in your members?[74] ² You lust and do not have, so you commit murder. You desire, and yet you do not have, so you fight and quarrel. You do not have because you do not ask. ³ You ask and do not receive, because you ask with wrong motives,[75] so that you may spend it on your pleasures.

What is the source of wars and fights among you? (4:1a)

It should be noted that James's readers were not literally involved in wars, but rather murderous hatred for others. Clearly, this letter was intended for an audience that lacked unity. Early on James dealt with those who were showing favoritism to the rich. This congregation or group of Christians did not possess the love that Jesus had spoken of when he said, "By this all men will know that you are my disciples, if you have love for one another." (John 13:35) A few in the congregation were wrongly judging some while a handful ignored the needs of others. Within this group of Christians, there was a spirit of contention that should not have been. Jealousy and selfish ambition had grown in the congregation. Consequently, peace was interrupted. Therefore, the question that begs to be asked is what is the basis of this infighting and aggression among these Christians?

Are they not from this source, your pleasures that wage war in your members? (4:1b)

James answers our question by naming the source of this warring and fighting among Christians, i.e., a battle within the heart. In other words, these ones were struggling with the desire for personal pleasure

---

[72] Or *quarrels*

[73] Or *conflicts*

[74] I.e., *a conflict within you*

[75] Lit., *wickedly* or *badly*

(Gr. *hēdonē*). From this Greek word, we get hedonism, which is devotion, especially a self-indulgence of pleasure and happiness as a way of life. These ones sought immediate gratification without any regard of whom it might affect.[76] We are imperfect, possessing human weaknesses and are mentally bent toward evil, with the natural desire toward wrongdoing. This creates turmoil within a Christian, as Paul put it,

Romans 7:21-23 Updated American Standard Version (UASV)

[21] I find then the law in me that when I want to do right, that evil is present in me. [22] For I delight in the law of God according to the inner man, [23] but I see a different law in my members, warring against the law of my mind and taking me captive in the law of sin which is in my members.

When a Christian fails to maintain control over his member, these cravings set in, causing conflicts within the Christian congregation. These Christians were craving the fleshly desires of self-importance, materialism and so on, which caused a tumultuous atmosphere with their brothers and sisters. Moreover, if there were any semblance of a conscience left within these battling their fleshly cravings, they would be struggling with a spiritual turmoil themselves.

You lust and do not have, so you commit murder. You desire, and yet you do not have, so you fight and quarrel. You do not have because you do not ask. (4:2)

These ones had desires for things for which they should not, and had no means of fulfilling that desire, at least not honorably anyway. These cravings were allowed to grow and fester within the congregation. This greedy, envious, longing in these Christians built up until it gave rise to an unbearable, murderous spirit. Again, these ones, lacked the love that Jesus said his disciples would have, ignoring fellow brothers in need, clinging to what they had while coveting things that were simply out of reach. The apostle John had this to say on the subject,

1 John 2:15-17 Updated American Standard Version (UASV)

[15] Do not love the world or the things in the world. If anyone loves the world, the love of the Father is not in him. [16] For all that is in the world, the lust of the flesh and the lust of the eyes and the boastful pride of life, is not from the Father, but is from the world. [17] The world is

---

[76] See Luke 8:14; Titus 3:3; 2 Peter 2:13

passing away, and its lusts; but the one who does the will of God lives forever.

More murders than we would like to count have been committed because of wrong desires. This holds true of secular history as well as God's people, both in the history of Nation of Israel and Christianity. Think of the desire of coveting another man's wife, another man's position, another man's wealth, and you can see by this one wrong desire millions of murders have taken place, from a robbery gone bad, to one nation trying to conquer another nation for its wealth. The wrong desire of hatred moved Cain to kill his brother Abel. Then, we have King Ahab being encouraged by his wife Jezebel to kill Naboth for his vineyard. (Gen. 4:8; 1 Ki. 21:2-16) Think of all the atrocities committed by the bishops, cardinals and the Popes throughout the Medieval Times because they lusted for the worship of others, or they wanted a higher position within the church hierarchy.

The congregation James wrote to was unable to acquire the things that they lusted after because they had wrong desires, and there was no way they were going to be blessed by God while acting in such a manner. Because their greediness and their malicious, detestable ways left their cravings unsatisfied, they kept on fighting and warring to attain the unattainable. The Christian congregation can suffer the same strife if heavenly wisdom, unity and peace are not pursued through the application of the Word of God. This is especially true of those who are chosen to take the lead. (Heb. 13:7, 17; Acts 20:28-30) Leaders are the backstop to the purity of the congregation, because those who slip into these wrong desires can go to the point where their formalistic prayers are not being heard by God and will need help to recover spiritually.

You ask and do not receive, because you ask with wrong motives, so that you may spend it on your pleasures. (4:3)

Their prayers were toward selfish ends, as they had the wrong motives. We think of Jesus' parable of the Prodigal Son, as he initially sought to waste his father's money on his selfish needs. (Lu 15:14) Paul tells us that there is a "constant friction among people, who are depraved in mind and deprived of the truth, imagining that godliness is a means of gain." (1 Tim. 6:5) Jesus said that our prayers should not extend beyond asking for "our daily bread." (Matt. 6:11) He went on to say, we should 'seek first the kingdom of God and his righteousness, and all these things will be added to us.' (Matt. 6:33) Many do not realize that God does not listen to everyone's prayers, just those of the righteous. Who are the righteous? They are those, who are doing their best in their circumstances to live by God's Word daily. (Pro. 15:29; 28:9) We must be humble when we are praying. (Lu 18:9-14) We need to evidence our prayers by working on behalf of those prayers. It would do very little good to pray to God to better understand the Bible and then never read the Bible or reading any books on how to understand the Bible correctly. It will do very little good to pray for a job when unemployed if we never fill out applications because we are sitting around waiting on God to find us a job. It evidences our faith when we work on behalf of what we pray for, as this is what God expects.–Hebrews 11:6.

We are fooling ourselves if we are using God in our prayers simply for what we can get out of him. This sort of prayer is actually idolatry. How, we may ask, is it idolatry? The pagans believe they can force a god to give them whatever they want by using special words or phrases in their prayers. Jesus told us plainly, "your Father knows what you need before you ask him." (Matt. 6:8) We can pray for things, but what we pray for must be in harmony with God's will and purposes. If we are praying for a job that is going to require us to work 65 hours a week, causing us to have no family life, and miss our Christian meetings, do we believe that God is going to bless our efforts?

James 4:4-6 Updated American Standard Version (UASV)

⁴ You adulteresses,[77] do you not know that friendship with the world is enmity[78] toward God? Therefore whoever wishes to be a friend of the world makes himself an enemy of God. ⁵ Or do you think that the Scripture speaks to no purpose, "The spirit that dwells in us strongly desires to envy"? ⁶ But he gives more grace. Therefore it says, "God opposes the proud, but gives grace to the humble."

You adulteresses (4:4a)

James is not one to hold anything back just as he had done at 2:20, where he called his readers, who said that they had faith but had no works that should result from that faith claim, "O foolish man." James here in his standard denunciation style called out his readers once more with the charge, "adulteresses!" Scripture refers to those who abandon God as "an adulterer," i.e., a spiritual adultery. (Isa. 57:3; Matt. 12:39) Conversely, Paul said of the Christian congregation, "I betrothed you

---

[77] Or "unfaithful ones"

[78] Or "hostility"

[Christians] to one husband so that to Christ I might present you as a pure virgin." (2 Cor. 11:2) Therefore, James' admonition to these ones makes it all too clear that they are no longer spiritually pure and clean in the eyes of God.

do you not know that friendship with the world is enmity toward God? (4:4b)

Christians should be very cautious as to whom they have as a friend. A friend (Gr. *philos*) is defined as an intimate relationship or bond with another. Christians would not have a close friend whose habits God would detest, who's thinking, and worldview is contrary to God's Word. If we as humans were exacting about people we would have as an intimate friend, would this not also be the case with our sovereign Creator of the heavens, earth, and humanity. The apostle John wrote of "all that is in the world, the lust of the flesh and the lust of the eyes and the boastful pride of life, is not from the Father, but is from the world." (1 John 2:16) The spirit of this world is like poisonous gas, which is next to impossible to escape, as it is within the air of humanity that is alienated from God. This contaminated air proceeds from the ruler of the world, Satan, and if we breathe it in regularly, we will begin to adopt their goals, beliefs, attitude, thinking, speech, conduct, and worldview. This spirit controls the world without them ever knowing; it is demonic and separate from God. Satan controls humanity by his catering to the fallen flesh, our human weaknesses, resulting in enmity toward God. The world's way of thinking and resultant conduct is in opposition to the Holy Spirit.—1 Corinthians 2:6-16.

Many Christians have believed that they can be friends with the above person and not be affected by their worldly personality, thinking that they will win him over to the faith. As Edward D. Andrews has written elsewhere, 'if a dirty glove and a clean glove come into contact, dirt comes off on the clean glove, and the clean glove does not make the dirty glove cleaner.' How then can we win one over to the faith? We do so by keeping a controlled distance. We will study the Bible with one from the world. We will invite them to the meetings. We will invite them to Christian gatherings. After they have turned toward the truth, taking steps in that direction, we will invite them places that we would go as Christians. Once they are regularly attending meetings, studying the Bible regularly and moving toward abandoning bad habits, we will then bond with them more intimately. However, we never do worldly things, in order to attract ones from the world, ever.[79]

Therefore whoever wishes to be a friend of the world makes himself an enemy of God. (4:4c)

Continuing his point, James writes, "Whoever wishes to be a friend of the world makes himself an enemy of God." These ones reject God because his standards and values would get in the way of the self-indulgent, pleasure-seeking lifestyle. They know that choosing God is also choosing to obey him, choosing to live by his Word. Those of the world have a devotion, especially to a life of debauchery, to wrong desires, seeking happiness as a way of life, by feeding their fallen flesh. (I John 2:3-6) When we choose to follow God, it is the whole heart, whole soul, whole mind and whole strength. (Mark 12:30) Not only can we not walk on both sides of this choice, but also there is no walking on the line, or even seeing how close we can get to the line without going over to the other side. Jesus said in prayer to his Father, "they are not of the world, just as I am not of the world." (John 17:14) If we are to truly be no part of the world, he must make sacrifices on his part, never lacking, or wavering in his loyalty to Christ.

Or do you think that the Scripture speaks to no purpose, "The spirit that dwells in us strongly desires to envy"? (4:5)

Or do you think that the Scripture speaks to no purpose, introduces the reader to the bent toward envy? There is no text in the Hebrew Old Testament that the quoted words come from. Clearly, James was reflecting on what was being taught, or the sense of the entirety of the Hebrew Old Testament,[80] as opposed to quoting a specific text. Another alternative is that we know New Testament writers tend to paraphrase the Old Testament. On this Edward Andrews writes,

> On many occasions, a New Testament writer would quote or cite an Old Testament Scripture. Many times the New Testament writer would be using the Old Testament text

---

[79] There was actually a minister, who felt that it would be okay to go to bars, to drink and evangelize. There are young ones who have started heavy metal Christian bands (oxymoron), believing they can reach young ones by using the things of the world. Andrews wrote elsewhere that this merely makes Christians 'nine parts world and one part Christian.'

[80] See, Genesis 6:5; 8:21; Proverb 21:10; and Galatians 5:17.

104

contextually, according to the setting, and intent of the Old Testament writer (observing the grammatical-historical sense). However, at times the New Testament writer would add to or apply the text differently than what was meant by the Old Testament writer (**not** observing the grammatical-historical sense). This is either a new or a progressive revelation of God, where he has inspired the New Testament writer to go beyond the intended meaning of the Old Testament writer, and carry out what is known as *Inspired Sensus Plenior Application* (ISPA). In this latter case, the New Testament writer is using the Old Testament text to convey another meaning to another circumstance. This does not violate the principle that all texts have just one single meaning. The Old Testament text has one meaning, and the New Testament writer's adaptation of that text is not a second meaning, but another meaning.[81]

Here is what God said to man right after the flood, "I will never again curse the soil because of man though the bent of man's mind may be evil from his very youth ..." (Gen. 8:21, AT)[82] Yes, we are mentally bent toward evil, and part of that evil is that we can be inclined to envy. Such a spirit will lead toward conflict and augments within the congregation. The love shown to Jesus made the Jewish religious leaders envious in the extreme, to the point of handing the Son of God over to Pilate to be executed. (Matt. 27:1-2, 18; Mark 15:10) The envious spirit that James speaks of is made all too clear throughout the entirety of the Hebrew Old Testament.

Envy is a product of selfishness. Solomon writes, "The soul of the wicked desires evil; his neighbor finds no mercy in his eyes." (Prov. 21:10) In other words, If one is envious, even of his best friend, he will resort to evil, to acquire what his friend has. The envious one's main objective is to tear down the one who has what he wants so that he can undermine his accomplishments. Again, Solomon writes, "Then I saw that all toil and all skill in work come from a man's envy of his neighbor. This also is vanity and a striving after wind." What did Solomon mean? The Holman Old Testament Commentary,

---

[81] **New Testament Writers Use of the Old Testament**

http://www.christianpublishers.org/nt-writers-use-of-the-ot

[82] *The Bible–An American Translation* (1935), J. M. Powis Smith and Edgar J. Goodspeed.

Some people determine that the way to "make it" in this sin-saturated world is to allow the competitive juices to flow. Competition per se is not evil, especially the type that seeks to make personal goals. But competition that seeks to overpower another or to make that person look stupid or inferior is sinful. This type of competition is common in our world. As Solomon will graphically demonstrate, this leads to heartache and loneliness.

In case we don't "feel" that we are very competitive, it is time for honest evaluation. How do we respond inwardly when someone does a better job at something we value? Do we feel "beat"? If we feel that we "lost," we know where the competitive spirit is coming from![83]

James 4:5 does present problems when it comes to translation. On this, A Textual Commentary on the Greek New Testament writes, "The two verbal forms, which, because of itacism, were pronounced alike, have slightly different meanings: [katókᵻsen] is causative ("the spirit which he [God] has made to dwell in us"), whereas [katókēsen] is intransitive ("the spirit [or, Spirit] which dwells in us"). The causative reading katókᵻsen has better textual support, which suggests that God placed the Spirit within the believers, as God wanted us to be protected against losing our love for him. In other words, "the Spirit is jealous for the believers' affection." (Comfort 2008, 730) The intransitive katókēsen can convey two different thoughts: (1) the Spirit is jealous for our affection but does not convey that God placed it there, or (2) the spirit is a disposition (inclination or tendency), an inborn, imperfect human desire to do wrong, like envy another.[84] Kurt Richardson offers another interpretation,

The more likely reading is based upon God as Creator and as lawgiver and as the one who is giving new life to his dying creation. Humans are his perishing creatures. The spirit of life

---

[83] Moore, David; Anders, Max; Akin, Daniel (2003-07-01). Holman Old Testament Commentary Volume 14 - Ecclesiastes, Song of Songs (p. 56). B&H Publishing. Kindle Edition.

[84] "There is really no pneumatology, that is, doctrine of the Holy Spirit, in the Epistle of James. His specific doctrinal and practical concerns evidently did not warrant such a discussion. So the verse is probably not concerned with God either desiring his Holy Spirit to indwell believers or what Paul called grieving the Holy Spirit (Eph. 4:30). A second interpretive option understands the Holy Spirit as desiring believers. But both these options, while not contrary to scriptural truth at all, are not likely interpretations." (Richardson 1997, 180)

that transformed the newly formed body of the first man into a "living being" (Gen 2:7) is likely what is meant here. God is the giver of the spirit of life; it belongs to him. Moreover, the human spirit is not merely the vitality of the body (cf. 2:26) but also that which communes with God on the one hand or adulterates itself with idols on the other (cf. 1 Cor 6:17). The most natural understanding of "spirit" then is the human spirit, which gives us life and makes us spiritual beings. (Richardson 1997, 180)

However, this commentary interprets it as the spirit, inclination or disposition, which leans toward evil, of which one of the behaviors is envy. This envious spirit lies within imperfect humans and is not a behavior that God had intended for Adam and Eve, or their prospective perfect offspring prior to their choosing to rebel. It was their sin, which came into the world through Adam, and death through sin, and so death spread to all men because all sinned." (Rom. 5:12) Our inherited imperfection brings about this tendency to envy. It is not something God tolerates. Scripture clearly condemns envies, and "those who do such things will not inherit the kingdom of God." – Galatians 5:19-21.

But he gives more grace. Therefore it says, "God opposes the proud, but gives grace to the humble." (4:6)

Although humans are living in imperfection, being mentally bent toward evil, and possess such harmful behaviors as envy, we are not abandoned in a difficult position without help. Yes, God's grace is far greater but should never be taken as an excuse for badness. God makes allowances for our imperfections. God "is compassionate and gracious, slow to anger and rich in faithful love. He will not always accuse us or be angry forever. He has not dealt with us as our sins deserve or repaid us according to our offenses." (Psa. 103:8-10, HCSB) King David goes on to write, "As far as the east is from the west, so far has He removed our transgressions from us." (Psa. 103:12) Plainly, the distance from the East to the West is the greatest distance something can be removed. Isaiah says God has "thrown all my sins behind your back." (Isa. 38:17) The sense is that if our sins are behind God's back he can no longer see them and will call them to mind no more. Micah says God "will hurl all their sins in the depths of the sea." In those days, whatever is thrown into the sea will never be recovered. All of the above is based on how we deal with our inherited sin. If we were unrepentant, it would not apply. If we were not working toward getting our envious spirit under control, it would not apply. If we are using Spirit inspired Scripture in our lives in a correct and balanced manner, the above will apply. The apostle Paul tells us "walk by the Spirit, and you will not gratify the desires of the flesh."–Galatians 5:16.

If our envy has moved us to seek out persons in the world, who are influential and prominent, hoping that their success will become our success, we will be making ourselves a friend of the world. Rather, we should humbly walk with God and his people, as any perceived losses that we have suffered due to the faith will never be missed upon Christ's return. We need to give of ourselves fully, knowing that God's grace is abundantly available to help us conquer the world.

"God opposes the proud, but gives grace to the humble," is a quote from a Greek translation of the Hebrew Old Testament (c. 280-150 B.C.E.), known as the Septuagint. It is a translation of Proverbs 3:34. The humble one will seek God, looking for help through prayer, as well as acting on behalf of that prayer. In other words, he will apply God's inspired Word, and if necessary, seek the counseling from the pastor. Whatever is needed in order to overcome an envious spirit, he will do with the help of God and God's people. The apostle Peter tells us "God opposes the proud but gives grace to the humble."– 1 Peter 5:5.

James 4:7-10 Updated American Standard Version (UASV)

⁷ Submit therefore to God. Stand against[85] the devil and he will flee from you. ⁸ Draw near to God, and he will draw near to you. Cleanse your hands, you sinners, and purify your hearts, you double-minded. ⁹ Be miserable and mourn and weep; let your laughter be turned into mourning and your joy to gloom. ¹⁰ Humble yourselves in the eyes of[86] the Lord, and he will exalt you.

Submit therefore to God. Stand against the devil and he will flee from you. (4:7)

How can Christians receive the grace of God mentioned in verse 6? They can do so by **submitting themselves to God**. To submit to God means that we place ourselves under his sovereignty, in which we fully commit ourselves to obeying him in all things. The Greek verb (*hypotasso*) means 'to submit, be subject, and, in general, communicates some sense

---

[85] I.e., *resist* or *oppose*

[86] Or *in the presence of* or *before*

of hierarchy.' (Mounce 2006, 695) This submission to God is voluntary in every aspect of the Christian life. This includes the does and don'ts of Scripture, and also the things that God provides for us or allows us to go through, knowing his way is always best. Peter tells us "Humble yourselves, therefore, under the mighty hand of God so that at the proper time he may exalt you." (1 Pet. 5:6) In this, we are placing our will under the control of the Father.

Part of our submission to God is that we take a **stand against** the Satan the Devil. (See Eph. 4:27; 6:11-12; 1 Tim. 3:6-7; 1 Pet. 5:8-9) As Satan is actually the god of this world at this time (2 Cor. 4:3-4; John 14:30), to resist him is to be no part of the world. As we saw, to be a part of the world would make us an enemy of God. Satan's world caters to the fallen flesh, such as individuality, absolute freedom, self-importance, self-interest, love of self, fame, reputation, covetousness, and the like. The word "devil" translates the Greek *diabolos*, which means "slanderer." The Devil brought humanity into the current turmoil by originally slandering God. The main objective of the Devil is to separate us from God by his deception. Many times this is also accomplished through false religious leaders as well.

When we stand against the devil, we are told by James that **he will flee from us**. This is the case because we have help from the one who conquered the world, Jesus Christ (John 16:33), as well as the helper he sent us, the Holy Spirit. (John 14:26; 15:26; 16:7) The Devil tried to tempt Jesus as well. However, when Jesus used the Scriptures against him, he fled from Jesus. (Matt 4:1-11) In the book of Job, we learned that God put a hedge around Job and his house and all that he had, blessing him. (Job 1:10) Why did God protect Job in this way? If there were no protective wall around the righteous, the Devil and his demons could just arbitrarily kill every faithful person: Enoch, Noah, Abraham, Moses, David, John, Peter, and Paul, to mention just a few. In fact, Peter wrote, "Now who is there to harm you if you are zealous for what is good?" (1 Pet. 3:13) Therefore, Christians can conquer the Devil through the power of the Father, the Son, and the Holy Spirit.

Draw near to God, and he will draw near to you. (4:8a)

James first addressed the fact that one must not be a friend of the world if he is going to **draw near to God**. The Hebrew Old Testament spoke of God's people, the Israelites, 'coming near to Jehovah.' (Ex. 19:22; Jer. 30:21; Ez. 44:13) In the New Testament, we have the Father sending humanity his only-begotten Son. (John 3:16) The apostle John tells us, "the Word became flesh and dwelt among us, and we have seen his glory, glory as of the only-begotten *one* from the Father, full of grace and truth." As we learn from the example Christ set while on earth, it is by prayer, repentance, obedience and exclusive devotion to God that Christians can draw near to God. "Now the Spirit of God came upon Azariah, the son of Oded, and he went out before Asa and said to him, 'hear me, Asa, and all Judah and Benjamin: Jehovah is with you while you are with him. If you seek him, he will be found by you, but if you forsake him, he will forsake you.'" (2 Chron. 15:1-2) As we 'get to know the only true God, and Jesus Christ whom he sent' (John 17:3), we will learn more fully of his love, power, wisdom and justice, which will guide us in the way that we should go, as he draws near us as well.

Cleanse your hands, you sinners, and purify your hearts, you double-minded. (4:8b)

The book of James accuses his readers of being guilty of wars at 4:1 and murder at 2:11. Obviously, as was mentioned earlier, James was not talking about literal wars and murder. Rather, he was speaking of ones that were guilty of murderous hatred for others, infighting, slander, and the like. This is why he told them to **cleanse their hands**. This would have sounded familiar to those familiar with Isaiah, which reads,

Isaiah 1:15-16 Updated American Standard Version (UASV)

[15] When you spread out your hands,
    I will hide my eyes from you;
Yes, even though you make many prayers,
    I will not listen.
    Your hands are full[87] of blood.
[16] Wash yourselves; make yourselves clean;
    remove the evil of your deeds from before my eyes;
cease to do evil,

James' readers were **sinners** in more ways than inherited sin or just occasionally committing a sin, they were living in sin and needed to repent, i.e., turnaround from their bad ways. Hands in a figurative sense had many different meanings, but James is using them to symbolize deeds, as almost all work, especially in Bible times, was carried out with the hands. The sinful actions that these ones were carrying out spiritually polluted their hands. Many times within Scripture, the heart is used

---

[87] Or *covered with*

figuratively for "the center of the self, of its feeling and willing, has purity as one of its chief virtues (cf. Matt 5:8; 1 Tim 1:5)." (Richardson 1997, 187) Jesus said, "For out of the heart come evil thoughts, murder, adultery, sexual immorality, theft, false witness, slander." (Matt. 15:19) Our heart "is deceitful above all things, and desperately sick" (Jer. 17:9), which brings forth sinful thinking, leading to sinful works if cultivated. Therefore, we must cleanse the inner person, which will result in good works, which also is facilitated by the power of the Holy Spirit.

James is the only writer to use the expression double-minded, which refers to their impurity of heart and their failure to trust in God. The Greek is literally speaking of two-souled ones, meaning they are trusting in both God and something else: self, world, money, and the like. We likely recall that James said the one who asks God for wisdom and doubts was a double-minded man. In other words, he is an indecisive man, namely, wavering in mind. This one fails to ask God because he is not certain God will or can answer him. Another aspect of this is, one who may ask, but does not have faith either, so he depends on his own wisdom; and then, blames God when things do not go as he had hoped. James said of this man; he is "unstable in all his ways." James' readers were wavering between being a friend to God and being friends with the world, that is, figuratively, adultery.

We need to be every vigilant in our relationship with God. Our inherited sin and human weaknesses, coupled with Satan's world catering to our fallen flesh, will contribute to our drifting away (Heb. 2:1), drawing away (3:12-13), falling away (6:6), becoming sluggish (6:12), grow weary or fainthearted (12:3), or turning away (12:25). One can move away from the Christian faith for many different reasons, and it can be sudden, or so slow that we do not even realize it is taking place. (See Rom. 7:18-19) Therefore, we must employ constant, unending watchfulness.

Be miserable and mourn and weep; (4:9a)

James tells his readers to **be miserable and mourn and weep**, when we know that Christians are not to Christians to be miserable, continuously having some sad view of life, bringing about sad expressions. In fact, Paul said Christian were to "Rejoice in the Lord always; again I will say, rejoice!" (Phil. 4:2) If a Christian is evidencing sadness, it should be the result of a repentant heart. (2 Cor. 7:10-11) Some claiming to be Christian are, in fact, friends with the world and have very little recognizable traits that they are Christian, except when they are at

Christian meetings. If we are heading in that direction, we should be saddened by our spiritually weak state, which should motivate us to make the needed corrections. When we pray and then act on our prayers, knowing that God has forgiven us, we have a clean conscience and find the joy that we were lacking.

let your laughter be turned to mourning, and your joy to gloom. (4:9b)

James wants his readers to realize fully the weightiness of their sins, when he writes, **let your laughter be turned to mourning, and your joy to gloom**. The Old Testament often refers to the laughter of the stupid one or the fool, i.e., the stupid one who ridicules the notion of living a righteous life and without a care in the world goes along in a life of idleness and desire of the fallen flesh. (See Pro. 10:23; Eccl. 7:6) Jesus even commented on such a fool, "Woe to you who laugh now, for you shall mourn and weep." (Lu 6:25b) James and Jesus were rebuking those who believe that they can be friends of the world while saying they are also a servant of God. James wanted them to wake up from their path, this free from care, lighthearted approach to life, and notice it is not the path to salvation. Rather, they need to feel disappointed and mourn over their plight, realizing their need to improve their spirituality. – Matthew 5:3-4.

Humble yourselves in the eyes of the Lord, and he will exalt you. (4:10)

Jesus Christ said, "Whoever exalts himself will be humbled, and whoever humbles himself will be exalted." (Matt. 23:12) Sin means missing the mark of perfection, which we simply do from birth. However, sin is also anything not in agreement with, conflicting with, God's character, values, moral, ethics and ideals, as well as his will and purposes; i.e., anything that can stain our relationship with God. Therefore, we must humble ourselves before God, not thinking more of ourselves than necessary. King David said, "The sacrifices of God are a broken spirit; a broken and contrite heart, O God, you will not despise." (Ps. 51:17) There is nothing that we can do, which will restore our relationship with God, aside from confessing our sins to him and accepting our human weaknesses. Thus, we need to remove the self-important or carefree attitude toward our sinful nature. We must come to the realization that our self-worth is in the fact that God created our parents and loves faithful humanity; then, we will find favor. If we do this, we will have a feeling of intense or extreme happiness or exhilaration, knowing the sin has been removed by Jesus' ransom sacrifice. (Matt 20:28; Rom 5:12; 1 John 2:1) Yes, God will renew our disposition, and we can then feel free from any hypocrisy in our sharing of God's loving-kindness, as well as of his will and purposes.

James 4:11-12 Updated American Standard Version (UASV)

¹¹ Do not speak against one another, brothers. He who speaks against a brother or judges his brother, speaks against the law and judges the law; but if you judge the law, you are not a doer of the law but a judge. ¹² There is only one lawgiver and judge, he who is able to save and to destroy. But who are you to judge your neighbor?

Do not speak against one another, brothers. He who speaks against a brother or judges his brother, speaks against the law and judges the law; but if you judge the law, you are not a doer of the law but a judge. (4:11)

Three times within this one verse, James talks of "speaking against. The Greek term (katalaleo) describes 'speaking against, often involving speaking evil of, to speak evil of, to slander, slander.' (Louw and and Nida 1996, LN 33.388) Moreover, it describes one who accuses someone, with a suggestion of the false and exaggerated.'[88] (Bromiley and Friedrich 1964-, TDNT Volume 4, Page 3) We must keep in mind that Scripture does not say that it is wrong to speak out against wrongdoing, or anything that is contrary to God's Word. For example, the overseers within a congregation counsel on that quite often. Moreover, Christians are to report any serious sin or practice of sin to the church leaders. In addition, if one has been personally wronged,[89] a specific approach needs to take place. In other words, the one who has been personally wronged would go to the person privately. If unsuccessful, they would take another as a witness. If there were still not progress, she or he would take it to the church leaders.

James has already warned against anger (James 1:19–20), favoritism (James 2:1–13), cursing (James 3:9–10), and wars and fights (James 4:1–2). Here James is dealing with another aspect of an incorrect attitude toward

---

[88] See 1 Peter 2:12

[89] Being personally wronged is dealing with minor things, such as bad behavior toward another. This is not dealing with spiritual, mental or physical abuse, or crimes against another. These should be reported to the church leaders, and if a crime, to the police.

one's brother. It is a powerfully grave personal view that is now being considered. Here again, James refers to his readers as "brothers," because this will let them know just how egregious their wrongdoing is. Many times in life, one who lacks love and compassion for another will seek to elevate himself by slandering another, seeking to make him look inferior by comparison. The psalmist describes such a person, "You sit and speak against your brother; you slander your own mother's son." (Ps. 50:20) In addition, a sanctimonious, smug and haughty attitude can make a person disposed toward being critical of others and their human weaknesses, even to the point of accusing them or inferring they are guilty of wrongdoing. (John 9:13-16, 28, 34) Regardless of why, the slander of another has no place within the Christian congregation. (See Lev. 19:16; Pro. 3:29-30) "For all have sinned and fall short of the glory of God" (Rom. 3:23); therefore, the tendency to backbite, gossip or even slander is within us all, so James' counsel is very beneficial.

We can internally evaluate the conduct of another because we must be able to determine who is a good or bad association for our children or us. However, we are not to judge one as to their standing before God, as a righteous one or an unrighteous one. Jesus said, "Do not judge so that you will not be judged." (Matt. 7:1; See Rom. 2:1; 14:1–3) We are not to be overly critical of others, always finding fault, being opinionated. This is true of our perception of nonChristians, and especially of our spiritual brothers and sisters. This is the gossip, backbiting and judging, which James condemns. This wrongful speak toward our brothers is speaking against the law, judging the law, i.e., "the law of liberty." (Jam. 2:8, 12) Again, this "law of liberty" is a reference not to the Mosaic Law, but to the new covenant, in which the Father declared, "I will put my law within them, and I will write it on their hearts. And I will be their God, and they shall be my people." (Jer. 31:33) Christians are under the principles behind the Mosaic Law, not some lengthy code of rules and regulations, but rather under the inspired, inerrant Word of God, which enables them to know the will of the Father. (Matt. 7:21-23; 1 John 2:15-17; Gal. 5:1, 13-14) With a critical and judgmental attitude, we place ourselves in the judgment seat. In this, we are setting aside God's laws, inferring that they need not be obeyed. Christians are obligated to obey God's Word, not be judgmental of it so that we begin to rationalize or justify our violation of it. When we slander others, we are in opposition to the God of love (1 John 4:8) and suggest that we need not obey.

There is only one lawgiver and judge, he who is able to save and to destroy. But who are you to judge your neighbor? (4:12)

The Scripture makes it clear whom the **lawgiver and judge** is, the Father, who is spoken of at Isaiah 33:22, "For Jehovah is our judge; Jehovah is our lawgiver; Jehovah is our king; he will save us." He is the sovereign of the universe, the life giver to spirit creatures, to humans and to animals, which means it is his standards and rules. It is he who determines who does and who does not receive salvation. James spells out what sort of judging is being discussed when he adds, **he who is able to save and to destroy.** One day before Jesus' ascension to heaven, the Son said to his disciples, "All authority has been given to me in heaven and on earth." Who gave the Son this authority? Jesus had said it was the Father earlier to the Pharisees

The Authority of the Son

John 5:19-23 Updated American Standard Version (UASV)

So Jesus answered and was saying to them, "Truly, truly, I say to you, the Son can do nothing of his own accord, but only what he sees the Father doing. For whatever things that One does, these things the Son does likewise. 20For the Father loves the Son and shows him all the things he himself does. And greater works than these will he show him, so that you may marvel. 21For just as the Father raises the dead and makes *them* alive, so also the Son makes alive whom he wants to. 22 For the Father judges no one, but has given all judgment to the Son, 23in order that all may honor the Son, just as they honor the Father. The one who does not honor the Son does not honor the Father who sent him.

The Son said, "Do not fear those who kill the body but are unable to kill the soul; but rather fear Him who is able to destroy both soul and body in Gehenna." (Matt. 10:28) The ones that James is referring to, those that are slandering and judging their brother, most likely are not fully aware of the seriousness of placing themselves on the judgment seat, trying to assume the authority that was given to the Son by the Father! Why would we ever want to live by our human imperfection when we have the perfect lawgiver and judge? The Psalmist wrote, "The law of the Lord is blameless, restoring the soul; the testimony of Jehovah is sure, making wise the simple." (Ps. 19:7) Let us walk through the Bible from beginning to end and see exactly why James' counsel is so very important.

Deuteronomy 12:32 (UASV)	Proverbs 30:5-6 (UASV)	Revelation 22:18 (UASV)

"Everything that I command you, you shall be careful to do; you shall not add to nor take away from it.	5 Every word of God proves true;
	    he is a shield to those who take refuge in him.
	6 Do not add to his words,
	    lest he reprove you and you be found a liar.
		18 I testify to everyone who hears the words of the prophecy of this book: if anyone adds to them, God will add to him the plagues which are written in this book;

While no created has the authority to determine for themselves that something is acceptable when God's Word condemns it, it is just as egregious for any created being to suggest that God's law prohibits something, when it is acceptable. On this Isaiah writes, "Woe to those who call evil good, and good evil, who put darkness for light and light for darkness; who put bitter for sweet and sweet for bitter!" (Isa. 5:20) Wise King Solomon said, "He who justifies the wicked and he who condemns the righteous, both of them alike are an abomination to Jehovah." (Pro. 17:15) Jesus condemned the Jewish religious leaders for just this thing, as their over zealousness of the Law moved them to add hundreds of rules that the common people had to carry out, which were not an obligation and hundreds of rules that prohibited things, when in it was, in fact, acceptable under the Law. James did not want his brothers making this same error of going beyond what the Scriptures said.

Warning Against Pride

James 4:13-17 Updated American Standard Version (UASV)

13 Come now, you who say, "Today or tomorrow we will go into such and such a town and spend a year there and trade and make a profit." 14 Yet you do not know what your life will be like tomorrow.[90] For you are a mist appearing for a little while and then vanishing 15 Instead you ought to say,[91] "If the Lord wills, we will live and do this or that." 16 As it is, you boast in your arrogance. All such boasting is evil.

---

[90] Or *what* will happen *tomorrow. What kind of life is yours?*

[91] Lit *Instead of your saying*

¹⁷ Therefore, to one who knows the right thing to do and does not do it, to him it is sin.

Come now, you who says, "Today or tomorrow we go into such and such a town and spend a year there and trade and make a profit." (4:13)

We should never make any plans without having considered the Word of God, for we should be biblically minded. Bible principles should be embedded in our thinking to the point that what we think is what God would have wanted us to think. Such persons would never make plans that did not involve God, as they are servants of him and in essence, their lives are his. The context is as follows: verses 1-10 speaks of those who set God aside for friendship with the world. Then, verses 11-12 speak of those who have set God aside as the lawgiver and judge for their independent decisions. Now, these same ones act as though their future is absolute, so they can make business plans at the disregard of God. They are self-centered that they have broken down their plans to the point of how long they will stay and just how much profit they will make.

We must understand that James is not suggesting that a person cannot travel until they have some manifestation of proof from God that it is permissible. Rather, what he is reproving is the approach by their arrogant, disrespectful, and self-assured statements. They have not considered God in their plans. For a modern day example, suppose a husband and Father decided that he would get his family out of poverty by taking a long-haul team truck-driving job, which would have him on the road months at a time over a few years. A father is obligated to provide for his family's needs. He is obligated to provide food, clothing, and housing for his wife and children. (1 Tim. 5:8) However, how many other Scriptures would this violate? Aside from financial means, the father is also obligated to take care of his family's mental, spiritual and emotional needs. He is obligated to make Christian meetings, to carry out a personal Bible study with the family, spend quality time with his family, and far more. Therefore, taking such a job would evidence a lack of faith in God and an independent spirit, disregarding the Word of God in his decision.

Yet you do not know what your life will be like tomorrow. For you are a mist appearing for a little while and then vanishing. (4:14)

Solomon writes, "Do not boast about tomorrow, for you do not know what a day may bring." No human can know what the future holds, even a few minutes from the present, let alone a year from the moment of decision-making. God, on the other hand, knows what is going to take place every second into the eternal future. In fact, Solomon warns us, "Again I saw that under the sun the race is not to the swift, nor the battle to the strong, nor bread to the wise, nor riches to men of understanding, nor favor to those with knowledge, **but time and unexpected events happen** to them all."—Ecclesiastes 9:11.

In this imperfect age of Satan, human life is both unclear and short-lived. For we **"are a mist appearing for a little while and then vanishing**." Therefore, we are foolish if we think for a moment that anything other than God is secure to the point that we can build on it. (Eccl. 1:2; 2:17-18) In the business of today, we are making thousands of decisions every day, and it is quite easy to allow God to fade out of our decisions. Therefore, we should have a biblical worldview[92] because we are a serious student of God's Word. We should never ignore that biblical mind, the mind of Christ, the whispering of the Scriptures in our ear, telling us, 'this is the way that you should go.'

Instead you ought to say, "If the Lord wills, we will live and do this or that." (4:15)

As the father and the husband, the wife and mother, or a single Christian, male or female, we have dreams of the kind of work we want to do, the type of job, our church life, or our family life. This is perfectly fine; James is simply recommending that God be at the forefront of any decisions we make. James wants us to say, **"If the Lord wills, we will live and do this or that**." This does not mean that everything that we think, do, feel, or believe in our life is the will of God, because we are imperfect humans, and we are living in a wicked world that is ruled by Satan the Devil. This is not to say that human weaknesses, a fallen world, or Satan can foil God's will. It means that we will not perfectly follow the lords will at every moment of our life. If we did, we would be perfect.

Being imperfect humans, who are 'mentally bent toward evil,' possessing a deceitful heart that is desperately sick, and a natural desire for wrongdoing, we can do but one thing. We need to heed the following verses,

---

[92] A biblical world view is ideas and beliefs through which a Christian interprets the world and interacts with it.

Matthew 7:21-23 Updated American Standard Version (UASV)

21 "Not everyone who says to me, 'Lord, Lord,' will enter the kingdom of heaven, but **the one <u>who does the will</u> of my Father** who is in heaven. **22** On that day many will say to me, 'Lord, Lord, did we not prophesy in your name, and cast out demons in your name, and do many mighty works in your name?' **23** And then I will declare to them, 'I never knew you; depart from me, you who practice lawlessness.'

1 John 2:15-17 Updated American Standard Version (UASV)

15 Do not love the world or the things in the world. If anyone loves the world, the love of the Father is not in him. **16** For all that is in the world, the lust of the flesh and the lust of the eyes and the boastful pride of life, is not from the Father, but is from the world. **17** The world is passing away, and its lusts; but **the one <u>who does the will</u> of God** lives forever.

How are we to know the **will of God**? We do so through the inspired, fully inerrant Word of God. If we have a biblical worldview and we follow Scripture, interpreting it correctly, we will do the will of the Father. What we do not want to do is to adopt some cliché, repeatedly saying, 'if the Lord wills it.' This makes it superstitious, some routine or habit, which is using it to be noticed by others. This becomes insincere or phony and a mockery of the principle behind James' words. We need not say it out loud, but know in our heart of hearts that we seek God's will and purposes in every decision in life, and when we fail to do so in a case of human weakness, we will correct it most it most of the time when it comes to our attention.

As it is, you boast in your arrogance. All such boasting is evil. (4:16)

Those who have had success in business tend to boast of those successes. However, this is not the way of a true Christian. James is saying that these ones were boasting of the successes they would have in their future to the disregard of God, the very person that holds their eternal future in his hands. Yes, this is arrogant indeed. The bright lights of life have blinded these ones. They are as the apostle John said, "For all that is in the world, the lust of the flesh and the lust of the eyes and the boastful pride of life, is not from the Father, but is from the world." (1 John 2:16) Our boasting is to result from our relationship with God. His presence has been a blessing to our lives and will continue to do so. Paul wrote, "My power is made perfect in weakness." (2 Cor. 12:9) Paul knew that when

119

he was weak, the power of God protected him, and this is where the boasting should lay.

The boasting and arrogance are evil because it is of the world, which is under the rulership of Satan, and this one is fooling himself if he believes it will be lasting. Oh, he may be a successful businessman his entire life, but if this arrogance remains it will end at death. He rather should return to his dependence on God.

Jeremiah 9:23-24 Updated American Standard Version (UASV)

23 Thus says Jehovah: "Let not the **wise** man boast in his wisdom, let not the **mighty** man boast in his might, let not the **rich** man boast in his riches, **24** but let him who boasts boast in this, that he understands and knows me, that I am Jehovah who exercises loving kindness, justice and righteousness on earth, for I delight in these things," declares Jehovah.

God is not saying that one cannot be wise, mighty or rich, but rather he should not fall into the wrong way of thinking, by bragging about them. To do so, would be to ignore his dependence on God. Such an attitude would be the result of a self-fantasy and arrogance. In the end, it will result in condemnation.

Therefore, to one who knows the right thing to do and does not do it, to him it is sin. (4:17)

These words of James in verse 17 are contextually related to what had been said in verses 14-16, i.e., boasting in ignorance as to their future successes when they have failed to consider God. If a person understands that they can indeed not accomplish anything eternally successful without God's help and yet fails or refuses to depend on God, this is a sin. However, James' words can by implication apply to sins of omission as well.

Thus, one who offers himself to God must carry out that commitment. He has an obligation to carry out his Christian duties, responsibilities to the best of his abilities. It is a sin if he does not do the right thing. How can this be you may ask? Well, picture him coming out of a store when he sees a very young child running into traffic. What if he has every opportunity to grab the child before it is run over, but instead, he turns his back and walks away? True, there will be no legal consequences in the human legal system. However, as a Christian before the one lawgiver and judge, the fact that he could have done what was right, what was obligated and did nothing, it would be a sin. Are there times when we failed to express Christian love toward another, especially a spiritual brother or sister, or toward God? Each time we failed to do so, it was a sin for us. Every Christian should humbly recognize his dependence on God.

Review Question

(1) **[vs 1]** What is the source of wars and fights among you?

(2) **[vs 1]** Just how bad is the sinful nature of fallen human?

(3) **[vs 2]** How are we to understand James' words in verse 2?

(4) **[vs 3]** Why were these ones prayers not being answered?

(5) **[vs 4]** How is friendship with the world enmity toward God?

(6) **[vs 5]** How prevalent is envy in the world today?

(7) **[vs 6]** The words, "God opposes the proud, but gives grace to the humble," should move us do what?

(8) **[vs 7]** How complete should a Christians subjection to God be?

(9) **[vs 8]** How can Christians draw close to God?

(10) **[vs 9]** How are we to understand James' words here?

(11) **[vs 10]** How are we to humble ourselves in the eyes of God?

(12) **[vs 11]** What does James mean when he says, "He who speaks against a brother or judges his brother"?

(13) **[vs 12]** "But who are you to judge your neighbor?" Who is your neighbor?

(14) **[vs 13]** What does James mean here?

(15) **[vs 14]** Why should we not view the life we have now as being so special?

(16) **[vs 15]** What attitude should we have?

(17) **[vs 16]** Why is pride so wicked?

(18) **[vs 17]** Explain what James means here.

JAMES CHAPTER 5 Warning to the Rich

Misuse of Riches

James 5:1-6 Updated American Standard Version (UASV)

¹Come now, you rich, weep and howl for your miseries which are coming upon you. ² Your riches have rotted and your garments are moth-eaten. ³ Your gold and your silver have rusted; and their rust will be a witness against you and will eat your flesh like fire. You have laid up treasure in the last days. ⁴ Behold, the wages of the laborers who mowed your fields, which you kept back by fraud, are crying out against you, and the cries of the harvesters have reached the ears of the Lord of Sabaoth.[93] ⁵ You have lived on the earth in luxury and in sensual indulgence. You have fattened[94] your hearts in a day of slaughter. ⁶ You have condemned, and you have murdered[95] the righteous one; he does not resist you.

Come now, you rich, weep and howl (5:1a)

James is calling for the rich to take heed to what follows. In the above passage, James singles out the rich saying **you rich weep and howl**, in their need for urgency to take heed to his words. This is not because the rich are more sinful than others are. However, the rich have the greater temptation to let their earthly riches surpass their need for the incredible riches in Christ. The rich have more of a tendency to perceive that they have no need for God but can depend on the security of their wealth. James is warning them that they need to not be overly concerned about their riches in light of what is about to happen to them.

James has already talked about the emotions of weeping and mourning in connection with repentance in chapter four. Now again, James uses these terms for the rich man as a means to say that they too need to repent due to what is about to happen to their riches that cannot save them. James tells them to take heed of the fact that they are to weep and to howl. The word here that James uses for weep means to wail and lament and is not just the shedding of tears but an outward expression of grief as if wailing over someone who has died. James also says the word

---

[93] I.e. Hosts

[94] Lit., *nourished*

[95] Or *put to death*

howl means to shriek. The word also means to cry aloud as if one would cry aloud to a god. James adds that the reasoning for the weeping and howling is for the miseries that are about to come upon them.

for your miseries which are coming upon you. (5:1b)

James here now gives the reason as to why he writes to these rich that they were to weep and mourn for their miseries that were going to come upon them. Under the influence of the Holy Spirit, James gives a great warning for these rich to repent because of the soon coming devastation upon their city. The rich with all their wealth and luxuries were thinking that they were secure with no fears. They felt that they could hide behind their wealth, and since they lived in the Great City of God in Jerusalem, nothing would ever happen to them. They feared little because their riches appeared to protect them from the difficulties of daily life.

However, they would find that the words of James would come true when the Roman army under the leadership of General Titus came into the city of Jerusalem and destroyed it. James wrote his book most likely about 62 C.E.

James wrote the letter to "the twelve tribes in the Dispersion."[96] (1:1) James is addressing the letter to his spiritual brothers, who should have been 'holding their faith in our glorious Lord Jesus Christ.' (2:1; 5:7) In other words, he was writing to Christian congregations that were outside of Palestine. Much of the counsel offered throughout the letter comes from the Hebrew Scriptures, which does not necessarily mean the letter was meant for Jewish Christians alone. He made a reference to Abraham as being "our father," similar to Paul's words at Galatians 3:28-29, where Paul makes it clear that the true seed of Abraham is not determined by whether one is a Jew or a Greek. Therefore, James is addressing the "the Israel of God" (Gal 6:15-16), i.e., spiritual Israel, not some natural Israel.

Two years after James wrote his letter, the Christians living in Rome would receive the blame by Roman Emperor Nero for burning down much of Rome in 64 C.E., and a great persecution of Christians throughout the empire would be under way. Just six years later, in 70 C.E., the Roman General Titus would destroy the city of Jerusalem, and devastate the land of Judah. Over 1,100,00 Jews would be slaughtered,

---

[96] Jewish people scattered throughout Gentile lands

with an additional 97,000 being taken captive, many going into slavery in Egypt and others to Rome to be killed by beasts in the theaters. Therefore, obeying the counsel in the whole of James' letter was paramount, but especially those who felt their wealth would protect them from the coming persecution. For example, the Roman General Cestius Gallus had come to Jerusalem in 66 C.E. to quash an uprising. He surrounded the city with Roman troops and was in the verge of taking it, when he pulled away for some unknown reason. This left an open window for the Christians to recall Jesus' words and act. (Matt 24:1-2; Lu 21:20-22) If the rich hesitated over their wealth, they would be there when Titus came back in 70 C.E. Yes, they need to flee the city, if lives were to be saved, even if it meant leaving possessions behind.

Your riches have rotted and your garments are moth-eaten. Your gold and your silver have rusted; and their rust will be a witness against you and will eat your flesh like fire. You have laid up treasure in the last days. (5:2-3)

Items that could make one wealthy or appear wealthy in James' day were food (Luke 12:18; Joel 2:19), expensive clothing, and precious metals (Acts 20:33). The point that James is making here is not that riches are perishable, which would be true had that been his point. Rather, his point is that in the end they are worthless when set beside what God has offered his servants. Is there any amount of money that can buy perfection or eternal life? – Proverbs 11:28.

Expensive clothing was evidence of one's riches, or like today was a means of trying to appear wealthy. In James' day, the wealthy could have hundreds or even thousands of expensive garments, many of which had already suffered an attack by moths. Such high numbers were not for personal use alone but were for banquets. Other wealthy and powerful guests would be offered these expensive garments during certain gatherings. – Matthew 22:11; see Matthew 6:19.

Actually, gold and silver cannot rust, so James is figuratively saying that gold and silver are as worthless as something that has rusted. What do we do with something that is completely rusted through? We throw it in the garbage. These ones had placed all of their hopes in wealth as opposed to placing their hopes in God up unto the last days. Now, theses ones wealth were witnesses against them before God, condemning them.

Jesus came to offer all repentant ones an opportunity to act on the good news of the kingdom, by evidencing trust in his ransom sacrifice.

(Matt. 20:28; John 3:16) Speaking to the philosophers at Athens, Paul said, "The times of ignorance God overlooked, but now he commands all people everywhere to repent." (Acts 17:30) Just two years after James' letter, Christians suffered under the persecution of the Roman Emperor Nero in 64 C.E. while the Roman General Titus in 70 C.E. decimated Jerusalem and Judea. When we have no idea of the day and the hour of Jesus' return, which should not be our motivating factor anyway, we should not have wealth as the primary factor in our life. We should not store up and rely on our riches to save the day, as they will only serve as a witness against us, bringing the fire of God's anger. (Isaiah 30:27) It should be noted that wealth is not the enemy, but rather it is the love of wealth, the pursuit of wealth, the reliance upon wealth, over our trust in God.

Behold, the wages of the laborers who mowed your fields, which you kept back by fraud, are crying out against you, (5:4a)

Here is the real crime, as it is not as if the wealthy had earned their riches through wise business practices, but rather had done so by fraudulently withholding to from their workers. Think of those earning minimum wages to day, because they are living from one paycheck to the next, and to have just one withheld could cause their entire world to crumble. In ancient times, the laborer was paid at the end of each day and the wages were barely enough for food and housing to get through the next day. Therefore, to withhold his pay was one of the greatest crimes that one could commit, literally life and death. (Lev. 19:13; Deut. 24:14–15; Jer. 22:13) Both Jesus and Paul made it very clear that "the laborer deserves his wages." (Lu 10:7; Rom. 4:4; 1 Tim. 5:18) This stolen money of the wealthy is worthless in the end, as it will only serve as a witness to their crimes before God.—See Malachi 3:5.

and the cries of the harvesters have reached the ears of the Lord of the Sabaoth. (5:4b)

These workers, whether servants of God or not, are crying out over their miscarriage of just. Jesus heard the cries of the harvesters and came to the aid of the oppressed, as it is he does not forget, and when he returns all will be held accountable. The Mosaic Law stated, "You shall not oppress a hired worker who is poor and needy, whether he is one of your brothers or one of the sojourners who are in your land within your towns. You shall give him his wages on the same day, before the sun sets (for he is poor and counts on it), lest he cry against you to the Lord, and you be guilty of sin." (Deut. 24:14-15) The Almighty will not let the injustices of the wicked go unanswered forever. The day is coming, when the lovers of money will be held accountable for their wrongs. (See Genesis 18:20) Into what great danger the ones who have deprived the day workers of their money by dishonest means find themselves!

You have lived on the earth in luxury and in sensual indulgence. You have fattened your hearts in a day of slaughter. (5:5)

These wealthy ones have failed to treat their workers justly, let alone helping the downtrodden; rather they **have lived on the earth in luxury and in sensual indulgence**. These ones were living sensual and indulgent lives, who have unnecessary excesses that evidenced no regard for those they had to take from to live such a life. The mindset of these ones was enveloped in the fleshly living as opposed to a spiritual life. The apostle Paul also showed where such a lifestyle would lead when talking of widows, "she who is self-indulgent is dead even while she lives." A person with this mindset and who seeks his own self-gratification over and other, will eventually lead to immorality as well. This is not just sexual but includes many things that are contrary to accepted moral principles (See 2 Timothy 3:2-6) For example, one who is focused only on his sensual indulgences could commit acts of cruelty, persecution and brutality to gain and retain riches to continue one's luxurious lifestyle.

You have fattened your hearts in a day of slaughter, describes taking in enormous amounts of something with no regard, not even considering there will be a day of slaughter that awaits them. In ancient times, fatness was actually considered a positive quality because it was a sign of wealth, as it meant that the person had enough money to eat enough to be fat. When fattening a pig, we know that it will eat both meat and vegetables. It will consume anything, including bones, fish heads and table scraps.[97] Think of the parallel, the pig gorges himself not knowing that there is a day of slaughter at the end of all of his self-indulgence. One would think that the wealthy would have used the intelligence that made them rich to see that things were not going to end well, but they acted like senseless, oblivious animals. While they lived out this luxurious lifestyle, the day of slaughter (divine judgment) was watching, waiting and would soon condemn them for their evil ways.

---

[97] http://www.ehow.com/how_4798050_put-weight-pig.html

You have condemned, and you have murdered the righteous one; he does not resist you. (5:6)

The rich **have condemned** and **have murdered the righteous one**. The word that James uses here for condemn is a legal term, which means to bring an accusation against another. The righteous man that the rich were putting to death were the Christians, they were refusing to pay though **he does not resist you**. They were killing innocent Christians in the fact that they were causing great devastation in the lives of the believers by not giving them their pay. James had already mentioned earlier in his letter that the rich were dragging them into the courts. The rich would have had the ability with their finances to be able to try to condemn these Christians. The rich were coming against Christians that were not even resisting them in the first place and had no ground for their behavior against them. The fact that these poor Christians did not retaliate against these landowners could be due to the application of the Lords commands in Matthew 5:38-39.

At times, the life of the righteous one's may have appeared to be in vain because they walked a life of one difficulty after another, while the rich were just getting richer. (Psalm 73) However, this just was not the case, nor is it today. Yes, for a time, the rich who attained their wealth through dishonest gain seem to have it all. In addition, until the poor Christian can come to appreciate that drawing near to God was in his best interests, the potential of envy setting in is possible. It can get to the point where the worshiper begins to doubt the value of worshiping God. However, if he would just ponder for a moment, he would realize that devotion to God is the only way to eternal happiness, as opposed to immediate gratification. He will come to realize that God hates the evil far more than he ever could, and in due time, the wicked will be punished. In fact, it is the life of suffering that this righteous one had to go through that will serve as a witness against the evil one.

Persecution of Disciples Predicted

Mark 13:9-11 English Standard Version (ESV)

[9] "But be on your guard. For they will deliver you over to councils, and you will be beaten in synagogues, and you will stand before governors and kings [and the wealthy] for my sake, to bear witness before them. [10] And the gospel must first be proclaimed to all nations. [11] And when they bring you to trial and deliver you over, do not

be anxious beforehand what you are to say, but say whatever is given you in that hour, for it is not you who speak, but the Holy Spirit.

James 5:7-11 Updated American Standard Version (UASV)

⁷ Be patient, therefore, brothers, until the coming of the Lord. See how the farmer waits for the precious fruit of the earth, being patient about it, until it receives the early and the late rains. ⁸ You also, be patient. Establish your hearts,[98] for the coming of the Lord is at hand. ⁹ Do not grumble against one another, brothers, so that you may not be judged; behold, the Judge is standing at the door. ¹⁰ As an example, brothers, of suffering and patience, take the prophets who spoke in the name of the Lord. ¹¹ We count those blessed who endured. You have heard of the endurance[99] of Job and have seen the outcome of the Lord, that the Lord is full of compassion and is merciful.

Be patient, therefore, brothers, until the coming of the Lord. (5:7a)

In review, James laid out a case against the evil rich over the righteous poor:

(1) collecting and storing large amounts of food or money for their future use, which could have been used to help the poor,

(2) withholding the wages of workers, which they needed to survive from day to day,

(3) living in luxury and in sensual indulgence, while

(4) condemning and murdering the righteous one.

Now James turns his attention to the burdened Christians, to reassure them that their long-suffering spirit will not be in vain. He encourages them to not become envious, irritated, resentful, or to tire out, but rather to be steadfast in their carrying out the will of God. James urges the brothers to be patient in the face of these adversities as well as whatever else this imperfect world has to offer, until the coming of the Lord. Of course, looking back, those first century Christians would die before the second coming of Christ. Nevertheless, a lifetime of patience and endurance in a righteous standing before God would get them

---

[98] Or *strengthen your hearts*

[99] Or *steadfastness*

written in the book of remembrance, i.e., the book of life. (Ex. 32:32; Mal. 3:16; Phil 4:3; Rev. 3:5; 20:15) In the end, they will receive "the resurrection of life, and those who have done evil to the resurrection of judgment." – John 5:28-29.

See how the farmer waits for the precious fruit of the earth, being patient about it, until it receives the early and the late rains. (5:7b)

Zondervan Bible Background writes, "In Palestine, the growth of crops was particularly dependent on the rain that came in late autumn and early spring. Note, for example, Deuteronomy 11:14, where God, in response to his people's obedience, promises: 'Then I will send rain on your land in its season, both autumn and spring rains, so that you may gather in your grain, new wine and oil.' Every passage in which the language of "early and late rains" appears in the Old Testament affirms God's faithfulness to his people. James's readers may well have detected an "echo" of this faithfulness theme in the illustration here." (Arnold 2002, p. 116) The farmer cannot control the weather, or how his plants will turn out, but he is very familiar with the different seasons and how they progress. The farmer knows that it is God, who set in motion, the components of weather, seasons, seeds, soil and so on, and the day of harvest will come when it comes. Therefore, while he highly anticipates the harvest, which brings life-sustaining food for his family, he must patiently await the day.

You also, be patient. Establish your hearts, for the coming of the Lord is at hand. (5:8)

Regardless of what takes place in a world that is ruled by imperfect humans that are alienated from God and are under the control of Satan, Christians should never lose their trust in Christ. To the contrary, we need to 'be prepared to make a defense to anyone who asks you for a reason for the hope that is in us.' (1 Pet. 3:15) Not only are we sure that relief from sin, suffering, old age and death will come, but that there will be an accounting for all. (Rom. 9:28; Matt. 16:27) Even if they have passed on into death, God will remember their lifetime of patient endurance. James was writing to some, who needed to get back on track spiritually, as they were not acting as ones who have implicit trust in Jesus Christ. For example, some had allowed bad desires to creep within their hearts. They needed to be patient and prayerful.

Do not grumble against one another, brothers, so that you may not be judged; behold, the Judge is standing at the door. (5:9)

Zondervan Bible Background writes, "The word "grumble" translates a word (stenazō) that often connotes the frustration of God's people at the oppression that they are suffering. Exodus 2:23 is a classic example: 'During that long period, the king of Egypt died. The Israelites groaned in their slavery and cried out, and their cry for help because of their slavery went up to God.' James, of course, here prohibits believers from grumbling against each other. But his use of this word may hint at the fact that their impatience with one another is the product of the persecution they are enduring." (Arnold 2002, p. 117)

Christians are advised to **not grumble against one another**. The Greek word (stenazō) implies inner sighing or groaning, as opposed to openly complaining against another. Earlier in the letter, James dealt with brothers that were openly speaking against and judging others in the congregation. In this instance, he is getting at the feeling behind those outward complaining judgments, which can ruin relationships; even those not directly involved causing a rift within the congregation. Consider that the one grumbling internally has close friends and the one those grumbles are directed against has close friends as well. Thus, friends tend to side with friends.

Within the congregation, someone is bound to let us down, maybe even numerous times, which can move us toward sighing or groaning internally, as they failed to live up to our expectations. Thus, James is letting the brothers know that we live in imperfect flesh, within a fallen humanity, having Satan cater to our human weaknesses, all the while being mentally bent toward bad. In other words, Christians being aware of these conditions need to make allowances for one another. (See Gal. 6:10) Instead of sighing or groaning over perceived slights against us, we get back to the need of being **patient until the coming of the Lord.** (5:7) In fact, if they carry on in sighing or groaning against their brother, it is they that will be guilty before the judgment seat of God, as he can read their heart, the seat of motivation. We should be cautious here because it is not sighing or groaning themselves that is being condemned because Jesus did so. (Mark 7:34) Rather, sighing or groaning that comes about from a wrong inner attitude toward one's brother.

When James says, **behold, the Judge is standing at the door**, he is inferring that the second coming of Jesus is near. For example, Jesus said about the end of this wicked age, "so, you too, when you see these things happening, recognize that He is near, right at the door." (Mark 13:29, NASB) Thus, if James were warning the first century Christians about the nearness of the second coming of Christ, should not the Christians of the 21st century be even more concerned. As Edward Andrews has written elsewhere, 'we need to live as though Jesus is returning tomorrow, but plan as though it is fifty years from now.' In other words, we maintain our righteous standing before God, because the second coming could come at any time, but we plan a long life of carrying out his will and purposes. However, let it be said that we do not maintain a righteous standing for fear of a return at any time, but because it is the right thing to do. We must certainly not let our desire for relief through Jesus' return slowly give way to a lack of patience, resulting in feeling displeasure concerning our Christian brothers. Though we do not complain outwardly, the sighing and groaning of the inner person can condemn him.

As an example, brothers, of suffering and patience, take the prophets who spoke in the name of the Lord. (5:10)

Being moved along by Holy Spirit, the prophets of the Old Testament were the mouth of God as what they spoke was directly from God himself. James wants these brothers to recall the difficult times that some of these prophets had to endure patiently. These prophets lived through the savage Assyrian and Babylonian Empires, but also wicked rulers from their people, who were known to kill prophets with a message they did not like. God's prophets were about faith and endurance. In other words, these men from old have successfully faced what James' readers were facing and what we have to face. Jeremiah, for example, suffered all kinds of afflictions but faithfully and patiently continued to serve as God's prophet. (Jer. 20:8-11) Just before being martyred by the Jewish religious leaders, Stephen said, "Which of the prophets did your fathers not persecute?" – Acts 7:52.

These faithful prophets on occasion felt disheartened, confounded at why this or that was not happening. Some, like Habakkuk, went to God in prayers, asking him why he continued to allow these rich, powerful men and corrupt kings to rule. In all of this, they by no means abandoned their path of endurance in favor of sighing and groaning against God or their fellow brothers. Rather, they tried to use their office as God's spokesmen to lovingly help those who were persecuting them. For example, Jeremiah warned, "They will not give you over. Please obey

Jehovah in what I am saying to you, that it may go well with you and you may live." – Jeremiah 38:20

We count those blessed who endured. (5:11a)

Certainly, anyone who has endured in the face of serious trials has the blessing of God. Jesus said, "Blessed are you when others revile you and persecute you and utter all kinds of evil against you falsely on my account. Rejoice and be glad, for your reward is great in heaven, for so they persecuted the prophets who were before you." (Matt. 5:11-12) The brothers should be comforted by past examples of those who have faithfully endured as well as by Jesus' words. It should enable them to walk faithfully through their own hardships, serving God with patience. If we can see in our heart the blessing of serving faithfully, we can be comforted as well.

You have heard of the endurance of Job (5:11b)

This is the only place in the New Testament Job is mentioned. If we have had an opportunity to read the book of Job, we might be thinking that Job is a bad example of patient endurance, as he complained to God quite a bit. However, the endurance James had in mind is one of a hero to the faith, one who faithfully survived the greatest trial when Satan had complete access to him. In this case, Job is an exceptional example of courageous endurance, especially in the fact that he was not even an Israelite. Moreover, the book of Job itself is a major part of the answer as to why God has allowed sin to enter into the world, placing mankind into an object lesson.—Job 1:7-22; 2:6-10

and have seen the outcome of the Lord, that the Lord is full of compassion and is merciful. (5:11c)

After God had allowed Job to go through extreme difficulties and to suffer at the hands of Satan, with Job evidencing that he could patiently endure anything, he was rewarded for his loyalty. Job now had a better understanding of God's will and purposes. He could now see God's sovereignty, holiness, power, love, justice, faithfulness, righteousness, mercifulness, and wisdom. (Job 40:6-14; 42:2) Also, God stated his approval of Job before the three false comforters, who were supposed to be his friends. God made the reproved friends pray for Job. (Job 42:7, 8) Job had his health restored, and his life was extended another 140 years, during which he had another ten children and doubling his material possessions. (Job 42:10-17) Moreover, the respect, dignity and good name that Job had possessed before was now restored. Job became the symbol of righteousness. He and his family will receive a resurrection. – Job 14:13-15.

Because Job did not fully understand why God would allow him to go through these trials, he allowed wrong conclusions to come into his thinking. However, he remained faithful to God, unwaveringly rejecting any idea of denying God or accusing him of being unrighteous. (Job 1:21, 22; 2:9, 10) The way God dealt with Job throughout evidenced his great attributes of compassion and mercy. (Ex. 34:6; Ps. 103:8) In the end, Job repented over the mistaken things that he said during his conversation with the false comforters. – Job 42:1-7.

This should have brought comfort to James' readers and should do so for Christians today, as God will be faithful to those who are faithful to him. We simply need to endure with patience and keep our inner thinking clean and firmly fixed on the coming of the Lord. We can know with certainty that God will walk with us through this evil age in which we live, helping us to be faithful to the end, just as he had done with the faithful men of old. – Micah 7:18-19.

James 5:12 Updated American Standard Version (UASV)

¹² But above all, my brothers, do not swear, either by heaven or by earth or by any other oath, but let your "yes" be yes and your "no" be no,¹⁰⁰ so that you may not fall under judgment.

But above all, my brothers, do not swear, either by heaven or by earth or by any other oath, but let your "yes" be yes and your "no" be no, so that you may not fall under judgment. (5:12)

James likely had the words of Jesus in mind,

Matthew 5:34-37 New American Standard Bible (NASB)

³⁴ But I say to you, make no oath at all, either by heaven, for it is the throne of God, ³⁵ or by the earth, for it is the footstool of His feet, or by Jerusalem, for it is the city of the great King. ³⁶ Nor shall you make an oath by your head, for you cannot make one hair white or black. ³⁷ But let your statement be, 'Yes, yes' or 'No, no'; anything beyond these is of evil.

---

¹⁰⁰ Lit., *yours is to be yes, yes, and no, no*

Douglas J. Moo writes, "When James says *Do not swear*, it is not coarse or vulgar speech he prohibits but invoking God's name to guarantee the reliability of what a person says."[101] When James says "above all," he is not suggesting that refraining from swearing is the most important thing of all. He simply meant that aside from anything else they were doing, they should not be swearing. As swearing would be a misuse of the tongue that would result in more sinning, by using unproductive and worthless words. Likely, too, he was suggesting that it was worse than grumbling against one another. James is not referring to oaths that would be required of witnesses in a court of law, or at times when dealing with a very significant or severe nature.

The reason both James and Jesus spoke of swearing by "heaven and earth" specifically is, because the Pharisees had no problem swearing by anything except God. When Jesus covered this issue, he was clear that to swear by the things that God created is worthless, and worse still, it is displeasing to God. Swearing by such things was simply a pretense or convenience, avoiding the use of God's name in a worthless way. The person swearing on insignificant things was simply trying to make his words carry more weight than they did. Kistemaker and Hendriksen write, "The people knew the commandment, 'You shall not misuse the name of [Jehovah][102] your God, for [Jehovah] will not hold anyone guiltless who misuses his name' (Exod. 20:7; Deut. 5:11, [ASV]). To remain guiltless, the Jews had made a distinction between binding and nonbinding oaths. Instead of using the divine name (which would be binding), they swore "by heaven or by earth or by anything else." In their opinion, that would be nonbinding and would not incur the wrath of God.[103] Both Jesus and James denounce this practice; the intention of appealing to God remains the same, even though one pretends to avoid

---

[101] Douglas J. Moo, *The Letter of James*, The Pillar New Testament Commentary (Grand Rapids, MI; Leicester, England: Eerdmans; Apollos, 2000), 232.

[102] Christian Publishing House finds it a bit insulting when modern translations remove the personal name of God for a title (i.e., "the Lord"), and verses such as this makes our position even clearer. How can one have a verse that speaks of misusing God's name (not title), and the translators remove that name and replace it with an impersonal title? The irony is that these translators are following a Jewish tradition by removing God's personal name, and what did Jesus say about the traditions of the Jewish leaders? He said they were 'making void the word of God by their tradition that they had handed down.'–Mark 7:13.

[103] Refer to SB, vol. 1, pp. 332–37, for rabbinic sources. Also see D. Edmond Hiebert, *The Epistle of James: Tests of a Living Faith* (Chicago: Moody, 1979), p. 310; D. Edmond Hiebert, "The Worldliness of Self-Serving Oaths," *Direction* 6 (1977): 39–43.

using God's name.[104] Persons, who are always saying, "I swear by ..." are only evidencing that they are impulsive, unsteady and undependable persons. – Matthew 23:16-22.

When James says that we should let our "yes" be yes and your "no" be no, he is referring to forthright, straight, simple and certain answers. If our word has always been one that can be trusted there is no need to go through extra steps to be convincing, or impressive, or to come off as being honest because everyone knows that our "yes" is yes and our "no" is no. If we cannot be trusted to be honest and forthright in oaths or vows that do not involve God, how are we to be taken seriously when our word does involve God? If we are constantly invoking God, "I swear to God," in every little thing that we say, we come off as a person that cannot be trusted, and why would anyone want to be involved in a religion of a person that cannot be trusted, meaning our witnessing about Christ would be impeded.

Helping Through Prayer and Forgiveness

James 5:13-18 Updated American Standard Version (UASV)

[13] Is anyone among you suffering? Let him pray. Is anyone cheerful? Let him sing praise.[105] [14] Is anyone among you sick? Let him call for the elders of the church, and let them pray over him, anointing him with oil in the name of the Lord. [15] And the prayer of faith will save the one who is sick,[106] and the Lord will raise him up. And if he has committed sins, he will be forgiven. [16] Therefore, confess your sins to one another, and pray

---

[104] Simon J. Kistemaker and William Hendriksen, *Exposition of James and the Epistles of John*, vol. 14, New Testament Commentary (Grand Rapids: Baker Book House, 1953–2001), 172.

[105] Lit., *sing psalms*

[106] The "sickness" here is a reference to spiritual weakness or sickness, not some physical sickness. The J. P. Lang Commentary says, 1. The calling for the presbyters of the congregation in the Plural; 2. the general direction concerning their prayer accompanying unction with oil; 3. and especially the confident promise that the prayer of faith shall restore the sick apart from his restoration being connected with the forgiveness of his sins. Was the Apostle warranted to promise bodily recovery in every case in which a sick individual complied with his directions? This misgiving urges us to adopt the symbolical construction of the passage, which would be as follows: if any man as a Christian has been hurt or become sick in his Christianity, let him seek healing from the presbyters, the kernel of the congregation. Let these pray with and for him and anoint him with the oil of the Spirit; such a course wherever taken, will surely restore him and his transgressions will be forgiven him. - John Peter Lange, Philip Schaff, et al., *A Commentary on the Holy Scriptures: James* (Bellingham, WA: Logos Bible Software, 2008), 138.

for one another so that you may be healed. The supplication[107] of a righteous man can accomplish much. **¹⁷** Elijah was a man with a nature like ours, and he prayed fervently that it might not rain, and for three years and six months it did not rain on the earth. **¹⁸** Then he prayed again, and heaven gave rain, and the earth produced its fruit.

Is any among you suffering? Let him pray. (5:13a)

We may recall back in chapter 5 verse 10, James wrote, "As an example, brothers, of suffering and patience, take the prophets." He may have had the prophets in mind here just three verses later. Recall too that Paul told Timothy, "you, be sober-minded in all things, **endure hardship**, do the work of an evangelist, fulfill your ministry." (2 Tim. 4:5) No affliction should discourage any Christian. If ever, we are discouraged, it is our irrational worldly thinking because we have set aside our biblical mindset, the mind of Christ. We need to know that it is the sin of Adam, which has brought us suffering, not God. We need to know that it is inherited sin, missing the mark of perfection, human weaknesses, being mentally bent toward evil, having a deceitful heart, having a natural desire toward wrong, and an imperfect world run by Satan that causes us any suffering. We need to know that in the end, God wins, so we win. (Rom. 8:28) We simply need to draw close to God and the God of comfort will draw close to us.–2 Corinthians 1:3-5; James 4:8

If we were to look to the faithful biblical persons and our primary example Jesus Christ, we see that it is prayer, talking with the Father over the challenging decisions we must make, the difficulties that this life of imperfection throws at us, which gets us through the suffering. (Luke 6:12-13) The night before his death, in the Garden of Gethsemane, Jesus prayed with loud cries and tears to the Father. Peter informed his readers that "the eyes of the Lord are on the righteous, and his ears are open to their prayer." (1 Pet. 3:12) The apostle Paul wrote, "Rejoice in hope, be patient in tribulation, be constant in prayer." (Rom. 12:12) No matter the circumstance, praying is always available and we know that Jesus will entreat the Father on our behalf. Jesus tells us, "In that day you will ask in my name, and I do not say to you that I will ask the Father on your behalf; for the Father himself loves you, because you have loved me and have believed that I came from God." (John 16:26-27) Paul wrote, "For we do not have a high priest who is unable to sympathize with our weaknesses, but one who in every respect has been tempted as we are,

---

[107] I.e., *prayer*

yet without sin. Let us then with confidence draw near to the throne of grace, that we may receive mercy and find grace to help in time of need." – Hebrews 4:15-16

Is any cheerful? Let him sing praise. (5:13b)

James now goes from how one who suffers, to asking **is any cheerful?** James has just stated that the response for the one suffering is to pray. Here now James expresses that the response to the one who is cheerful is that he should **sing praise**. At times, we are quick to pray in the midst of our sufferings but so slow to praise the Father when the outcome is good. In addition, at times, we are quick to pray for God to deliver us out of our situations but so slow to thank him when we are delivered. We see a great example of singing praises to God for the trials that he has brought them through in the writings of David in the Psalms. When David was close to being killed by Saul and God spared him, he writes

Psalm 40:1-3 Updated American Standard Version (UASV)

¹ I waited patiently for Jehovah;
   and he inclined to me and heard my cry.
² He brought me up out of the pit of destruction,
   out of the miry clay,
and set my feet upon a rock,
   making my steps secure.
³ He put a new song in my mouth,
   a song of praise to our God.
Many will see and fear,
   and trust in Jehovah.

The psalms are full of David's praises to God for all the sufferings God had sustained him through during the course of his life. To sing praises to God is a reflection of the gratitude of the heart for what God has done or gives, which creates the joy within the heart. Paul wrote, "Let the peace of Christ rule in your hearts, to which indeed you were called in one body; and be thankful. Let the word of Christ richly dwell within you, with all wisdom teaching and admonishing one another with psalms and hymns and spiritual songs, singing with thankfulness in your hearts to God. Whatever you do in word or deed, do all in the name of the Lord Jesus, giving thanks through Him to God the Father." Col. 3:15-17) Similar words were echoed by Paul, "addressing one another in psalms and hymns and spiritual songs, singing and making melody to the Lord with your heart, 20 giving thanks always and for everything to God the Father in the name of our Lord Jesus Christ." – Ephesians 5:19-20

Is anyone among you sick? Let him call for the elders of the church, (5:14a)

James has covered the subject of how all Christians undergo evil in a general sense, because of inherited sin, human weaknesses and the world ruled by Satan. Now, he turns his attention to what has resulted and can result from having to deal with a bombardment of suffering through the evils of this fallen would, i.e., spiritual weakness or sickness. Almost all modern commentaries believe James is talking about physical sickness. However, Christian Publishing House does not, and it should be noted that the majority does not equal correct, as history has shown many times over that the majority can be wrong. It is the evidence that determines what is correct. We are in agreement with an older commentary, by a noted Bible scholar,

> Here is the culminating point of the question whether the language of James is to be uniformly taken in a literal sense, or whether it uniformly bears a figurative character. The literal construction involves these surprising moments: 1. The calling for the presbyters of the congregation in the Plural; 2. the general direction concerning their prayer accompanying unction with oil; 3. and especially the confident promise that the prayer of faith shall restore the sick apart from his restoration being connected with the forgiveness of his sins. Was the Apostle warranted to promise bodily recovery in every case in which a sick individual complied with his directions? This misgiving urges us to adopt the symbolical construction of the passage, which would be as follows: if any man as a Christian has been hurt or become sick in his Christianity, let him seek healing from the presbyters, the kernel of the congregation. Let these pray with and for him and anoint him with the oil of the Spirit; such a course wherever taken, will surely restore him and his transgressions will be forgiven him.[108]

The spiritual sickness spoken of by James can be a direct result of continued suffering of evil, i.e., his not understanding why God has allowed evil. Or, it may be a result of his human weaknesses in that he

---

[108] John Peter Lange, Philip Schaff, et al., *A Commentary on the Holy Scriptures: James* (Bellingham, WA: Logos Bible Software, 2008), 138.

has committed some serious sin, or is living in sin, which has him distraught to the point he feels his unrighteous condition prevents his prayers from being heard by God (Pro. 15:29; 28:9), and has sought the righteous prayers of the elders. Then again, he might have drifted away from the faith to an extent (Heb. 2:1), or he may have developed an unbelieving heart, leading him to fall away from the living God. (Heb. 3:12-13) Then again, maybe he has become sluggish in his Christian walk. (Heb. 6:12) Maybe he has endured hostility from sinners, so that he has grown weary or fainthearted. (Heb. 12:3) Moreover, some had grown weary of doing good, living in miserable, wretched, hopeless poverty, while those doing bad, lived in wealth. (Gal. (6:9) It is also true that prolonged anguish can bring about physical sicknesses as well. No one, who has suffered spiritual weaknesses should be ashamed to seek out the congregation elders, as they will be able to strengthen and fortify him with biblical counseling and prayer, so that there will be no future irrational thinking, which can lead to wrongdoing.

Acts 20:28 Revised Standard Version (RSV)

[28] Take heed to yourselves and to all the flock, in which the Holy Spirit has made you overseers, to care for the church of God which he obtained with the blood of his own Son.

and let them pray over him, anointing him with oil in the name of the Lord. (5:14b)

The father does not hear the prayers of the wicked, but he does the prayer of the righteous one. (Pro. 15:29) The loving biblical counsel and prayers from the elders (the righteous), would be like calming oil, alleviating the fears and quieting the doubts of the spiritually weak one, enabling him to feel at peace (cheerful even), in that, God is hearing the prayers. (Ps. 23:5; Jer. 8:22) The "word of God is living and active, sharper than any two-edged sword, piercing to the division of soul and of spirit, of joints and of marrow, and discerning the thoughts and intentions of the heart." (Heb. 4:12) Scripture can be likened to the rubbing in of soothing oils. (Isa. 61:3) The soothing heartfelt voice of the elder as he prays to the Father will enable this weakened one to draw close to God once more. He can feel a relief of the weight he has been carrying lifted off his shoulders. He will come to realize that "Jehovah [i.e., the Father] is near to the brokenhearted and saves the crushed in spirit." – Psalm 34:18, UASV.

This meeting with the elders would not be a onetime deal, as the weakened one would be helped over time so he could make a full recovery. This would include assigning someone to shepherd him in making a full spiritual recovery. This could include rides to meetings, visiting his home once a week, and so on. The one shepherding would do so in a biblical manner and would not depend on the wisdom of this fallen world, which is foolishness to God, but rather on the Word of God. – 2 Timothy 3:16-17

And the prayer of faith will save the one who is sick, and the Lord will raise him up. And if he has committed sins, he will be forgiven. (5:15)

Here is another reason to believe that we are talking about spiritual sickness or weakness over against the idea of physical sickness. This verse is an absolute guarantee that if the conditions are met, he will be restored. If it was physical, there could be no such guarantee, as God only miraculously heals those who have a role to play in his will and purposes. We all know of thousands that had tremendous faith, even the apostle Paul, and they still did not receive a physical healing. However, there can be an absolute guarantee when it comes to spiritual weaknesses. If a person receives prayers of faith from the elders and counsel from the Word of God, that they then apply, they can fully recover spiritually. The apostle John said, "If we ask anything **according to his <u>will</u>** he hears us." (1 John 5:14) What we have here is the fact that it must be according to God's will and purposes, and we only have the promise that he hears us, not that he will act on it. However, if it is spiritual weakness, God will bless anyone that comes to him in faith and with a repentant heart.

Jesus said, "And whatever you ask in prayer, you will receive, if you have faith." (Matt. 21:22) Jesus also promised, "If you ask me anything in my name, I will do it." (John 14:14) We will get what we ask for **if** it is according to God's will and purposes.

Philippians 4:13 English Standard Version (ESV)

¹³ I can do all things through him who strengthens me.

Bible scholar J. Vernon McGee writes:

Whatever Christ has for you to do, He will supply the power. Whatever gift He gives you, He will give the power to exercise that gift. A gift is a manifestation of the Spirit of God in the life of the believer. As long as you function in Christ, you will have power. He certainly does not mean that he is putting into your hand unlimited power to do anything you want to do. Rather, He will give you the enablement to do all things in the context of His will for you (McGee, Thru the Bible, V:327–8).

Matthew 6:30-33 English Standard Version (ESV)

[30] But if God so clothes the grass of the field, which today is alive and tomorrow is thrown into the oven, will he not much more clothe you, O you of little faith? [31] Therefore do not be anxious, saying, 'What shall we eat?' or 'What shall we drink?' or 'What shall we wear?' [32] For the Gentiles seek after all these things, and your heavenly Father knows that you need them all. [33] But seek first the kingdom of God and his righteousness, and all these things will be added to you.

Edward D. Andrews writes,

Have not faithful Christians gone hungry, even starved to death? Do not tens of thousands of Christian Children go to bed hungry every night around the world? Are not many Christian homes in this world lacking water? Do not many thousands of Christian families live in rundown homes, having only dirty clothes and in some cases not even having shoes?[109]

Let us also add that "the prayer of faith" alone by the elders is not going to help one recover their spiritual health. The spiritually weak one will have to evidence faith in the elder's words and the wise counsel from the Word of God. Therefore, if one is to recover spiritually, the following conditions must be met:

(1) "the prayer of faith" must be by elders

(2) According to God's will and purposes

(3) In Jesus name

(4) The elders must offer comfort and guidance from God's Word

(5) The spiritually weak one must trust in the words of the elder and Scripture, acting on both

How do serious spiritual weaknesses come about? Generally, it is by irrational thinking or some behavior that had deteriorated. It can be a

---

[109] http://www.christianpublishers.org/bible-absolutes-in-this-age

minor sin, which has gone on to become a serious sin, like flirting to fornication. It can be a person, who is practicing some sin, which he alone has been unable to get control over, like pornography. Living with a secret sin can be so weighty that it causes one to stumble out of the faith. Then, there are those that allow doubts about their faith, God, or the Bible to grow to the point that they fall away from the faith into apostasy, or simply just abandon the faith. Once the weight has gotten so heavy, this one does not feel worthy of approaching God in prayer, because he believes he is beyond repentance. Thus, the loving prayers from an elder combined with corrective counsel from God's Word will calm his spirit.

Once the elders have some idea of the depth of what lead to this spiritual sickness, they can apply Bible counsel like soothing oils. Even if the spiritually weak one has committed some very serious sin (like David's adultery with Bathsheba and the murder of Uriah her husband), the elders can show him how God views the matter and Scripture on how he can make a recovery. This would come from the elders as a reproof for correction and for training in righteousness of the sick one. On this point David wrote, "Let a righteous man strike me, it is a kindness; let him rebuke me, it is oil for my head; let my head not refuse it." God will look approvingly upon such a humble person, who is able to bring his sins to another, as well as the prayers of the righteous elders. He will be willing to remove his sins as though they never were and call them to mind no more.

Psalm 6:2-4 English Standard Version (ESV)

² Be gracious to me, O Lord, for I am languishing;
   heal me, O Lord, for my bones are troubled.
³ My soul also is greatly troubled.
   But you, O Lord—how long?

⁴ Turn, O Lord, deliver my life;
   save me for the sake of your steadfast love.

Therefore confess your sins to one another, and pray for one another so that you may be healed. (5:16a)

There is nothing in the verse, which would suggest that the spiritually weak one must confess his sin to the entire congregation to have them pray for him. "Confess your sins to one another" is speaking of person to person. If one has committed a wrong against another in the congregation, they may be moved to confess that wrongdoing, asking for forgiveness, and they may pray together. Then, again, it might be the one who was wronged, who goes to the one who wronged him, and the sin is confessed, followed by prayer. On the other hand, the wronged one may take a spiritually mature person along with him, maybe an elder. There is the possibility that a person who has sinned or is practicing sin may simply seek a spiritually mature one, to talk with about his sin, which ends in prayer. The Christian congregation should be a family-like atmosphere, where we can feel comfortable sharing our difficulties with others, knowing we will get comforting, even corrective advice and prayer.

If this sinner thought that the result is that they would be exposed to the whole congregation for something they are ashamed of and have not had any control over, this would be a deterrent from coming forward. On the other hand, knowing that the elders would keep one's transgressions in confidence, while helping him overcome his weaknesses, this would encourage him to contact the elders. Again, in looking at the expression "one another," this is not suggesting that we air out our sins before the while congregation, but rather that we all are sinners and none are exempt from having to seek help from others. Even the spiritually mature one, who has been sought out by someone who has sinned, they too one day may need to go to another. The beauty is in the fact that if we confess our sins to one another, it will serve as a protection from our continuing to sin, because someone is now aware of our secret.

Lastly, when we think of "confessing" our sin, **it should not be thought of** as though it were a confessional, where congregation members regularly come in and confess their sins, attaining some kind of absolution. Again, the elders are not the only ones where a person can go to confess their sins.[110] Nevertheless, the one being sought out to hear the sins should be a spiritually mature one, because along with the confession comes a prayer and counsel from God's Word. For example, a younger sister may seek the help of an older sister in the congregation. (Titus 2:3-5) Therefore, the one being sought for help is not limited but should be qualified to offer the level of help being sought. That person needs to be able to offer the healing help of prayer because the one seeking help has such a troubled conscience; he is unable to go to God in prayer. Just as the continued distress and anxiety of his sin could have caused physical sickness, the words and prayer of the one sought for help can just as easily remove the physical sickness once the tension is gone.

---

[110] Therefore, it would be fine if a sister in the congregation, who was struggling spiritually or with problems, chose to go to a mature female sister in the congregation.

The supplication of a righteous man can accomplish much. (5:16b)

James is strongly advocating intercessory prayers for others, i.e., praying for one another. The apostle Paul encourages supplicatory prayers for others. He says, "I urge that supplications, prayers, intercessions, and thanksgivings be made for all people" (1 Tim. 2:1) Paul exhorted the Thessalonica congregation, "brothers, pray for us, that the word of the Lord may speed ahead and be honored, as happened among you." Paul urged the Colossian congregation, "Continue steadfastly in prayer, being watchful in it with thanksgiving. At the same time, pray also for us, that God may open to us a door for the word, to declare the mystery of Christ, on account of which I am in prison, that I may make it clear, which is how I ought to speak." (Col. 4:2-4) Here James speaks of "a righteous man," meaning anyone whom God counted as righteous because he has trusted in Jesus Christ and is living a life reflective of the Word of God.

Prayer is part of our worship. Prayer is very powerful because we have access to the Almighty any time of the day. If a person has a righteous standing before God, he will have his prayers heard. The apostle Peter wrote, "For the eyes of the Lord are on the righteous, and his ears are open to their prayer." (1 Pet. 3:12) The apostle John helps to understand the effectiveness of our prayers. He wrote, "And this is the confidence that we have toward him, that if we ask anything according to his will he hears us. And if we know that he hears us in whatever we ask, we know that we have the requests that we have asked of him." Regarding praying in behalf of others, John continued, "If anyone sees his brother committing a sin not leading to death, he shall ask, and God will give him life, to those who commit sins that do not lead to death. There is sin that leads to death; I do not say that one should pray for that." (1 John 5:15-16) In other words, we would not pray for one that has committed sin that leads to death. Jesus also spoke of sin that "will not be forgiven," that is, "blasphemy against the Spirit." – Matthew 12:31-32

Only Jesus can judge if one has committed the unforgiveable sin, so we should show loving concern for all erring ones, going to God in prayer in their behalf. A good example is King Manasseh of Judah, who sacrificed to false gods, even sacrificing his son to the god Molech. He also practiced spiritism and put a carved image in God's temple. He literally caused thousands to die and was punished by being taken captive to Babylon. Did King Manasseh commit the unforgivable sin, i.e., sin that leads to death? No, because he eventually humbled himself, repented and went to God in prayer, and God restored him as king over Judah. – 2 Kings 21:1-9; 2 Chronicles 33:1-13.

Elijah was a man with a nature like ours, (5:17a)

James gives an example of how a righteous man's prayer in faith is effective and can accomplish much using Elijah as an example. Once again, James uses another Old Testament figure to make his point, which seems to be a common theme now in the book of James. Elijah like Abraham, the prophets and Job, was very much respected among all Christians and held in high esteem. It was for this reason that James would use him as an example of a righteous man's prayer being effective. Elijah was a mighty prophet used of God and the account of his life and working can be found in I Kings chapters 17-22 and 2 Kings Chapters 1-4.

James makes the case that although Elijah was a great prophet used of God; he was also a man just like the rest of us. That is why James says that **Elijah was a man with a nature like ours,** to signify the fact that Elijah has flesh, bones, and a spirit like everybody else. James wanted his readers to understand that it was not Elijah himself, who was powerful, but rather it was God, who worked through him. James wanted his readers to understand the fact that Elijah was a man just as they were, so they should consider what was accomplished through his prayers because he was a righteous man.

and he prayed fervently that it might not rain, and for three years and six months it did not rain on the earth. Then he prayed again, and heaven gave rain, and the earth produced its fruit. (5:17b-18)

We do not know much of the life of Elijah apart from what is written in First and Second Kings and he seems to burst onto the scene of scriptures in First Kings chapter 17. We first meet Elijah during the reign of the evil king Ahab. It was during his reign that the great prophet Elijah was sent to speak the words of God. First Kings 17:1 reads, "Now Elijah the Tishbite, who was of the settlers of Gilead, said to Ahab, 'As the Lord, the God of Israel lives, before whom I stand, surely there shall be neither dew nor rain these years, except by my word.'"

Elijah tells Ahab upon meeting him that in accordance with God's power as judgment upon the land that there would be a famine in the land for the next three years. Shortly after Elijah spoke those words to Ahab, God allowed a great famine to strike the land for three years. Then

Elijah was called to go back to Ahab again with another message, which is recorded in I Kings 18:1, informing Ahab that he was going to send rain on the earth.

It should be mentioned that James here specifically speaks of three and a half years of no rain. Jesus gives us the same information in the sermon he delivered in his hometown synagogue in Nazareth, "I tell you, there were many widows in Israel in the days of Elijah, when the heavens were shut up three years and six months, and a great famine came over all the land." (Luke 4:25) Did James and Jesus have a source that gave them some greater detail than the author of Kings, as the account in 1 Kings 18:1 refers to the rain "coming in the third year"? That certainly is not the same as three and a half years. Of course, the Bible critic would say we have an error in the form of a contradiction. There are absolutely no errors in the originals and if there is a reasonable answer; then, there is no issue at all. We should note first that Jesus was in heaven when the account took place and when the book if Kings was written, so he would know that his comment was not worded the exact same way.

1 Kings 18:1 saying the rain came "in the third year," could have meant the third year of actual drought. First, we must consider the dry summer season of ancient Israel, which ran from April to September, i.e., six months. If the three years of drought spoken of in First Kings followed this, both Jesus and James could speak of three and a half years, being more specific in their reference. On this, Kistemaker and Hendriksen offer another possibility when they write, "From Jewish sources we learn that the expression *three and a half years* is an idiom which, because of frequent usage, came to mean 'for quite some time.'[111] Therefore, we ought to take the expression figuratively, not literally. Furthermore, the Jewish custom of counting part of a unit of time as a full unit sheds additional light on our understanding of the text."[112] On this, apologist Norman L. Geisler writes, "There are three possible solutions here. First, the three years may be a round number. Second, the third year in Kings may be reckoned from the time of Elijah's stay with the widow of Zarephthah, not the full time of the drought. Third, it is possible that the drought began six months before the famine did, making both passages

---

[111] Refer to SB, vol. 3, pp. 760–61. For additional information consult Mayor, *James*, pp. 180–81; and Ropes, *James*, p. 311.

[112] Simon J. Kistemaker and William Hendriksen, *Exposition of James and the Epistles of John*, vol. 14, New Testament Commentary (Grand Rapids: Baker Book House, 1953–2001), 181.

precise but referring to different things."[113] Therefore, we have no error within Scripture, as there are several reasonable and logical explanations.

After having a showdown with the Baal prophets in I Kings 18:20-35, Elijah goes to the top of Mt. Carmel to pray for the rains to fall. God listened to Elijah's prayer and the rains came ending the drought across the land. Although the account from I Kings 18 does not specifically say that Elijah prayed for it not to rain and then to rain again as James says, it is implied. It was the prayer of Elijah, a righteous man, who brought about the judgment of God on the land through the famine and the rain to alleviate the drought after three and a half years. Again, James confirms what Jesus had already said some thirty years earlier in Luke 4:25, "But I say to you in truth, there were many widows in Israel in the days of Elijah, when the sky was shut up for three years and six months, when a great famine came over all the land." Yes, we have the greatest authority of all in Christ Jesus, the Son of God.

That Elijah did pray is implied at 1 Kings 18:42, which reads, "Elijah went up to the top of Mount Carmel. And he bowed himself down on the earth and put his face between his knees." The key here to Elijah's prayer beside the fact that he was a righteous man was also the fact that Elijah **prayed fervently that it might not rain**. Elijah truly believed in what he was praying for **and for three years and six months it did not rain on the earth.** He believed God again, in the fact, that **he prayed again, and heaven gave rain, and the earth produced its fruit.** It was not that Elijah was better than any other Bible person was at having his prayer answered, but rather he was earnest in petitioning God for his answer. Elijah's righteous life unto God and his earnestness in prayer accomplished much through God's working through this man.

The example of Elijah and his praying for withholding rain is a very powerful one. On this, Gary Holloway offers a very important point to keep in mind: "This verse does not mean God will grant all the requests of the righteous, for he did not give Elijah all he prayed for (see 1 Kings 19:4). It is a call for confidence in the power of prayer, or better still, confidence in the power of the Lord to whom we pray."[114]

---

[113] Thomas Howe; Norman L. Geisler. The Big Book of Bible Difficulties: Clear and Concise Answers from Genesis to Revelation (Kindle Locations 6186-6188). Kindle Edition.

[114] Gary Holloway, *James & Jude*, The College Press NIV Commentary (Joplin, MO: College Press Pub., 1996), Jas 5:17–18.

Helping a Sinner to Return

James 5:19-20 Updated American Standard Version (UASV)

[19] My brothers, if any among you strays from the truth and one turns him back, [20] let him know that he who turns a sinner from the error of his way will save his soul from death and will cover a multitude of sins.

My brothers, if any among you strays from the truth and one turns him back, let him know that he who turns a sinner from the error of his way will save a soul from death and will cover a multitude of sins. (5:19-20)

The truth referred to here by James includes Bible doctrines or Christian beliefs as well as Christian ethics.[115] Over 41,000 different denominations call themselves Christian, all claiming to be the truth and the way. However, all of them believe differently, meaning that they are not just different roads leading to the same place. What we believe about God and his Word is what can make us a part of **the truth** or not. A new one, i.e., an unbeliever coming into **the truth** must first be taught the Word of God, and the Christian morals will follow. "This is eternal life that they may know you, the only true God, and Jesus Christ whom you have sent." (John 17:3) James did not have all twenty-seven books of the New Testament, as the apostle John had not yet written the Gospel of John, his three epistles and the book of Revelation. In addition, James would not have been aware of Peter's epistles either, or a couple of Paul's letters. Nevertheless, like all New Testament authors, James used the Old Testament extensively, and he viewed God's Word as the foundation of **the truth**. Today, we have all sixty-six books of the Bible, thirty-nine of the Old Testament and twenty-seven of the New Testament, which contain all that is necessary for the truth. James says of God in 1:18, "Of his own will he brought us forth by **the word of truth**, that we should be a kind of firstfruits of his creatures."

"We know that we have passed over from death into life" (1 John 3:14), but it is also just as possible to pass over from life to death, if we stray too far from **the truth**. Every Christian not just the elders has the obligation, to help a brother back to the path of the truth. The apostle Paul tells us, "Brothers, if anyone is caught in any transgression, you who

---

[115] **Christian ethics** is a branch of Christian theology that defines concepts of right (virtuous) and wrong (sinful) behavior from a Christian perspective. (http://en.wikipedia.org/wiki/Christian_ethics)

are spiritual should restore him in a spirit of gentleness. Keep watch on yourself, lest you too be tempted." (Gal. 6:1) When we think of James informing us of our obligation of helping those who have stumbled in **the truth**, we think back on the power of prayer. Remember, James had just written, "the prayer of faith will save the one who is sick." (5:15) For there to be success, one must diligently apply God's Word and deep prayer to achieve the regaining of the one who has stumbled from the path of **the truth**. If the erring one does not receive the needed help, he can go beyond repentance. Being beyond repentance refers being beyond the desire to repent, or to return to **the truth**. In some cases, he will be lost to Satan's world and no one will be able to reawaken his former desire. – Hebrews 6:4-8; 10:26-29

Every year we have tens of thousands of Christians who stray from the truth because they have misinterpreted or misunderstood scripture, as they have been reading misleading information, or they have drifted away, turned away, or fallen away because they had become sluggish, so they grew weary or fainthearted. Many others have fallen away because they have stumbled morally. All of these find themselves in a very dangerous position. When we ponder the phrase "turns him back [Gr *epistrepsas*, having returned]," it helps us to appreciate that we are talking about a Christian, not one who has never accepted the truth. Yes, we are dealing with a fallen brother, who has strayed from **the truth** that he accepted but now rejects by behavior or belief.

When Jesus knew one of his most intimate disciples was going to stumble spiritually, to the point of betraying Jesus three times after boasting that he never would do such a thing, what did Jesus say? He said to Peter, "but I have prayed for you, that your faith may not fail; and you, when once you have turned again [Gr *epistrepsas*, having returned], strengthen your brothers." (Lu 22:32) In both texts, we are talking about the recovery of an erring person, with Jesus' great love for Peter and our great love for our bothers, like Jesus, we can lovingly help someone back on the path.

The word "know" stresses the significance of our restoration ministry. When a military unit is in the heat of battle, their senses are heightened by the perilous situation they find themselves in, and are mindful of where every team member is, as it could mean the difference between life and death. Christians find themselves in the heat of a serious battle with inherited sin, human weakness, being mentally bent toward evil, a deceptive heart, Satan and his demons, the world of mankind alienated from God, all working toward our demise. We need to be mindful of where every Christian team member is in his walk with God. Would it not be prudent to assist a brother when he simply trips over something rather than trying to help him up once he has fallen? When we err in certain ways, we are literally tripping toward death and this spiritual death can lead to eternal death for him, if someone does not **turn him back**. Our help can come in the form of loving guidance, prayer, the opportunity to give some helpful service; we assist the erring one in receiving the atonement of Jesus' ransom sacrifice. If we commit a sin, we have Jesus' ransom sacrifice (Matt 20:28; 1 John 2:1), which covers human weaknesses and Adamic sin (Rom. 5:12, 18). However, if we enter into the practice of sin or are living in sin, we no longer receive that ransom sacrifice of Jesus Christ (1 John 3:8-10), unless we have returned again [Gr *epistrepsas*, having returned].

When we think of turning one back from their sin, it might be best to use the example of the Father in his dealing with the Israelites.

Isaiah 1:18 Updated American Standard Version (UASV)

18 "Come now, let us reason together, says Jehovah:
"though your sins are like scarlet,
    they shall be as white as snow;
though they are red like crimson,
    they shall become like wool.

First, it should be noted that the phrase, "let us reason together," does not suggest a give and take conversation, where both sides are going to argue their case, with both making concessions. We need not worry, the Father is the most generous and compassionate Judge. His forgiveness is unmatched. (Ps. 86:5) He has appointed his Son, Jesus Christ to do the judging. Jesus tells us constantly in the Gospel of John about his relationship with the Father. Jesus said, "Truly, truly, I say to you, the Son can do nothing of his own accord, but only what he sees the Father doing. For whatever the Father does, that the Son does likewise." (John 5:19) Jesus as the appointed judge can take the sins of Israel that "are like scarlet" and make them "as white as snow." The sins of Israel were the worship of false gods, orgies under trees, sacrificing sons to the god of Molech, the murder of prophets and so much more. Yes, their sins were "red like crimson" and Jesus as appointed judge has the authority (Matt. 28:18), to make them "like wool." No human can do this. There is no number of works that can remove any sin, let alone this level of egregiousness. Only the Father, through his appointed Son can wash away sin. The forgiveness of sins is based on God's standards, not some reasoning back and forth. There must be genuine heartfelt repentance. On the phrase "To "reason together" A Commentary on the Book of Isaiah says that it "implies the background of the court of appeal mentioned at Isa. 1:2. God appeals to Israel with the hope that they are still reasonable beings who can discuss matters without prejudice. The very nature of forgiveness is of grace alone." (Apranawa 1990, p. 8)

The commentary goes on to make some very good observations, "The very nature of forgiveness is of grace alone. It is *sola gratia*, radical but also conditional—radical because it is complete and perfect, conditional because it requires an honest response from Israel. There are only two alternatives for Israel: either to be willing and obey, resulting in new life and in eating the good of the land—and this includes the promise of the renewal of the land (v. 7); or to refuse and rebel, resulting in total destruction by the sword of the Assyrians. This is indeed the essence of the gospel message (cf. John 3:16, 18). "Between life and death there is no compromise!" (Apranawa 1990, p. 8)

Thus, if God can forgive 1,500 years of Israelite history that was so sinful, he will cover the missteps of a brother that has stumbled in either belief or behavior. However, we must acknowledge that God's patience does not go on forever, as Israel went on to reject the Son of God, so God rejected Israel as his chosen people.[116] Thus, we would want to assist our brother in his return to the fold [Gr *epistrepsas*, having returned]," before it becomes an all-out rejection of the truth, i.e., a rejection of Jesus Christ. One way that we help our brother is not making his missteps known to others. Yes, if the situation seems beyond our abilities, we might seek the help of another, but we would never tell other congregation members of his sins. (Pro. 10:12) When this erring one has returned, the words of King David will be realized. David wrote, "Blessed is the one whose transgression is forgiven, **whose sin is <u>covered</u>**. Blessed is the man against whom the Lord counts no iniquity, and in whose spirit there is no deceit." (Ps. 32:1-2) We know that God sees the living concern we have for our brothers and it will not go unrewarded. – 2 Corinthians 5:10; See Colossians 3:23, 24; Luke 14:13, 14

Review Question

(1) **[vs 1]** Why is materialism so consuming?

(2) **[vs 2]** What did James mean here?

---

[116] http://www.christianpublishers.org/the-jews-chosen-people

(3) **[vs 3]** How is this true?

(4) **[vs 4]** How are the laborers crying out?

(5) **[vs 5]** What is sensual indulgence?

(6) **[vs 6]** In what sense had they condemned and murdered the righteous one?

(7) **[vs 7]** Why is patience highly important as we await the return of Christ?

(8) **[vs 8]** How can we be patient?

(9) **[vs 9]** How may we grumble against one another and not even realize?

(10) **[vs 10]** In considering suffering and patience, why should we look to the prophets?

(11) **[vs 11]** Why should the endurance of other bring us happiness and make us stronger?

(12) **[vs 12]** Just how important is our word, as to oir relationships with others?

(13) **[vs 13]** Why do bad things befall us all?

(14) **[vs 14-15]** How do we know that the "sickness" here is a reference to spiritual weakness or sickness, not some physical sickness?

(15) **[vs 16]** Why does the spiritually weak or sick need the prayers of a righteous one?

(16) **[vs 17]** Why does James point to Elijah?

(17) **[vs 18]** What does this prove? Does it prove that we should expect a miraculous answer on everything we pray for simply because we are faithful?[117]

(18) **[vs 19]** What is required of us, if we are to be skilled enough to turn someone back?

(19) **[vs 20]** How are we to understand this verse?

---

[117] See DIGGING DEEPER Does God Step in and Solve Our Every Problem Because We are Faithful?

DIGGING DEEPER Why Has God Permitted Suffering and Evil?

Edward D. Andrews

"God has morally sufficient reasons for permitting the evil and suffering in the world."—William Lane Craig

That morally sufficient reason lies below.

"The significant issue that drove me to Agnostcism [Bible Scholar Dr. Bart D. Ehrman is now an Agnostic] has to do not with the Bible, but with the pain and suffering in the world." He writes, "I eventually found it impossible to explain the evil so rampant among us—whether in terms of genocides (which continue), unspeakable human cruelty, war disease, hurricanes, tsunamis, mudslides, the starvation of millions of innocent children, you name it—if there was a good and loving God who was actively involved in this world." *Misquoting Jesus* (p. 248)

As you will see below, Ehrman's issue is simply a matter of starting with the wrong assumption. **Point One**: He starts with 'if God is a God of love, who has the power to fix anything, how can there have been such horrific pain and suffering in imperfection over the last 6,000 years?' **Point Two**: He also likely begins with the premise that 'God is responsible for everything that happens.' If one starts with the wrong assumption, there is no doubt that he will reach the wrong conclusion(s). **Point One** is dealt with below, but let it be said that Ehrman is looking through the binoculars from the opposite end, the big side through the small. When we do that, we get a narrow, focused outlook. God looks through the binoculars the correct way, and can see the big picture. Ehrman can only see but a fraction and a moment of time, 70 – 80 years, while God has seen everything that has happened over these past 6,000 plus years in the greatest of detail, and can see what the outcome would be if he had handled things in a variety of ways.

Point Two is certainly one reason suffering and evil is often misunderstood. God is responsible for everything, but not always directly. If he started the human race, and we end up with what we now have, in essence, he is responsible. Just as parents, who have a child are similarly responsible for the child committing murder 21 years into his life, because they procreated and gave birth to the child. The mother and father are indirectly responsible. King David commits adultery with Bathsheba and has her husband Uriah killed to cover things up, and impregnates

Bathsheba, but the adulterine child, who remains nameless, died. Is God responsible for the death of that child? We can answer yes and no to that question. He is responsible in two ways: **(1)** He created humankind, so there would have been no affair, murder, adulterine child if he had not. **(2)** He did not step in and save the child, when he had the power to do so. However, he is not directly responsible, because he did not make King David and Bathsheba commit the acts that led to the child being born, nor did he bring an illness on the adulterine child, he just did not move in to protect the child, in a time that had a high rate of infant deaths.

The reason people think that God does not care about us is the words of some religious leaders, which have made them, feel this way. When a tragedy strikes, what do some pastors and Bible scholars often say? When 9/11 took place, with thousands dying in the twin towers of New York, many ministers said: "It was God's will. God must have had some good reason for doing this." When religious leaders make such comments or similar ones, they are actually blaming God for the bad things that happened. Yet, the disciple James wrote, "Let no one say when he is tempted, 'I am being tempted by God,' for God cannot be tempted with evil, and he himself tempts no one." (James 1:13) God never directly causes what is bad. Indeed, "far be it from God that he should do wickedness, and from the Almighty that he should do wrong." Job 34:10.

The history of humans has been inundated with pain and suffering on an unprecedented scale, much of which they have brought on themselves. The problem/question that has plagued many persons is, 'why if there is a loving God, would he allow it to start with, and worse still, why allow it to go on for over 6,000 years?' Some apologist scholars have struggled to answer this question, because they are over analyzing, as opposed to just looking for the answer in God's Word. Therefore, if we are to answer this question, we must go back to Adam and Eve at the time of the first sin. Many have read this account, but I will list the texts as a refresher.

Genesis 2:17 (English Standard Version)

[17] but of the tree of the knowledge of good and evil you shall not eat, for in the day that you eat of it <u>you shall surely die</u>."

As you can see, humankind's continued existence in a paradise, with perfection, was dependent upon obedience, his continued acceptance of God as his sovereign.

Genesis 3:1-5 (English Standard Version)

¹ Now the serpent was more crafty than any other beast of the field that the LORD God had made. He said to the woman, "Did God actually say, 'You shall not eat of any tree in the garden'?" ² And the woman said to the serpent, "We may eat of the fruit of the trees in the garden, ³ but God said, 'You shall not eat of the fruit of the tree that is in the midst of the garden, neither shall you touch it, lest you die.'" ⁴ But the serpent said to the woman, "<u>You will not surely die</u>. ⁵ For God knows that when you eat of it your eyes will be opened, and you will be like God, knowing good and evil."

Later Bible texts establish Satan the Devil as the one using a serpent as his mouthpiece, like a ventriloquist would a dummy. Anyway, take note that Satan contradicts the clear statement made to Adam at Genesis 2:17, "you will not surely die." Backing up a little, we see Satan asking an inferential question, "Did God actually say, 'You shall not eat of any tree in the garden'?" First, he is overstating what he knows to be true, not "any tree," just one tree. Second, Satan is inferring, 'I can't believe that God would say . . . how dare he say such.' Notice too that Eve has been told so thoroughly about the tree that she even goes beyond what Adam told her, not just that you 'do not eat from it,' no, 'you do not even touch it!' Then, Satan out and out lied and slandered God as a liar, saying that 'they would not die.' To make matters much worse, he infers that God is withholding good from them, and by rebelling they would be better off, being like God, 'knowing good and bad.' This latter point is not knowledge of; it is the self-sovereignty of choosing good and bad for oneself, an act of rebellion for created creatures. What was symbolized by the tree is well expressed in a footnote on Genesis 2:17, in The Jerusalem Bible (1966):

> This knowledge is a privilege, which God reserves to himself and which man, by sinning, is to lay hands on, 3:5, 22. Hence it does not mean omniscience, which fallen man does not possess; nor is it moral discrimination, for unfallen man already had it and God could not refuse it to a rational being. It is the power of deciding for himself what is good and what is evil and of acting accordingly, a claim to complete moral independence by which man refuses to recognize his status as a created being. The first sin was an attack on God's sovereignty, a sin of pride.

The Issues at Hand

(1) Satan called God a liar and said he was not to be trusted, as to the life or death issue.

(2) Satan's challenge, therefore, took into question the right and legitimacy of God's rightful place as the Universal Sovereign.

(3) Satan also suggested that people would remain obedient to God only as long as their submitting to God was to their benefit.

(4) Satan all but said that humankind was able to walk on his own, there being no need for dependence on God.

(5) Satan argued that man could be like God, choosing for himself what is right and wrong.

(6) Satan claimed that God's way of ruling was not in the best interests of humans, and they could do better without God.

Job 1:6-11 (English Standard Version)

⁶ Now there was a day when the sons of God came to present themselves before the LORD, and Satan also came among them. ⁷ The LORD said to Satan, "From where have you come?" Satan answered the LORD and said, "From(C) going to and fro on the earth, and from walking up and down on it." ⁸ And the LORD said to Satan, "Have you considered my servant Job, that there is none like him on the earth, a blameless and upright man, who fears God and turns away from evil?" ⁹ Then Satan answered the LORD and said, "<u>Does Job fear God for no reason</u>? ¹⁰ Have you not put a hedge around him and his house and all that he has, on every side? You have blessed the work of his hands, and his possessions have increased in the land. 11 But <u>stretch out your hand and touch all that he has, and he will curse you to your face</u>."

Job 2:4-5 (English Standard Version)

⁴ Then Satan answered the LORD and said, "Skin for skin! All that <u>a man</u> has he will give for his life. ⁵ But stretch out your hand and touch his bone and his flesh, and he will curse you to your face."

This general reference to "a man," as opposed to explicitly naming Job, is suggesting that all men [and women] will only obey God when things are good, but when the slightest difficulty arises, he will not obey. If you were put to the test, would you prove your love for your heavenly Father and show that you preferred His rule to that of any other?

God Settles the Issues

There is one thing that Satan did not challenge, namely, the power of God. Satan did not suggest that God was unable to destroy him as an opposer. However, he did challenge God's way of ruling, not His right to rule. Therefore, it is a moral issue that must be settled.

An illustration of how God chose to deal with the issue can be demonstrated in human terms. A neighbor down the street slandered a man, who had a son and daughter. The slanderer said that he was not a good father, i.e., he withheld good from his children, and was so overbearing, to the point of being abusive. The slanderer stated that the children would be better off without the father. He further argued that the children had no real love for their father, and only obeyed him because of the food and shelter. How should the father deal with these false, slanderous accusations? If he were to go down the road and pummel the slanderer, it would only validate the lies, making the neighbors believe he is telling the truth.

The answer lies within his family as they can serve as his witnesses. (Pro 27:11; Isa 43:10) If the children stay obedient and grow to be successful adults, turning out to be loving, caring, honest people with spotless character, it proves the accusations false. If the children accept the lies and rebel, and grow up to be despicable people, it just further validates that they would have been better off by staying with the father. This is how God chose to deal with the issues. The issues that were raised must be settled beyond all reasonable doubt.

If God had destroyed the rebellious three: Satan, Adam and Eve; he would not have resolved the issues of

(1) whether man could walk on his own,

(2) if he would be better off without his Creator,

(3) if God's rulership were not best, and

(4) if God were hiding good from man.

(5) In addition, there was an audience of untold billions of angelic spirit creatures looking on.

If God destroyed without settling things, these spirit persons would be following God out of dreadful fear, not love, fear of displeasing God. Moreover, say He did kill them and start over, and ten thousand years down the road (with billions of humans now on earth) the issues were raised again. He would have to destroy billions of people again, and again, and again all throughout time, until these issues were laid to rest.

What God has done is allow time to pass and the issues to be resolved. Man thought he was better off without God and could walk on his own. In addition, man has attempted every kind of rulership imaginable, and one must ask, 'have they proven themselves better than rulership under the sovereignty of their Creator?' (Proverbs 1:30-33; Isaiah 59:4, 8) Sadly, the issues must be taken up to the brink of destroying man (Rev. 11:18), otherwise, the argument would be that if given enough time, they could have turned things around. If man goes up to the point of destroying himself and Armageddon comes at the last minute, it will have set a case law, solved the issue, and the Bible can serve as the example forever. If the issues of God's sovereignty or the loyalty of His created creatures, angelic or human, is ever questioned again, we would have the Holy Bible that will serve as a law established based on previous verdicts of not guilty. Please see below.

What Have the Results Been?

(1) God does not cause evil and suffering. Romans 9:14.

(2) That fact that God has allowed evil, pain and suffering has shown that independence from God has not brought about a better world. Jeremiah 8:5, 6, 9.

(3) God's permission of evil, pain and suffering has also proved that Satan has not been able to turn all humans away from God. Exodus 9:16; 1 Samuel 12:22; Hebrews 12:1.

(4) The fact that God has permitted evil, pain and suffering to continue has provided proof that only God, the Creator, has the capability and the right to rule over humankind for their eternal blessing and happiness. Ecclesiastes 8:9.

(5) Satan has been the god of this world since the sin in Eden (over 6,000 years), and how has that worked out for man, and what has been the result of man's course of independence from God and his rule? Matthew 4:8-9; John 16:11; 2 Corinthians 4:3-4; 1 John 5:19; Psalm 127:1.

Satan's impact on the earth's activities has carried with it conflict, evil and death, and his rulership has been by means of deception, power and his own self-interest. He has demonstrated himself an unfit ruler of everything. Therefore, God is now completely vindicated in putting an

158

end to this corrupted rebel along with all who have shared in his evil deeds. (Romans 16:20)

God has tolerated evil, sickness, pain, suffering and death until our day in order to resolve all the issues raised by Satan. We are self-centered in thinking that this has only pained us. Imagine that you are holding a rope on a sinking ship that 20 other men, women and children are clinging to, when your child loses her grip and falls into the ocean. You can either hold the rope, saving 20 people, or you can let go and attempt to rescue your daughter. God has been watching the suffering of billions from the day of Adam and Eve's sin. Moreover, it has been His great love for us, which causes Him to cling to the rope of issues, saving us from a future of repeated issues. Nevertheless, he will not allow this evil to remain forever. He has set a fixed time when He will end this wicked system of Satan's rule.

Daniel 11:27 (Holman Christian Standard Bible)

[27] The two kings, whose hearts are bent on evil, will speak lies at the same table but to no avail, for still the end will come <u>at the appointed time</u>.

Unlike what many people of the world may think (the world that lies in the hands of Satan), being obedient to God is not difficult. We simply must set our pride aside and accept that the wisdom of God is so far greater than our own, and accept that He has worked for the good of obedient humankind, as He loves each one of us.

Matthew 7:21 (Holman Christian Standard Bible)

21 "Not everyone who says to Me, 'Lord, Lord!' will enter the kingdom of heaven, but [only] the one who does the will of My Father in heaven.

1 John 2:15-17 (Holman Christian Standard Bible)

15 Do not love the world or the things that belong to the world. If anyone loves the world, love for the Father is not in him. Because everything that belongs to the world,16the lust of the flesh, the lust of the eyes, and the pride in one's lifestyle, is not from the Father, but is from the world. 17And the world with its lust is passing away, but the one who does God's will remains forever.

As Christians, there is a love we must not have. We must 'not love the world or anything in it.' Instead, we need to keep from becoming infected by the corruption of unrighteous human society that is alienated from God and must not breathe in its mental disposition or be moved by its sinful dominant attitude. (Ephesians 2:1, 2; James 1:27) If we were to have the views of those in the world that are in opposition to God, "the love of the Father" would not be in us. (James 4:4)

DIGGING DEEPER Why Is Life So Unfair?

Edward D. Andrews

On December 14, 2012, 20-year-old Adam Lanza fatally shot twenty children and six adult staff members in a mass murder at Sandy Hook Elementary School, in the village of Sandy Hook in Newtown, Connecticut. Before driving to the school, Lanza shot and killed his mother Nancy at their Newtown home. As first responders arrived, he committed suicide by shooting himself in the head.[118]

Parents, who sent their children to school that morning, never expected that by the end of the day, Adam Lanza would have murdered them. Worse still, there were signs that, if paid attention to, things may have not turned out the way they did. These parents are certainly what comes to mind when we think of life being unfair.

Unfairness the World Over

The world is full of these type of accounts the world over. We have social depravities everywhere we look. In the United States, there are hundreds of thousands living in homeless shelters, under bridges, eating at soup kitchens, and many have young children with them as well. On the other hand, the United States throws away more food than any other country. Sadly, the hungry in the United States, while truly unfair, rates very low when one considers the inhumane conditions of other countries. In some countries, like Mexico, you have a millionaire living in a mansion, with a poor person living in a shack next door, and a person living in a car, living next door to him. Almost two billion people live in such hopeless poverty and inhumane conditions that those in the Western part of the world could never relate.

Poverty is defined as a state of want; lacking means; inadequacy. Poverty "brings hunger, disease, high infant mortality, homelessness, and even war." Poverty "falls on the more vulnerable groups in society, such as women, the elderly, minority groups, and children." About 1 billion people around the world live on less than $1 a day.[119]

---

[118] http://en.wikipedia.org/wiki/Sandy_Hook_Elementary_School_shooting

[119] ttp://prezi.com/8duqy_es2rmu/inadequate-living-conditions-around-the-world/

God's View of Fairness

Leviticus 19:15 English Standard Version (ESV)

[15] "You shall do no injustice in court. You shall not be partial to the poor or defer to the great, but in righteousness shall you judge your neighbor.

Deuteronomy 32:4 English Standard Version (ESV)

[4] "The Rock, his work is perfect,
   for all his ways are justice.
A God of faithfulness and without iniquity,
   just and upright is he.

Acts 10:34-35 English Standard Version (ESV)

[34] So Peter opened his mouth and said: "Truly I understand that God shows no partiality, [35] but in every nation anyone who fears him and does what is right is acceptable to him.

From Where Does Unfairness Stem?

Genesis 2:17 Updated American Standard Version (UASV)

[17] "but from the tree of the knowledge of good and evil you shall not eat, for in the day that you eat from it you shall surely die."

Genesis 3:4-5 Updated American Standard Version (UASV)

[4] And the serpent **[Satan the Devil]** said to the woman, "You shall not surely die. [5] For God knows that when you eat of it your eyes will be opened, and you will be like God, knowing good and evil." [knowing good and evil is there taking for themselves the right to choose what is good and bad, which is a rebellion against the sovereignty of God, i.e., God's right to rule, his right to determine what is good and what is bad.]

[6] So when the woman saw that the tree was good for food, and that it was a delight to the eyes, and that the tree was to be desirable to make one wise, and she took of its fruit and ate, then she also gave some to her husband when with her, and he ate.

Genesis 3:24 Updated American Standard Version (UASV)

[24] So he drove the man out, and at the east of the garden of Eden he placed the cherubim and a flaming sword that turned every way to guard the way to the tree of life.

John 8:44 English Standard Version (ESV)

⁴⁴ You are of your father the devil, and your will is to do your father's desires. He was a murderer from the beginning, and does not stand in the truth, because there is no truth in him. When he lies, he speaks out of his own character, for he is a liar and the father of lies.

Revelation 12:9 English Standard Version (ESV)

⁹ And the great dragon was thrown down, that ancient serpent, who is called the devil and Satan, the deceiver of the whole world, he was thrown down to the earth, and his angels were thrown down with him.

Unfairness in the Last Days

Revelation 12:12 English Standard Version (ESV)

¹² Therefore, rejoice, O heavens and you who dwell in them! But woe to you, O earth and sea, for the devil has come down to you in great wrath, because he knows that his time is short!"

Daniel 12:4 English Standard Version (ESV)

⁴ But you, Daniel, shut up the words and seal the book, until the time of the end. Many shall run to and fro, and knowledge shall increase."

2 Timothy 3:1-5 English Standard Version (ESV)

¹ But understand this, that in the last days there will come times of difficulty. ² For people will be lovers of self, lovers of money, proud, arrogant, abusive, disobedient to their parents, ungrateful, unholy, ³ heartless, unappeasable, slanderous, without self-control, brutal, not loving good, ⁴ treacherous, reckless, swollen with conceit, lovers of pleasure rather than lovers of God, ⁵ having the appearance of godliness, but denying its power. Avoid such people.

Unfairness Removed

Romans 16:20 English Standard Version (ESV)

20 The God of peace will soon crush Satan under your feet. The grace of our Lord Jesus Christ be with you.

Do Not Love the World

1 John 2:15-17 English Standard Version (ESV)

[15] Do not love the world or the things in the world. If anyone loves the world, the love of the Father is not in him. [16] For all that is in the world, the desires of the flesh and the desires of the eyes and pride of life, is not from the Father but is from the world. [17] And the world is passing away along with its desires, but whoever does the will of God abides forever.

The End of the Age

Matthew 24:1-3 English Standard Version (ESV)

[1] Jesus left the temple and was going away, when his disciples came to point out to him the buildings of the temple. [2] But he answered them, "You see all these, do you not? Truly, I say to you, there will not be left here one stone upon another that will not be thrown down." [3] As he sat on the Mount of Olives, the disciples came to him privately, saying, "Tell us, when will these things be, and what will be the sign of your coming and of the end of the age?"

Here in verse three, we have Jesus and the disciples taking a seat on the Mount of Olives, looking down on the temple below. The temple compound was the ninth wonder of the ancient world. Jesus had just told the disciples that this marvel was going to be so devastated in a coming destruction, "there will not be left here one stone upon another that will not be thrown down." Looking down, the disciples asked Jesus what they thought to be but one question, not knowing the answer that Jesus would give, showed it to be three separate questions. Of course, the initial question **(1)** was their wondering when the destruction that Jesus spoke of was coming. There second portion of that question was **(2)** what will be the sign of your coming. The third portion of the question was **(3)** the end of the age.[120] Herein, we will focus on questions **(2)** and **(3)**. In

---

[120] Whether one sees this as two questions or three questions is not that big of a difference. If it is two questions; then, the coming/presence of Christ and the end of the age are being treated as one event. However, if there are three; then, the coming/presence of Christ and the end of the age are being treated as two events. Either way, you have Christ's coming/presence and the end of the age. If the Greek word *parousia* carries the sense of both the arrival of Christ and his presence for a time before the end of the age, as explained by *Vine's Expository Dictionary*, this seems to better support it being a three part question. How long that interval is between the arrival, the presence and the conclusion, no one can truly know.

short, **(1)** the destruction of Jerusalem took place in 70 C.E., just 37-years after the death, resurrection, and ascension of Christ.

> They ask these questions about the destruction of Jerusalem and the temple, his own second coming (... [*parousia*], presence, common in the papyri for the visit of the emperor), and the end of the world. Did they think that they were all to take place simultaneously? There is no way to answer. At any rate Jesus treats all three in this great eschatological discourse, the most difficult problem in the Synoptic Gospels. ... It is sufficient for our purpose to think of Jesus as using the destruction of the temple and of Jerusalem which did happen in that generation in a.d. 70, as also a symbol of his own second coming and of the end of the world (... [*sunteleias tou aiōnos*]) or consummation of the age. In a painting the artist by skilful perspective may give on the same surface the inside of a room, the fields outside the window, and the sky far beyond. Certainly in this discourse Jesus blends in apocalyptic language the background of his death on the cross, the coming destruction of Jerusalem, his own second coming and the end of the world. He now touches one, now the other. It is not easy for us to separate clearly the various items.[121]

In "what will be the sign of your **coming**," the Greek word behind "coming" (*parousia*) needs a little more in-depth explaining.

> *Parousia* ... lit., "a presence," *para*, "with," and *ousia*, "being" (from *eimi*, "to be"), denotes both an "arrival" and a consequent "presence with." For instance, in a papyrus letter a lady speaks of the necessity of her parousia in a place in order to attend to matters relating to her property there. Paul speaks of his *parousia* in Philippi, Phil. 2:12 (in contrast to his *apousia*, "his absence"; see absence). Other words denote "the arrival" (see *eisodos* and *eleusis*, above). *Parousia* is used to describe the presence of Christ with His disciples on the Mount of Transfiguration, 2 Pet. 1:16. When used of the return of Christ, at the rapture of the church, it signifies, not merely His momentary "coming" for His saints, but His presence with them from that moment until His revelation and manifestation to the world. In some passages the word gives prominence to the

---

[121] A.T. Robertson, *Word Pictures in the New Testament* (Nashville, TN: Broadman Press, 1933), Mt 24:3.

beginning of that period, the course of the period being implied, 1 Cor. 15:23; 1 Thess. 4:15; 5:23; 2 Thess. 2:1; Jas. 5:7-8; 2 Pet. 3:4. In some, the course is prominent, Matt. 24:3, 37; 1 Thess. 3:13; 1 John 2:28; in others the conclusion of the period, Matt. 24:27; 2 Thess. 2:8.[122]

"What will be the sign of your coming" As we can see from the context of Matthew 24 and Vine's *Expository Dictionary*, parousia, describes not only the arrival of Christ, but his presence as well. This does not give us the sense of a coming and some swift departure. Rather, the presence aspect is a period of time that we cannot know the exact length of, so it does no good even to speculate by adding adjectives, like a "lengthy" or "short" presence.

"the end of the age" What is meant by the Greek word *aion*, which is translated "age"" It refers to a certain period of time, an epoch, or age.

> *aion* (αἰών, 165), "an age, era" (to be connected with *aei*, "ever," rather than with *ao*, "to breathe"), signifies a period of indefinite duration, or time viewed in relation to what takes place in the period.[123]

What period of time is being referred to here? If we look at God's use of Moses to help in the Exodus of his people from Egypt, and Moses penning of the Mosaic Law, we would say that from the Exodus to the sacrifice ransom death of Christ was an "age" (period of time or epoch) where the Israelite nation was the only way to God. Then, Jesus entered humanity into another age by his ransom sacrifice, which runs up unto his second coming/presence and the end of this age of Christianity.

Jesus answers this two or three-part question throughout the rest of Matthew 24 and chapter 25. Matthew gives us Jesus' presentation of the events that lead to Jesus coming and presence, to set up his kingdom to rule **over** the earth for a thousand years. Most will be shocked by my saying "over" the earth, as almost all translations render Revelation 5:10

---

[122] The reader should be aware that the Greek word parousia does mean presence, the word is derived from para (with) and ousia (being). However, it does not denote the idea of invisible as the Jehovah Witnesses attest to. See W. E. Vine, Merrill F. Unger, and William White Jr., *Vine's Complete Expository Dictionary of Old and New Testament Words* (Nashville, TN: T. Nelson, 1996), 111.

[123] W. E. Vine, Merrill F. Unger, and William White Jr., *Vine's Complete Expository Dictionary of Old and New Testament Words* (Nashville, TN: T. Nelson, 1996), 19.

166

as "and you have made them a kingdom and priests to our God, and they shall reign **on** the earth."

epí [2093] is in the genitive and can range from: "on, upon; over; at, by; before, in the presence of; when, under, at the time of;"[124] Below you are going to find a list of the genitive epi within Revelation that has a similar construction.

If we are to establish that some translations are choosing a rendering because it suits their doctrine, we must compare how they render the same thing elsewhere. I do believe that the English is a problem in trying to say, "They shall reign **on** the earth." First, because this is not a location issue: i.e., "where." The genitive *epi* is dealing not with where, but with authority over, which is expressed by having it over ... not on ...

Please also take special note that the context of all of these epi genitives that follow the active indicative verb and then are followed by the genitive definite article and noun are dealing with authority.

The verb "to reign" is properly used of kings and queens, and here implies complete power over the world and its inhabitants. So another way of expressing this is "and they shall rule over the world and its inhabitants" or "they shall have power over ...."[125]

Revelation 5:9-10 has a high level of theological content. It either says that Jesus and his co-rulers are going to over the earth, or on the earth. It is theological bias to have several cases of similar context and the same grammatical construction, rendering the verses the same every time, yet to then render one verse contrary to the others, simply because it aligns with one's theology. Please see Revelation 2:26; 6:8; 9:11; 11:6; 13:7; 14:18; 16:9; 17:18, and then look at Revelation **5:10**. Nowhere in Scripture does it say that Jesus is going to rule over the earth.

---

[124] William D. Mounce, Mounce's Complete Expository Dictionary of Old & New Testament Words (Grand Rapids, MI: Zondervan, 2006), 1150.

[125] Bratcher, Robert G.; Hatton, Howard: A Handbook on the Revelation to John. New York: United Bible Societies, 1993 (UBS Handbook Series; Helps for Translators), S. 105

Signs of the End of the Age

Matthew 24:4 New American Standard Bible (NASB)

⁴ And Jesus answered and said to them, "See to it that no one misleads you.

Jesus' disciples, like any other Jew of the day, would have seen the destruction of Jerusalem in 70 C.E., the first century Jewish historian, Josephus, tells us 1,100,000 Jews were killed in the destruction of Jerusalem, with another 97,000 taken captive. (War VI. 9.3)[126] Therefore, here in advance (33 C.E.), Jesus wanted his disciples to be on the watch, to not be misled, as though the destruction of Jerusalem (66-70 C.E.) also meant "the end of the age."

Matthew 24:5 English Standard Version (ESV)

⁵ For many will come in my name, saying, 'I am the Christ,' and they will lead many astray.

Yes, this would be one of the ways that many coming in Jesus' name would have led the disciples astray, claiming to be the Christ (Hebrew *Messiah*), namely the "anointed one." Therefore, it would not be Christians alone, who would be filling this role as false christs/messiahs/anointed ones.

"From Josephus it appears that in the first century before the destruction of the Temple [in 70 C.E.] a number of Messiahs arose promising relief from the Roman yoke, and finding ready followers ... Thus about 44, Josephus reports, a certain impostor, Theudas, who claimed to be a prophet, appeared and urged the people to follow him with their belongings to the Jordan, which he would divide for them. According to Acts v. 36 (which seems to refer to a different date), he secured about 400 followers. Cuspius Fadus sent a troop of horsemen after him and his band, slew many of them, and took captive others, together with their leader, beheading the latter ... Another, an Egyptian, is said to have gathered together 30,000 adherents, whom he summoned to the Mount of Olives, opposite Jerusalem, promising that at his command the walls of Jerusalem would fall down, and that he and his followers

---

[126] Flavius Josephus and William Whiston, *The Works of Josephus: Complete and Unabridged* (Peabody: Hendrickson, 1987).

would enter and possess themselves of the city. But Felix, the procurator (c. 55-60), met the throng with his soldiery. The prophet escaped, but those with him were killed or taken, and the multitude dispersed. Another, whom Josephus styles an impostor, promised the people "deliverance and freedom from their miseries" if they would follow him to the wilderness. Both leader and followers were killed by the troops of Festus, the procurator (60-62; "Ant." xx. 8, § 10). Even when Jerusalem was already in process of destruction by the Romans, a prophet, according to Josephus suborned by the defenders to keep the people from deserting announced that God commanded them to come to the Temple, there to receive miraculous signs of their deliverance. Those who came met death in the flames.

Unlike these Messiahs, who expected their people's deliverance to be achieved through divine intervention, Menahem, the son of Judas the Galilean and grandson of Hezekiah, the leader of the Zealots, who had troubled Herod, was a warrior. When the war broke out he attacked Masada with his band, armed his followers with the weapons stored there, and proceeded to Jerusalem, where he captured the fortress Antonia, overpowering the troops of Agrippa II. Emboldened by his success, he behaved as a king, and claimed the leadership of all the troops. Thereby he aroused the enmity of Eleazar, another Zealot leader, and met death as a result of a conspiracy against him (ib. ii. 17, § 9). He is probably identical with the Menahem b. Hezekiah mentioned in Sanh. 98b, and called, with reference to Lam. i. 17, "the comforter ["menaḥem"] that should relieve" (comp. Hamburger, "R. B. T." Supplement, iii. 80). With the destruction of the Temple the appearance of Messiahs ceased for a time. Sixty years later a politico-Messianic movement of large proportions took place with Bar Kokba at its head. This leader of the revolt against Rome was hailed as Messiah-king by Akiba, who referred to him. *The Jewish Encyclopedia* lists 28 false Messiahs between the years 132 C.E. and 1744 C.E.[127]

Matthew 24:6 English Standard Version (ESV)

[6] And you will hear of wars and rumors of wars. See that you are not alarmed, for this must take place, but the end is not yet.

---

[127] Vol. X, pp. 252-255.

There have been religious leaders that have been misled by the two Great Wars of the 20th century, World War I and II, associating each of them with the "end of the age." The First Jewish–Roman War (66–73 C.E.),[128] at times called The Great Revolt, could have misled the disciples into thinking that the end was imminent. Therefore, Jesus tells them that they should not be alarmed, and that the end is not yet. This counsel of Jesus has had to be applied from First Jewish–Roman War to the two Great Wars of the 20th century, every time a war came along, which seems to be an end all for humanity. Nevertheless, this one sign alone is not enough to signal the end because imperfect humans are prone to war.

Matthew 24:7 English Standard Version (ESV)

⁷ For nation will rise against nation, and kingdom against kingdom, and there will be famines and earthquakes in various places.

Here Jesus expounds on his previous comments about war, because the conflicts of humankind have been so pervasive that there was a need for a reference book, *Dictionary of Wars* by George C. Kohn. Therefore, while we should take note of current events, wars, rumors of wars and even kingdom against kingdom, this alone, is not enough to suppose that the end is here. Therefore, Jesus adds yet another two signs, famines and earthquakes. These two have been a part of humankind's history. Of course, the impact is going to be far greater with seven billion living people on earth, as opposed to a hundred million in 100 C.E. Nevertheless, these are just the beginning.

Matthew 24:8 English Standard Version (ESV)

⁸ All these are but the beginning of the birth pains.

Wars, rumors of wars, kingdoms again kingdom, famines and earthquakes are just the beginning of the things to come. However, they are not the goal post that the end is imminent. Such tragedies being merely a "beginning of the birth pains," the end was "not yet." Men likely cannot appreciate this verse because the woman only knows the pain of giving birth to a child. It is the most natural thing in her life and yet the most painful. Therefore, consider that what comes after this metaphorical concept is going to be far more painful for humankind. These pains will grow in severity until the birth of the end of the age and

---

[128] The Second Jewish–Roman War (132–135 C.E.) Simon Bar Kokba, who claimed to be the long awaited Messiah, led a revolt against Roman Emperor Hadrian (76-139), for setting up a shrine to Jupiter (supreme Roman god), on the temple site in Jerusalem, as well as outlawing circumcision and instruction of the Law in public.

the return of Jesus. Nevertheless, like any other birth that has finally reached the end, the joy of a newborn child makes one forget the prior pains. This is true after the tribulation; the joys from the Kingdom will outweigh the previous pains.

Matthew 24:9 English Standard Version (ESV)

⁹ "Then they will deliver you up to tribulation and put you to death, and you will be hated by all nations for my name's sake.

Verse 9 of the new section, 9-12, begins with "then" (Greek *tote*), which brings the reader into another section of signs, offering us more of the lines in the fingerprint, the full picture that we are in the time of the end. "Then" can have the meaning coming *after*, *or at the same time*, or it could mean simply *therefore*. It would seem that "then" is best understood as meaning 'at the same time,' because these signs, as well as those that we covered in 4-7, and those coming in verse 10 are of a composite sign. Meaning, you are looking for a time when they are all happening, and on a worldwide scale.

Who are "they" that deliver Christians up to tribulation? It would be those Christians of verse 5 of Matthew 24, who were led astray, abandoning the Christian faith. The last 30 years, this has truly seen the abandonment of Christianity, as well as much tribulation for those that have remained faithful. What I am primarily referring to is liberal Christianity (80 percent of Christianity), who has abandoned the biblical truth for the lie, so they can maintain a good relationship with the world and progressivism. Christianity has never been more hated than it is today. Sadly, conservative Christians have been deeply opposed and persecuted by liberal Christianity and atheists, not to mention Islam and other religions.

Verse 9 says they will deliver you over (ESV), or hand you over (HCSB), to tribulation. If one is handed over, he must first be seized and then delivered to those, who are seeking to do him harm, even death. Why are the Christians hated so? Jesus said, "If the world hates you, know that it has hated me before it hated you. If you were of the world, the world would love you as its own; but because you are not of the world, but I chose you out of the world, therefore the world hates you." (John 15:18-19, ESV) Former Christians and liberal Christians hate the stand that conservative Christians take by truly living by God's Word, in a world that is anything but. Radical Islamists are simply trying to impose themselves on everyone who stands in their way of dominating the world. Thus, being handed over is a result for one's true faith in Jesus Christ.

Matthew 24:10 English Standard Version (ESV)

[10] And then many will fall away and betray one another and hate one another.

While early Christianity suffered horrible deaths being martyred for simply being a Christian, the hatred today is just as vile by those that slaughter Christians around the world. Nevertheless, persecution through social media and news media, and by way of lawsuits, and by protests in the streets, has become the new form of persecution in the Western world. Many have fallen away from Jesus, becoming apostates toward their former brothers and sisters, loathing their very existence.

Matthew 24:11 English Standard Version (ESV)

[11] And many false prophets will arise and lead many astray.

What is a prophet? The primary meaning is one who proclaims the word of God, a spokesperson for God. Therefore, a false prophet would be a spokesperson giving the impression that he is a spokesman for God, but really he is far from it. These ones are very subtle and deceptive in their ability to present themselves as a person representing God. Some modern day examples would be Jim Bakker, Kenneth Copeland, Benny Hinn, T.D. Jakes, Joyce Meyer, Juanita Bynum, Creflo Dollar, Eddie Long, Pat Robertson, and Joel Olsteen. Of course, these are just some of the televangelists, who are false prophets, with tens of millions of followers. Other false prophet religious leaders have tens of millions of followers as well. Then, there are charismatic Christian denominations that numbered over 500 million followers. These ones claim gifts of God (faith healing, speaking in tongues, etc.), which clearly are anything but. The true Christians are falling away in great numbers, being led astray by these false prophets, and those who have not need to remain awake!

Matthew 24:12 English Standard Version (ESV)

[12] And because lawlessness will be increased, the love of many will grow cold.

The world we live in is overflowing with murders, rapes, armed robberies and assaults, not to mention war. It has grown so pervasive that many have grown callused to seeing the newspapers, websites and television news filled with one heinous crime one after another. In looking at just one city in the United States in 2012, 532 people were murdered in the city of Chicago, with a population of 2.7 million. However, in San Pedro Sula of the country Honduras, 1,143 people were murdered with only a population of 719,447. Statistics from the United Nations report 250,000 cases of rape or attempted rape annually. However, it must be kept in mind that because of the savagery of the times, in "many parts of the world, rape is very rarely reported, due to the extreme social stigma cast on women who have been raped, or the fear of being disowned by their families, or subjected to violence, including honor killings."[129]

Verse 12 says that "the love of many will **grow cold**," and indeed it has. There are atrocious crimes against individuals, groups, nations, which would cripple the mind of anyone living decades ago. However, because of seeing it every day, all day long, the world has grown hardened to the lawlessness that exists around them. Christians carry the hope of salvation in their heart, which Jesus addresses next.

Matthew 24:13 English Standard Version (ESV)

¹³ But the one who endures to the end will be saved.

What are we to endure? We are to endure while we maintain our walk with God through false Christs who will lead many astray, the wars, and the natural disasters. We are to endure while we maintain our walk with God through the loss of many of our spiritual brothers and sisters who fall away, the betrayal of former Christians, and the hatred of humankind who is alienated from God. We are to endure while we maintain our walk with God through false prophets that have arisen and lead many astray, the increase of the lawlessness in this world, and the love of humanity growing colder. Yes, each of us, who survives to the end of the Christian era, to the return of Christ, will be saved from Jesus' destruction of the wicked. However, we are not to simply sit around, we have a work to accomplish that is the last sign of the end of the age.

Matthew 24:14 English Standard Version (ESV)

¹⁴ And this gospel of the kingdom will be proclaimed throughout the whole world as a testimony to all nations, and then the end will come.

This is the last of the signs that Jesus gave that should concern us, as it is directly related to the end of the age, and the return of Christ, namely **'the gospel of the kingdom being proclaimed throughout the whole world.'** Jesus makes it very clear what he meant by "the whole

---

[129] http://en.wikipedia.org/wiki/Rape_statistics

world," by then saying "all nations" (Gk., *ethnos*). What Jesus meant here was more directed toward all races, not so much the "nations" that we know the world to be divided into today. Therefore, Jesus speaking of the whole world was a reference to "**a body of persons united by kinship, culture, and common traditions, *nation, people*.**"[130] Today, while for the most part, nations are made up of different races, the world is also becoming a melting pot.

In the phrase "**testimony** to all nations," we find the Greek word *martyrion*, which was a legal term for "**that which serves as testimony or proof, *testimony, proof*.**"[131] The testimony here that is to be shared by Christ's disciples has to do with Jesus and the kingdom. Evidence, proof, testimony has the ability to overcome the false reasoning of those in the world, to win them over as well as to convict those who refuse to see the evidence for what it is. Elsewhere Jesus said very clearly,

Matthew 11:15	Matthew 13:9	Matthew 13:43
English Standard Version (ESV)	English Standard Version (ESV)	English Standard Version (ESV)
[15] He who has ears to hear, let him hear.	[9] He who has ears, let him hear."	[43] Then the righteous will shine like the sun in the kingdom of their Father. He who has ears, let him hear.

No One Knows That Day and Hour

Matthew 24:36 English Standard Version (ESV)

[36] "But concerning that day and hour no one knows, not even the angels of heaven, nor the Son, but the Father only.

While none of us can know the precise time of Jesus' return, we do know that we are to be busy in the work that he has given us. Regardless of the time left, how will you use it? Here is how we should use our time before Christ's return. We should **live as though it is tomorrow**, but

---

[130] William Arndt, Frederick W. Danker, and Walter Bauer, *A Greek-English Lexicon of the New Testament and Other Early Christian Literature* (Chicago: University of Chicago Press, 2000), 276.

[131] IBID, 619.

plan as though it is 50-years away. What do we mean by this? We live as though Christ is returning tomorrow, by walking with God, having a righteous standing before him. We plan as though it is 50-years away by living a life that makes strategies for a long-term evangelism that fulfills our part of the great commission. – Matthew 24:14; 28:19-20; Acts 1:8.

Our sinful nature would not do well if we knew the exact day and hour. We do badly enough when we simply think Christ's return is close. There have been religions that set dates for Christ's return, or are constantly saying, 'the end is near!' The ones who set actual dates for Christ's return: quit their jobs, sell their homes, take all their money out of the bank, and take their kids out of school, either (1) to have a good time before the end, or (2) to spend the last couple years yelling from the rooftops that "the end is coming!"

Those who are constantly saying, 'the end is near,' are similar, in that they do not take job promotions, because it would cut into their evangelism. They do not allow their children to have university educations or plan careers because to them the end is near. Nevertheless, these groups are at least concerned about their evangelism, but fail to realize, we do not know when the end is coming.

We need to find a way in the time that remains, be it 5 years, 50 years, or 500 years, to encourage and foster "sincere brotherly love," and to display "obedience to the truth." What do we need to be obedient to? **(1)** We need to clean up the household of Christianity. **(2)** We need to then, carry out the great commission that Jesus assigned, to preach, to teach, and to make disciples! (Matt 24:14; 28:19-20; Ac 1:8) It is our assignment, in the time remaining, to assist God in helping those with a receptive heart, to accept the good news of the kingdom. Yes, we are offering those of the world, the hope of getting on the path of salvation, an opportunity at everlasting life. Just because we do not know the day or the hour, does not mean that we should be less urgent about this assignment.

Remember Jesus' illustration,

Matthew 24:43 English Standard Version (ESV)

[43] But know this, that if the master of the house had known in what part of the night the thief was coming, he would have stayed awake and would not have let his house be broken into.

Moreover, remember Jesus' question below, as it is a wakeup call, for we could not answer yet at this time.

Luke 18:8 English Standard Version (ESV)

⁸ I tell you, he will give justice to them speedily. Nevertheless, when the Son of Man comes, will he find faith on earth?"

If we were to consider the chaos within Christianity today, the 41,000 different denominations of Christianity, all believing differently, could we honestly say that Jesus would truly find the faith?

Fairness Restored

Isaiah 2:1-4 English Standard Version (ESV)

¹ The word that Isaiah the son of Amoz saw concerning Judah and Jerusalem.

² It shall come to pass in the latter days
   that the mountain of the house of the Lord
shall be established as the highest of the mountains,
   and shall be lifted up above the hills;
and all the nations shall flow to it,
³   and many peoples shall come, and say:
"Come, let us go up to the mountain of the Lord,
   to the house of the God of Jacob,
that he may teach us his ways
   and that we may walk in his paths."
For out of Zion shall go the law,
   and the word of the Lord from Jerusalem.
⁴ He shall judge between the nations,
   and shall decide disputes for many peoples;
and they shall beat their swords into plowshares,
   and their spears into pruning hooks;
nation shall not lift up sword against nation,
   neither shall they learn war anymore.

On these verses, Trent C. Butler writes, "**2:1.** This section begins with another introduction much like Isaiah 1:1, but this one only introduces the following sermons, not the entire book. What follows is a vision, what Isaiah … saw. Interestingly, the first part of this vision also appears in Micah 4:1–5. The form of this sermon sounds like a call to worship introduced by a prophetic announcement of salvation. Apparently Isaiah and his younger contemporary Micah both used the same call to worship from the Jerusalem temple to speak to God's people. This would mean that God used the temple hymnody as a source for his inspired word."

"**2:2.** While the destruction of Jerusalem dominated chapter 1, the city's function as the center of salvation for all nations introduces this section. The last days are still within world history with separate nations acting. Israel used the same language as her Near Eastern neighbors in talking about the national temple as the highest mountain on earth where the deity fights battles for his people (cp. Pss. 46; 48). The prophet Isaiah applied this language to the temple in Jerusalem even though Jerusalem was obviously not the highest of the mountains Israel could see. Jerusalem would be high and lifted up because God was at work there, causing his purpose for the world to be realized in historical events. The emphasis is not on the height of Jerusalem. The emphasis is on the unheard-of foreign nations coming to Jerusalem to worship. God's hope always encompasses the world, not just one small nation (see Gen. 12:1–4)."

"**2:3–4**. The prophet, as he often did, took up the popular theology of the people's hymnody and subtly shifted it from present to future tense. Only in the last days would Zion occupy such an exalted position. God would no longer battle the nations. Jerusalem could no longer glory in the hope that nations would march to her with large gifts and tribute for her victorious king. The prophetic hope is that God's word will become the world's weapon. Military academies and weapons will vanish. People will learn to live according to God's ways. They will obey his teachings. Nations will come to Jerusalem, not because a victorious king forces them to, but because they are attracted to Jerusalem by the God who lives there and the wisdom he gives there. No longer will they have to fight to settle their differences. In Jerusalem God will be the great Mediator who settles all human disputes without battle. Military weapons will become obsolete. The world's only war will be on poverty and hunger."[132]

Isaiah 11:3-5 English Standard Version (ESV)

[3] And his delight shall be in the fear of the Lord.
He shall not judge by what his eyes see,
    or decide disputes by what his ears hear,
[4] but with righteousness he shall judge the poor,
    and decide with equity for the meek of the earth;
and he shall strike the earth with the rod of his mouth,
    and with the breath of his lips he shall kill the wicked.

---

[132] Anders, Max; Butler, Trent (2002-04-01). Holman Old Testament Commentary - Isaiah (p. 29-30). B&H Publishing.

⁵ Righteousness shall be the belt of his waist,
and faithfulness the belt of his loins.

On these verses, Trent C. Butler writes, "The wise king would enter the royal courtroom to judge his nation correctly. As judge, the king would be empowered with the breath of his lips, the same word translated "Spirit" in verse 2. By this he would protect the poor from the wicked, establishing the economic justice so central to prophetic preaching. The new age established by the new king would bring righteousness, a dominant theme for Isaiah. Coupled with faithfulness, this clothed the king for his royal reign."[133]

Isaiah 42:1 English Standard Version (ESV)

42 Behold my servant, whom I uphold,
my chosen, in whom my soul delights;
I have put my Spirit upon him;
he will bring forth justice to the nations.

On this verse, Trent C. Butler writes, "This is the first of four "Servant Songs" in Isaiah 40-55 (49:1–6; 50:4–9; 52:13–53:12). Here God formally presented the servant to an audience, although both the name of the servant and the nature of the audience remain mysteriously unclear. We do not have to find answers to all our questions about the servant. We need to understand that he is God's chosen one, God takes great delight in him, and God upholds or supports him."

"The servant's mission surprised Israel and it surprises us. His mission was not to deliver Israel from captivity and exile. The mission was for the nations. The servant gained power for his mission from the divine Spirit just as earlier rulers and prophets had. (For Spirit of God, see "Deeper Discoveries," chs. 62-64.) The servant's task was to bring justice to the nations. (For justice, see "Deeper Discoveries," ch. 1.) Justice involves a much broader meaning than the English term. In verse 4 it stands parallel to Torah, law or teaching. It is the verdict handed down by a judge (2 Kgs. 25:6); the whole court process (Isa. 3:14); the gracious and merciful judgment of God (Isa. 30:18); or the natural right and order claimed by a person or group of persons (Exod. 23:6)."

"In our text, the term for the servant's mission apparently encompasses a broad meaning. It refers to the natural world order and the rights expected by the nations of the earth within that order. God

---

[133] Anders, Max; Butler, Trent (2002-04-01). Holman Old Testament Commentary - Isaiah (p. 83). B&H Publishing.

restores that order with its natural rights through his gracious and merciful judgment on the basis of his law or teaching."[134]

Isaiah 35:3-7 English Standard Version (ESV)

[3] Strengthen the weak hands,
and make firm the feeble knees.
[4] Say to those who have an anxious heart,
"Be strong; fear not!
Behold, your God
will come with vengeance,
with the recompense of God.
He will come and save you."

[5] Then the eyes of the blind shall be opened,
and the ears of the deaf unstopped;
[6] then shall the lame man leap like a deer,
and the tongue of the mute sing for joy.
For waters break forth in the wilderness,
and streams in the desert;
[7] the burning sand shall become a pool,
and the thirsty ground springs of water;
in the haunt of jackals, where they lie down,
the grass shall become reeds and rushes.

On these verses, Trent C. Butler writes, "The revelation of God's glory provided the background for a new prophetic commission (vv. 3-4; cp. ch. 6). If God could change the dry wasteland so radically, how much more he could do so for humanity! The prophet was called to encourage the weak and feeble. Their reason for fear would vanish. God would come in vengeance. The divine appearance would destroy the enemy (34:8) but bring salvation to the people of God. Such salvation is not limited to a spiritual realm. The sick and disabled would find all their reasons for having an inferiority complex destroyed."[135]

Isaiah 65:20-23 English Standard Version (ESV)

[20] No more shall there be in it
an infant who lives but a few days,

---

[134] Anders, Max; Butler, Trent (2002-04-01). Holman Old Testament Commentary - Isaiah (p. 232). B&H Publishing.

[135] Anders, Max; Butler, Trent (2002-04-01). Holman Old Testament Commentary - Isaiah (p. 191). B&H Publishing.

179

or an old man who does not fill out his days,
for the young man shall die a hundred years old,
    and the sinner a hundred years old shall be accursed.
21 They shall build houses and inhabit them;
    they shall plant vineyards and eat their fruit.
22 They shall not build and another inhabit;
    they shall not plant and another eat;
for like the days of a tree shall the days of my people be,
    and my chosen shall long enjoy the work of their hands.
23 They shall not labor in vain
    or bear children for calamity,
for they shall be the offspring of the blessed of the Lord,
    and their descendants with them.

On these verses, Trent C. Butler writes, "The injustices of life would disappear. Long life would be the rule for God's people, death at a hundred being like an infant's death that could only be explained as the death of a sinner. All of God's people would live to a ripe old age and enjoy the fruits of their life. The age of Messiah would clearly have dawned (cp. 11:6–9). No longer would people lose their property and crops to foreign invaders. Each of God's faithful people would enjoy the works of their hands. Labor would be rewarded in the field and in the birth place. Every newborn would escape the "horror of sudden disaster" (author's translation; NIV, misfortune). Curses would disappear. Every generation would be blessed by God."[136]

Psalm 37:7-11 English Standard Version (ESV)

7 Be still before the Lord and wait patiently for him;
    fret not yourself over the one who prospers in his way,
    over the man who carries out evil devices!

    8 Refrain from anger, and forsake wrath!
Fret not yourself; it tends only to evil.
9 For the evildoers shall be cut off,
    but those who wait for the Lord shall inherit the land.

    10 In just a little while, the wicked will be no more;
though you look carefully at his place, he will not be there.
11 But the meek shall inherit the land
    and delight themselves in abundant peace.

---

[136] Anders, Max; Butler, Trent (2002-04-01). Holman Old Testament Commentary - Isaiah (p. 374). B&H Publishing.

On these verses, Stephen J. Lawson wrote, "David repeated his original advice: Do not fret when men succeed. He returned to the earlier thought of verse 2—sinners who seem to flourish for a season will eventually be destroyed (Eccl. 3:16–17). To point this out, he used a series of contrasts between the godly and the ungodly. **Refrain from anger**, he declared, because these **evil men** in the final day would be cut off and die before entering eternity damned. **But those who hope in the LORD**—the meek—**will inherit the land** (cp. Matt. 5:5). This indicated the fullness of God's blessing."[137]

Revelation 21:3-4 English Standard Version (ESV)

[3] And I heard a loud voice from the throne saying, "Behold, the dwelling place of God is with man. He will dwell with them, and they will be his people, and God himself will be with them as their God. [4] He will wipe away every tear from their eyes, and death shall be no more, neither shall there be mourning, nor crying, nor pain anymore, for the former things have passed away."

On these verses, Kendell Easley wrote, "For the third and final time John hears **a loud voice from the throne** (16:17; 19:5). The word for **dwelling** is traditionally translated "tabernacle" or "tent." When the Israelites had lived in the wilderness after the exodus, God's presence was evident through the tent (Exod. 40:34). Part of the reward for Israel's obedience to God was, "I will put my dwelling place [tabernacle] among you, and I will not abhor you. I will walk among you and be your God, and you will be my people" (Lev. 26:11–12). Israel's disobedience, of course, led finally to the destruction of the temple."

"The permanent remedy began when God became enfleshed in Jesus: "The Word became flesh and made his dwelling among us" (John 1:14). A form of the same verb translated "made his dwelling" in John 1:14 is now used by the heavenly voice: **he will live with them**. Here, then, is the final eternal fulfillment of Leviticus 26."

"They will be his people, and God himself will be with them and be their God is a divine promise often made, particularly in context of the new covenant (Jer. 31:33; 32:38; Ezek. 37:27; 2 Cor. 6:16). In eternity, it will find full completion in its most glorious sense. One striking note here is that the word translated "people," while often singular in

---

[137] Anders, Max; Lawson, Steven (2004-01-01). Holman Old Testament Commentary - Psalms: 11 (p. 199). B&H Publishing.

Revelation (for example, 18:4), here is plural, literally "peoples." This points to the great ethnic diversity of those in heaven."

"The great multitude who came out of the Great Tribulation received the pledge of many blessings including the final removal of any cause for **tears** (7:15–17). Now this promise extends to every citizen-saint of the New Jerusalem. The picture of God himself gently taking a handkerchief and wiping away all tears is overwhelming. It pictures the removal of four more enemies:

• **death**—destroyed and sent to the fiery lake (20:14; 1 Cor. 15:26)

• **mourning**—caused by death and sin, but also ironically the eternal experience of those who loved the prostitute (18:8)

• **crying**—one result of the prostitute's cruelty to the saints (18:24)

• **pain**—the first penalty inflicted on mankind at the Fall is finally lifted at last (Gen. 3:16)"

"All these belonged to **the old order of things** where sin and death were present. The last thought could also be translated, "The former things are gone." No greater statement of the end of one kind of existence and the beginning of a new one can be found in Scripture." (Easley 1998, p. 395)

Resurrection of Life and Judgment

John 5:28-29 English Standard Version (ESV)

[28] Do not marvel at this, for an hour is coming when all who are in the tombs will hear his voice [29] and come out, those who have done good to the resurrection of life, and those who have done evil to the resurrection of judgment.

When Jesus returns, he will bring many angels, and wipe out the wicked. However, the righteous will not be destroyed, and the righteous prior to Jesus first coming back in the first century, will receive a resurrection. The unrighteous, which had never had the opportunity to know God, will also be resurrected for a chance to hear the Good News, and then, they will be judged on what they do during the millennial reign of Christ. Acts 24:15) Therefore, the punishment for sin is death, the punishment for those, who "keep on sinning deliberately after receiving the knowledge of the truth, there no longer remains a sacrifice for sins," i.e., eternal death. However, "there will be a resurrection of both the just and the unjust [i.e., those who never heard the Good News]."--Acts 24:15

In death, Scripture shows us as being unable to praise God. The Psalmist tells us, "For in death there is no remembrance of you; in Sheol [gravedom] who will give you praise?" (Psa. 6:5) Isaiah the prophet writes, "For Sheol [gravedom] cannot thank you [God], death cannot praise you; those who go down to the pit cannot hope for your faithfulness. 'It is the living who give thanks to you, as I do today; a father tells his sons about your faithfulness.'" (Isa 38:18-19)

Passing Over from Death to Life

John 5:24 English Standard Version (ESV)

[24] Truly, truly, I say to you, whoever hears my word and believes him who sent me has eternal life. He does not come into judgment, but has passed from death to life.

Regeneration is God restoring and renewing somebody morally or spiritually, where the Christian receives a new quality of life. This one goes from the road of death over to the path of life. (John 5:24) Here he becomes a new person, with a new personality, having removed the old person. (Eph. 4:20-24) **This does not mean** that the imperfection is gone, and the sinful desires are removed, but that he now has the mind of Christ, the Spirit and the Word of God to gain control over his thinking and his fleshly desires. Therefore, if one has truly experienced a conversion it will be evident by the changes in one's new personality from the old personality, his life, and his actions. If this is the case, he will be fulfilling the words of Jesus, "let your light shine before others, so that they may see your good works and give glory to your Father who is in heaven." (Matt. 5:16)

Can we see one as truly a man of faith, a committed Christian, who attends the meetings, but never carries out any personal study, never shares the gospel with another, never helps his spiritual brothers or sisters (physically, materially, mentally, or spiritually), nor helps his neighbor, or any of the other things one would find within a man of faith? James had something to say about this back in chapter 1:26-27, "If anyone thinks he is religious and does not bridle his tongue but deceives his heart, this person's religion is worthless. Religion that is pure and undefiled before God, the Father, is this: to visit orphans and widows in their affliction, and to keep oneself unstained from the world." One who does not possess real faith, will not help the poor, he will not separate himself from worldly pursuits, he will favor those that he can benefit from (the powerful and wealthy), and ignore those than he cannot make gains from (orphans and widows), he will not know the love of God, nor his mercy. (Jas. 2:8, 9, 13)

Titus 3:5 Lexham English Bible (LEB)

[5] he saved us, not by deeds of righteousness that we have done, but because of his mercy, **through the washing of regeneration** and renewal by the Holy Spirit,

The Greek word *polingenesia* means to a renewal or rebirth of a new life in Christ, by the Holy Spirit. Jesus told Nicodemus, "unless someone is born of ... Spirit, he is not able to enter into the kingdom of God." (John 3:5). At the moment a person is converted, he is regenerated or renewed, passing over from death to life eternal. Jesus explains this at John 5:24, "the one who hears my word and who believes the one who sent me has eternal life, and does not come into judgment, but has passed from death into life." The principal feature of rebirth of a new life in Christ, by the Holy Spirit, regeneration, is the passing over from death to life eternal.

At that point, the Spirit dwells within this newly regenerated one. From the time of Adam and Eve, God has desired to dwell with man. God fellowshiped with Adam in the Garden of Eden. After Adam's rebellion, he chose faithful men, to walk with him in their life course, to communicate with them. Enoch, Noah, and Abraham walked with God. In the Hebrew language the tabernacle is called *mishkan* meaning "dwelling place." In both the tabernacle and the temple, God was represented as dwelling with the people in the Most Holy. He also dwelt with the people through the Son, "And the Word became flesh and dwelt among us, and we have seen his glory, glory as of the only Son from the Father, full of grace and truth." (John 1:14) After Jesus' ascension, God dwelt among the Christians by way of the Holy Spirit in the body of each individual Christian, which began at conversion.

DIGGING DEEPER Does God Step in and Solve Our Every Problem Because We are Faithful?

Edward D. Andrews

Praising God as the Grand Savior

Psalm 42 depicts for us the circumstances of a Levite, one of the offspring's of Korah, who found himself in exile. His inspired words can be very beneficial to us in preserving thankfulness for friendship with fellow Christians and continuing steadfastly while going through hostile conditions.

Thirsting for God as a Deer Thirsts for Water

The psalmist stated,

Psalm 42:1-2 English Standard Version (ESV)

¹ As a deer pants for flowing streams,
    so pants my soul for you, O God.
² My soul thirsts for God,
    for the living God.
When shall I come and appear before God?

A female deer cannot survive long without water. If water is low, the deer will risk its life going out of cover to get at the lifesaving water, even though she knows that the prey could attack at any moment. Like the deer that longs for water because it is a matter of life or death, the psalmist longed for God. The word "pants" in the Hebrew means "to have a keen, consuming desire for." His driving passion was not for people, possessions, or prosperity but for God."[138]

The Bible lands are a dry country, where the vegetation wastes away rapidly throughout the dry season, and water is a very valuable commodity, as it is limited in the extreme. That is why the Psalmist says that he was a 'soul thirsting for God.' He had been going without his essential spiritual needs being satisfied, that is the freedom of going to the sanctuary; therefore, he asks when he might again "appear before God."

---

[138] Anders, Max; Lawson, Steven (2004-01-01). *Holman Old Testament Commentary - Psalms: 11* (p. 224). B&H Publishing. Kindle Edition.

He had been confined because of persecution, which prevented him from having contact with his fellow believers, which resulted in intense sadness, unhappiness and hopelessness, as verse three indicates.

Psalm 42:3 English Standard Version (ESV)

³ My tears have been my food
   day and night,
while they say to me all the day long,
   "Where is your God?"

Because of this hostile situation, the Psalmist was depressed to the point of being unable to eat. Therefore, his 'tears were his food.' Yes, "day and night" tears would roll down his cheeks into his mouth. His isolation and distress were not enough, as his enemies aggravated his wounds by provoking, ridiculing, in a hurtful or mocking way, as they would say all day long, "Where is your God?" He needed to find a way to reassure himself during this time of difficulty, to not be overrun by sorrow and heartache.

Why am I in Despair?

Psalm 42:4-6 English Standard Version (ESV)

⁴ These things I remember,
   as I pour out my soul:
how I would go with the throng
   and lead them in procession to the house of God
with glad shouts and songs of praise,
   a multitude keeping festival.

⁵ Why are you cast down, O my soul,
   and why are you in turmoil within me?
Hope in God; for I shall again praise him,
   my salvation ⁶ and my God.

My soul is cast down within me;
   therefore I remember you
from the land of Jordan and of Hermon,
   from Mount Mizar.

Here we find the Psalmist not living in the moment of suffering, but rather remembering a time before he was in exile. He 'pours out his soul,' reaching the depths of his inner self with such passion, as he reminisces within about the former days. The Levite recalls in his mind what life was like when he was in his land, as he lived and worshiped with his brother and sister Israelites, as they walked "to the house of God," to celebrate the festival. Initially, these memories did not bring joy, but rather the pain of knowing they were a thing of the past, deeply missed.

Then, he asked himself, "Why are you cast down, O my soul and why are you in turmoil within me"? At that moment, he realized that his hope of salvation was not in himself but in God. Therefore, the sweet memories truly brought him relief! He knew that if he patiently waited, God would act in his behalf. He then knew that his unfavorable conditions were not going to define his faith that, in time God would aid him in his time of need. When that moment would happen, he would "praise him" for 'his salvation' and being 'his God.' He might have been far removed from the sanctuary, but the Psalmist kept his God at the forefront of his mind.

If we ever find ourselves in difficult times, unrelenting times, we need to follow the pattern set by the Psalmist. We need to remember that God is well aware of our circumstances, and he will not forsake us. We must realize that the issues that were raised by Satan in the Garden of Eden, the sovereignty of God and the rightfulness of his rulership, and the issues raised by Satan to God in the book of Job, the loyalty of God's creatures, are greater than we are.

Proverbs 3:25-26 Lexham English Bible (LEB)

25 Do not be afraid of sudden panic,
   or the storm of wickedness that will come.
26 [Jehovah] will be your confidence
   and guard your foot from capture.

Before delving into the rest of Psalm 42, let us take a moment to establish what these verses do not mean. Should we understand that these verses or any others in Scripture teach that because we are wisely walking with God that he will miraculously step in to protect each servant personally from difficult times, diseases, mental disorders, injury or death? No. These sorts of miracles are the extreme exception to the rule. Of the 4,000 plus years of Bible history, from Adam to Jesus, with tens of millions of people living and dying, we have but a few dozen miracles that we know of in Scripture. Even in Bible times, miracles were not typical but far from it. Hundreds of years may pass with no historical record of a miracle happening at all.

If we are wisely walking with God, we can be confident that bodily disease, mental disorders, injury or early death is far less likely than if we were not. Moreover, we can draw on the resurrection hope. Does God miraculously move events to save us out of difficult times or miraculously heal us? Yes, he certainly can, but it is an extreme exception to the rule. He miraculously heals those who are going to play a significant role in his settling of the issues that were raised in the Garden of Eden.

What God's Word teaches us is this, that if we walk by using discernment and exercising sound judgment from Scripture, unless unexpected events befall us, we can be sure that we will not stumble into the difficulties that the world of humankind alienated from God faces every day. Conversely, the wicked do not have this protection as they reject the Word of God as foolish. In other words, Christians live by the moral values of Scripture, which gives them an advantage over those who do not. Therefore, God answers our prayers by our faithfully acting in behalf of those prayers and by applying Scripture in a balanced manner. If we have not taken in a deep understanding of God's Word, how can we have the Spirit inspired wisdom, the very knowledge of God to guide and direct us in our ways? Just because we are not being rescued when we feel that we should, this does not mean that we have lost faith or that God is displeased. Even though the Psalmist had no doubt that Jehovah God was coming to his aid, he still experienced grief.

Psalm 42:7 English Standard Version (ESV)

7 Deep calls to deep
   at the roar of your waterfalls;
all your breakers and your waves
   have gone over me.

Yes, the Psalmist's surroundings of his exile were very beautiful; however, they brought him back to the reality of his difficulty! Verse 7 may very well be describing the snow on Mount Hermon when it melts. Marvelous waterfalls are fashioned, which pour into the Jordan, causing it to increase in size. It is as though one wave is speaking to another wave. This extraordinary spectacle of power brought to the Psalmist's mind that he had been consumed by distress as if being overcome by a flood. Nevertheless, his faith in God does not waiver.

Psalm 42:8 English Standard Version (ESV)

^{8} By day [Jehovah]^{139} commands his steadfast love,
  and at night his song is with me,
  a prayer to the God of my life.

There is no doubt in the Psalmist's mind that Jehovah God will engulf him with his steadfast love, freeing him of anxiety. This will empower him to praise God in song and to offer a prayer of thanks 'to the God of his life.'

The Korahite Levite thinks,

Psalm 42:9-10 English Standard Version (ESV)

^{9} I say to God, my rock:
  "Why have you forgotten me?
Why do I go mourning
  because of the oppression of the enemy?"
^{10} As with a deadly wound in my bones,
  my adversaries taunt me,
while they say to me all the day long,
  "Where is your God?"

Then, it seems that the Psalmist slips, even though he views God as 'his rock,' a place of protection from one's enemies. Yes, he now asks, "Why have you forgotten me?" Yes, the Psalmist was allowed to remain in his circumstances of sadness, feeling depressed, as his enemies took pleasure in what appeared to be a victory. The psalmist speaks of himself as being criticized in an unbearable way. So malicious was the mockery and disdain that it could be likened 'as with a deadly wound in his bones.' However, the Levite again comes to himself with self-talk, challenging his irrational thinking with rational thinking.

Wait for God

Psalm 42:11 English Standard Version (ESV)

^{11} Why are you cast down, O my soul,
  and why are you in turmoil within me?

---

^{139} Translations take liberties with God's personal name, by removing it and replacing it with the title LORD in all caps. There is no rational reason, or Scriptural grounds for doing so. In fact, Scripture shows just the opposite.—See the American Standard Version Isaiah 42:8; Malachi 3:16; Micah 4:5; Proverbs 18:10; Joel 2:32; Ezekiel 36:23; Exodus 9:16; Malachi 1:11; Psalm 8:1;148:3.

Hope in God; for I shall again praise him,
   my salvation and my God.

It is not the troubles of the Psalmist, which actually caused him to feel bad. It is what he told himself that contributed to how he felt. Self-talk is what we tell ourselves in our thoughts. In fact, self-talk is the words we tell ourselves about people, self, experiences, life in general, God, the future, the past, the present; it is specifically all the words we say to ourselves all the time. Destructive self-talk, even subconsciously, can be very harmful to our mood: causing mood slumps, our self-worth plummeting, our body feeling sluggish, our will to accomplish even the smallest of things is not to be realized and our actions defeat us.

Intense negative thinking of the Psalmist led to his feeling forsaken, resulting in painful emotions, and depressive state. However, his thoughts based on a good mood were entirely different from those based on his being upset. Negative thoughts that flooded his mind were the actual contributors of his self-defeating emotions. These very thoughts were what kept the Psalmist sluggish and contributed to his feeling abandoned. Therefore, his thinking was also the key to his relief.

Every time the Psalmist felt down because of his irrational self-talk, he attempted to locate the corresponding negative thought he had to this feeling. It was those thoughts that created his feelings of low self-worth. By offsetting them and replacing them with rational thoughts, he actually changed his mood. The negative thoughts that move through his mind did so with no effort and were the easiest course to follow, because imperfect human tendencies gave him that way of thinking, a pattern of thinking. However, the Psalmist challenged those irrational thoughts of being forsaken with rational ones, saying that he would hope in God and that he would continue to praise him as in the end God is his salvation, even if that salvation comes in the form of a resurrection.

The centerpiece to it all is our Christlike mind. Our moods, behaviors and body responses result from the way we view things (fleshly or spiritual). It is a proven fact that we cannot experience any event in any way, shape, or form unless we have processed it with our mind first. No event can depress us; it is our perception of that event that will contribute to intense sadness, even depression. If we are only sad over an event, our thoughts will be rational, but if we are depressed or anxious over an event, our thinking will be bent and irrational, distorted and utterly wrong.

If we are to remain rational in our thinking, we need to grasp the fact that God does not always step in when we believe he should, nor is he obligated to do so. As was stated earlier, he has greater issues that need resolving, which have eternal effects for the whole of humankind. There is far more times when God does not step in, which means that our relief may come in the hope of the resurrection. However, for his servants that apply his Word fully and in a balanced manner, God is acting in their best interest by way of his inspired, inerrant Word.

DIGGING DEEPER Does God Provide Bible Absolutes or Guarantees In This Age of Imperfect Humanity?

Edward D. Andrews

Many verses (esp. Proverbs) have caused some difficulty in many churches because they are treated like absolutes or guarantees; if we do **A** we will get **B**. Proverbs are not to be applied in this sense in an imperfect world, with imperfect people. The best phrase that we can put before the proverb is "generally speaking." Let us look at Proverbs 22:6 as our first example, it says, "train up a child in the way he should go; even when he is old he will not depart from it." (ESV) Let us look at a easy version of this, "direct your children onto the right path, and when they are older, they will not leave it." (NLT) Is this an absolute guarantee that, if I raise my children in the best way, when they get older they will not leave it? No. Let us place our phrase in front of it. 'Generally speaking,' if you direct your children onto the right path, and when they are older, they will not leave it.'

Again, we ask, is a Bible verse that promises imperfect humans will receive something in this imperfect age to be interpreted as a universal law? Is it as the ancient law of the Medes and the Persians, which could never be overruled (Esther 8:8)? Is it to be interpreted absolutely, like the laws of thermodynamics, which describe what must always take place? It is apparent when reading proverbs that many of them seem to be less than absolute in their applicability. Let us look at a few more examples,

Proverbs 1:33 (New Living Translation)

³³ But all who listen to me will live in peace, untroubled by fear of harm.

Is it not true, even some of the most spiritual people we know, have suffered a lack of peace in war-torn countries, or have had trouble in a bad neighborhood, as they fearfully walk to the store, or get in and out of their car, even walk out on their front porch? Was not Stephen of the first century a very spiritual Christian, and was he not martyred?

Proverbs 3:9-10 (New Living Translation)

⁹ Honor the Lord with your wealth and with the best part of everything you produce. ¹⁰ Then he will fill your barns with grain, and your vats will overflow with good wine.

Have not many good Christians given much monetarily as well as their time to the congregation out of their heart over the years, and yet suffered financial disaster during an economic downturn?

Matthew 6:30-33 English Standard Version (ESV)

³⁰ But if God so clothes the grass of the field, which today is alive and tomorrow is thrown into the oven, will he not much more clothe you, O you of little faith? ³¹ Therefore do not be anxious, saying, 'What shall we eat?' or 'What shall we drink?' or 'What shall we wear?' ³2 For the Gentiles seek after all these things, and your heavenly Father knows that you need them all. ³³ But seek first the kingdom of God and his righteousness, and all these things will be added to you.

Have not faithful Christians gone hungry, even starved to death? Do not tens of thousands of Christian Children go to bed hungry every night around the world? Are not many Christian homes in this world lacking water? Do not many thousands of Christian families live in rundown homes, having only dirty clothes and in some cases any shoes?

Proverbs 10:3-4 (New Living Translation)

³ The Lord will not let the godly go hungry, but he refuses to satisfy the craving of the wicked.

Are there not many godly Christians going to bed hungry each night?

⁴ Lazy people are soon poor; hard workers get rich.

Are there not poor Christians, who work hard at minimum wage jobs; while there are rich wicked people, who have never worked a day in their life? (See Psalm 73)

Proverbs 13:21 (New Living Translation)

²¹ Trouble chases sinners, while blessings reward the righteous.

Do we measure one's righteous by who is the most blessed? Are all righteous people rich?

Proverbs 17:2 (New Living Translation)

² A wise servant will rule over the master's disgraceful son and will share the inheritance of the master's children.

Are there not rich wicked people?

If We Do "A," i.e., Apply God's Word Correctly We Will, Generally Speaking, Get "B"

It is obvious that none of the above verses and many thousand more within Scripture are absolutes. However, if we follow the rule and place "generally speaking" before the proverb and other verses that appear to be absolutes or guarantees, it will be what the author meant. Generally speaking,

- all who listen to the principles of God, will have peace, untroubled by harm.

- Keeping physically clean contributes to good health. (Deuteronomy 23:12-13)

- God's servants must always speak the truth. (Ephesians 4:25) Sex before marriage, adultery, bestiality, incest, and homosexuality are all serious sins against God. (Leviticus 18:6; Romans 1:26, 27; 1 Corinthians 6:9-10)

- Christians must avoid lying. (Proverbs 6:16-19; Colossians 3:9, 10)

- They do not take part in any kind of gambling. (Proverbs 13:11; 28:22; Ecclesiastes 5:10; Matthew 6:24; Ephesians 5:3-5; 1 Timothy 6:9-10; and Hebrews 13:5)

- In addition, Christians do not steal.

- Additionally, they do not knowingly buy property that they know to be stolen, nor do they take things without the owner's permission. (Exodus 20:15; Ephesians 4:28)

- Christians have learned to control their anger, as uncontrolled anger can lead to acts of violence. (Genesis 4:5-8)

- Christians know that God does not accept a person that is violent, or even loves violence as His friend. (Psalm 11:5; Proverbs 22:24, 25)

Christians do not take revenge or return evil for the bad things that others might do to us. (Proverbs 24:29; Romans 12:17-21) There is nothing in the Bible that prohibits drinking alcoholic beverages. (Psalm 104:15; 1 Timothy 5:23) However, heavy drinking and drunkenness are condemned. (1 Corinthians 5:11-13; 1 Timothy 3:8) A person, who consumes too much alcohol will more than likely ruin their health and upset their family. Moreover, it will decrease one's spiritual thinking ability, causing them to give into temptations. (Proverbs 23:20, 21, 29-35)

DIGGING DEEPER The Work of the Holy Spirit

Edward D. Andrews

Before we begin unraveling one of the touchiest topics in religious circles, it might be best if we borrow the story from Dr. Robert Stein's book, *A Basic Guide to Interpreting the Bible*:

Tuesday night arrived. Dan and Charlene had invited several of their neighbors to a Bible study, and now they were wondering if anyone would come. Several people had agreed to come, but others had not committed themselves. At 8:00 P.M., beyond all their wildest hopes, everyone who had been invited arrived. After some introductions and neighborhood chit-chat, they all sat down in the living room. Dan explained that he and his wife would like to read through a book of the Bible and discuss the material with the group. He suggested that the book be a Gospel, and, since Mark was the shortest, he recommended it. Everyone agreed, although several said a bit nervously that they really did not know much about the Bible. Dan reassured them that this was all right, for no one present was a "theologian," and they would work together in trying to understand the Bible.

They then went around the room reading Mark 1:1–15 verse by verse. Because of some of the different translations used (the New International Version, the Revised Standard Version, the King James Version, and the Living Bible), Dan sought to reassure all present that although the wording of the various translations might be different, they all meant the same thing. After they finished reading the passage, each person was to think of a brief summary to describe what the passage meant. After thinking for a few minutes, they began to share their thoughts.

Sally was the first to speak. "What this passage means to me is that everyone needs to be baptized, and I believe that it should be by immersion." John responded, "That's not what I think it means. I think it means that everyone needs to be baptized by the Holy Spirit." Ralph said somewhat timidly, "I am not exactly sure what I should be doing. Should I try to understand what Jesus and John the Baptist meant, or what the passage means to me?" Dan told him that what was important was what the passage meant to him. Encouraged by this, Ralph replied, "Well, what it means to me is that when you really want to meet God you need to go out in the wilderness just as John the Baptist and Jesus did. Life is too busy and hectic. You have to get away and commune with nature. I have a friend who says that to experience God you have to go out in the woods and get in tune with the rocks."

It was Cory who brought the discussion to an abrupt halt. "The Holy Spirit has shown me," he said, "that this passage means that when a person is baptized in the name of Jesus the Holy Spirit will descend upon him like a dove. This is what is called the baptism of the Spirit." Jan replied meekly, "I don't think that's what the meaning is." Cory, however, reassured her that since the Holy Spirit had given him that meaning it must be correct. Jan did not respond to Cory, but it was obvious she did not agree with what he had said. Dan was uncomfortable about the way things were going and sought to resolve the situation. So he said, "Maybe what we are experiencing is an indication of the richness of the Bible. It can mean so many things!"

But does a text of the Bible mean many things? Can a text mean different, even contradictory things? Is there any control over the meaning of biblical texts? Is interpretation controlled by means of individual revelation given by the Holy Spirit? Do the words and grammar control the meaning of the text? If so, what text are we talking about? Is it a particular English translation such as the King James Version or the New International Version? Why not the New Revised Standard Version or the Living Bible? Or why not a German translation such as the Luther Bible? Or should it be the Greek, Hebrew, and Aramaic texts that best reflect what the original authors, such as Isaiah, Paul, and Luke, wrote? And what about the original authors? How are they related to the meaning of the text?

It is obvious that we cannot read the Bible for long before the question arises as to what the Bible "means" and who or what determines that meaning. Neither can we read the Bible without possessing some purpose in reading. In other words, using more technical terminology, everyone who reads the Bible does so with a "hermeneutical" theory in mind. The issue is not whether one has such a theory but whether one's "hermeneutics" is clear or unclear, adequate or inadequate, correct or incorrect.

2 Corinthians 4:3-4 English Standard Version (ESV)

³ And even if our gospel **is veiled**, it is **veiled** to those who are **perishing**. **⁴** In their case **the god** of this world has **blinded the minds of the unbelievers**,[140] to keep them from seeing the light of the gospel of the glory of Christ, who is the image of God.

2 Corinthians 3:12-18 English Standard Version (ESV)

¹² Since we have such a hope, we are very bold, **13** not like Moses, who would put a veil over his face so that the Israelites might not gaze at the outcome of what was being brought to an end.**¹⁴** But **their minds were <u>hardened</u>**. For to this day, when they read the old covenant, that same **veil remains unlifted**, because only **through Christ is it taken away. 15** Yes, to this day whenever Moses is read a **veil lies over their <u>hearts</u>. 16** But **<u>when one turns</u>** to the Lord, the **veil is removed**. 17 Now the Lord is the Spirit, and where the Spirit of the Lord is, there is freedom.**18** And we all, with unveiled face, beholding the glory of the Lord, are being transformed into the same image from one degree of glory to another. For this comes from the Lord who is the Spirit.

Let us start by looking at an example of blind minds within Scripture. This was not a case of physical blindness, but mental blindness. There was a Syrian military force coming after Elisha, and God **blinded them <u>mentally</u>**. If it had been physical blindness, then each of them would have to have been led by hand. However, what does the account say?

2 Kings 6:18-20 American Standard Version (ASV)

¹⁸ And when they came down to him, Elisha prayed to Jehovah, and said, Please strike this people with blindness. And he struck them with blindness according to the word of Elisha. **¹⁹** And Elisha said to them, This

---

[140] By **unbelievers** Paul has in view non-Christians (1 Cor. 6:6; 7:12–15; 10:27; 14:22–24). First, the unbelievers of verse 4 are a subset of those who are perishing in verse 3. In other words, the two are the same. Second, the unbelievers are not persons, who have never heard the truth. No, rather, they are persons who have heard the truth, and have rejected it as foolish rubble. This is how this writer is using the term "unbeliever" as well. Technically, how could one ever truly be an unbeliever if they had never heard and understood the truth, to say they did not believe the truth? Therefore, to be an unbeliever, one needs to hear the truth, understand the truth, and reject that truth (i.e., not believing the truth is just that, the truth).

is not the way, neither is this the city: follow me, and I will bring you to the man whom you seek. And he led them to Samaria. 20 And it came to pass, when they were come into Samaria, that Elisha said, Jehovah, open the eyes of these men, that they may see. And Jehovah opened their eyes, and they saw; and, behold, they were in the midst of Samaria.

Are we to believe that one man led the entire Syrian military force to Samaria? If they were physically blind, they would have to have all held hands. Were the Syrian military forces not able physically to see the images that were before them? No, rather, it was more of an inability to understand them. This must have been some form of mental blindness, where we see everything that everyone else sees, but something just does not register. Another example can be found in the account about the men of Sodom. When they were blinded, they did not become distressed, running into each other.

Definitely, Paul is speaking of people, who are not receptive to truth because their heart is hardened to it, callused, unfeeling. They are not responding, because their figurative heart is opposed. It is as though God handed them over to Satan, to be mentally blinded from the truth, not because he disliked them per se, but because they had closed their hearts and minds to the Gospel. Thus, no manner of argumentation is likely to bring them back to their senses.

HOWEVER, at one time Saul (Paul) was one of these. Until he met the risen Jesus on the road to Damascus, he was mentally blind to the truth. He was well aware of what the coming Messiah was to do, but Jesus did none of these things because it was not time. Thus, Paul was blinded by his love for the Law, Jewish tradition and history. So much so, he was unable to grasp the Gospel. Not to mention, he lived during the days of Jesus ministry and studied under Gamaliel, who was likely there in the area. He could have even been there when Jesus was amazing the Jewish religious leaders, at the age of twelve. Therefore, Saul (Paul) needed a real wake up call to get through the veil that blinded him.

Hence, a mentally blind person sees the same information as another, but the truth cannot or will not get down into their heart. I have had the privilege of talking to dozens of small groups of unbelievers, ranging from four people to ten people in my life. I saw this in action. As I spoke to these groups, inevitably, I would see the light going off in the eyes of some (they would be shaking their heads in agreement as I spoke), but others having a cynical look, a doubting look (they would be shaking their heads in disgust or disapproval), and they eventually walked away.

This is not saying that the unbeliever cannot understand the Bible; it is simply that they see no significance in it, as it is foolishness to them.

1 Corinthians 2:14 The Lexham English Bible (LEB)

14 But the natural man <u>does not accept</u> the things of the Spirit of God, for <u>they are foolishness</u> to him, and <u>he is **not able to**</u> <u>**understand**</u>[141] <u>them, because they are spiritually discerned</u>.

Hundreds of millions of Christians use this verse as support that without the "Holy Spirit," we can fully understand God's Word. They would argue that without the "Spirit" the Bible is nothing more than foolish nonsense to the reader. What we need to do before arriving at the correct meaning of what Paul meant, is grasp what he meant by his use of the word "understand," as to what is 'foolish.' In short, "the things of the Spirit of God" are the "Spirit" inspired Word of God. The natural man sees the inspired Word of God as foolish, and "he is not able to understand them."

Paul wrote, "But the natural man does not accept the things of the Spirit of God, for they are foolishness to him." What did Paul mean by this statement? Did he mean that if the Bible reader did not have the "Spirit" helping him, he would not be able to grasp the correct meaning of the text? Are we to understand Paul as saying that without the "Spirit," the Bible and its teachings are beyond our understanding?

We can gain a measure of understanding as to what Paul meant, by observing how he uses the term "foolishness" elsewhere in the very same letter. At 1 Corinthians 3:19, it is used in the following way, "For the wisdom of this world is foolishness with God." This verse helps us to arrive at the use in two stages: (1) the verse states that human wisdom is foolishness with God, (2) and we know that the use of foolishness here does not mean that God cannot understand (or grasp) human wisdom. The use is that He sees human wisdom as 'foolish' and rejects it as such.

Therefore, the term "foolishness" of 1 Corinthians 3:19 is not in reference to not "understanding," but as to one's view of the text, its significance, or better yet, lack of significance, or lack of value. We certainly know that God can understand the wisdom of the world but condemns it as being 'foolish.' The same holds true of 1 Corinthians 1:20,

---

[141] "The Greek word *ginosko* ("to understand") does not mean comprehend intellectually; it means know by experience. The unsaved obviously do not experience God's Word because they do not welcome it. Only the regenerate have the capacity to welcome and experience the Scriptures, by means of the Holy Spirit."— (Zuck 1991, 23)

where the verbal form of foolishness is used, "Has not God made foolish the wisdom of the world?" Thus, we have the term "foolishness" being used before and after 1 Corinthians 2:14, (1:20; 3:19). In all three cases, we are dealing with the significance, the value being attributed to something.

Thus, it seems obvious that we should attribute the same meaning to our text in question, 1 Corinthians 2:14. In other words, the Apostle Paul, by his use of the term "foolishness," is not saying that the unbeliever is unable to understand, to grasp the Word of God. If this were the case, why would we ever share the Word of God, the gospel message with an unbeliever? Unbelievers can understand the Word of God; however, unbelievers see it as foolish, having no value or significance. The resultant meaning of chapters 1-3 of 1 Corinthians is that the unbelieving world of mankind can understand the Word of God, but views it foolish (lacking value or significance), while God on the other hand understands the wisdom of the world of mankind, but views it foolish (lacking value or significance). Therefore, in both cases, the information is understood or grasped; however, it is rejected because to the party considering it, believes it lacks value or significance.

We pray for the guidance of the Holy Spirit, and our spirit, or mental disposition, needs to be attuned to God and His Spirit through study and application. If our mental disposition is not in tune with the Spirit, we will not come away with the right answer. As Ephesians shows, we can grieve the Spirit.

Ephesians 4:30 English Standard Version (ESV)

[30] And do not <u>grieve the Holy Spirit</u> of God, by whom you were sealed for the day of redemption.

How do we grieve the Holy Spirit? We do that by acting contrary to its leading through deception, human weaknesses, imperfections, setting our figurative heart on something other than the leading.

Ephesians 1:18 English Standard Version (ESV)

[18] having the <u>eyes of your hearts</u> enlightened, that you may know what is the hope to which he has called you, what are the riches of his glorious inheritance in the saints,

"Eyes of your heart" is a Hebrew Scripture expression, meaning spiritual insight, to grasp the truth of God's Word. So we could pray for the guidance of God's Spirit, and at the same time, we can explain why there are so many different understandings (many wrong answers), some

201

of which contradict each other. This is so because of human imperfection that is diluting some of those interpreters (biases, wrong worldview, etc.). The spirit guides us by the Spirit inspired Word of God. Therefore, if we do not know how to correctly interpret the Scriptures, or we come at them with doctrinal biases, a worldview that does not permit the miraculous, an incorrect preunderstanding, we will arrive at not what the author meant but what we think it means.

A person sits down to study and prays earnestly for the guidance of Holy Spirit, that his mental disposition be in harmony with God's Word [or simply that his heart be in harmony with . . .], and sets out to study a chapter, an article, something biblical. In the process of that study, he allows himself to be moved, not by a mental disposition in harmony with the Spirit, but by human imperfection, by way of his wrong worldview, his biases, his preunderstanding.[142] A fundamental of grammatical-historical interpretation is that we are to look for the simple meaning, the basic meaning, the obvious meaning. However, when this one comes to a text that does not say what he wants it to say, he rationalizes until he has the text in harmony with his preunderstanding. In other words, he reads his presuppositions into the text,[143] as opposed to discovering the meaning that was in the text. Even though his Christian conscience was tweaked at the true meaning, he ignored it, as well as his mental disposition that could have been in harmony with the Spirit, to get the outcome he wanted.

In another example, it may be that the text does mean what he wants, but this is only because the translation he is using is full of theological bias, which is **violating** grammar and syntax, or maybe textual criticism rules and principles that arrives at the correct reading. Therefore, when this student takes a deeper look, he discovers that it could very well read another way, and likely should because of the context. He buries that evidence beneath his conscience, and never mentions it when this text comes up in a Bible discussion. In other words, he is grieving the Holy Spirit, and loses it on this particular occasion.

Human imperfection, human weakness, theological bias, preunderstanding, and many other things could dilute the Spirit, or even grieve the Spirit, so that while one may be praying for assistance, he is not

---

[142] Preunderstanding is all of the knowledge and understanding that we possess before we begin the study of the text.

[143] Presupposition is to believe that a particular thing is so before there is any proof of it

getting it, or has lost it, because one, some, or all of these things he is doing has grieved the Spirit.

Again, it is not that an unbeliever cannot understand what the Bible means; otherwise, there would be no need to witness to him. Rather, he does not have the spiritual awareness to see the significance of studying Scripture. An unbeliever can look at "the setting in which the Bible books were written and the circumstances involved in the writing," as well as "studying the words and sentences of Scripture in their normal, plain sense," to arrive the meaning of a text. However, without having any spiritual awareness about themselves, they would not see the significance of applying it in their lives. 1 Corinthians 2:14 says, "The natural person does not **accept** [Gr., dechomai] the things of the Spirit of God." Dechomai means, "to welcome, accept or receive." Thus, the unbeliever may very well understand the meaning of a text, but just does not *accept, receive* or *welcome* it as truth.

Acts 17:10-11 English Standard Version (ESV)

¹⁰ The brothers immediately sent Paul and Silas away by night to Berea, and when they arrived they went into the Jewish synagogue. ¹¹ Now these Jews [the Beroeans] were more noble than those in Thessalonica; they received [dechomai] the word with all eagerness, examining the Scriptures daily to see if these things were so.

Unlike the natural person, the Beroeans accepted, received, or welcomed the Word of God eagerly. Paul said the Thessalonians "received [*dechomai*] the word in much affliction, with the joy of the Holy Spirit." (1 Thess. 1:6) In the beginning of a person's introduction to the good news, he will take in knowledge of the Scriptures (1 Tim. 2:3-4), which if his heart is receptive, and will begin to apply them in his life, taking off the old person and putting on the new person. (Eph. 4:22-24) Seeing how the Scriptures have begun to alter his life, he will start to have a genuine faith over the things he has learned (Heb. 11:6), repenting of his sins. (Acts 17:30-31) He will turn around his life, and his sins will be blotted out. (Acts 3:19) At some point, he will go to God in prayer, telling the Father that he is dedicating his life to him, to carry out his will and purposes. (Matt. 16:24; 22:37) This regeneration is the Holy Spirit working in his life, giving him a new nature, placing him on the path to salvation. – 2 Corinthians 5:17.

A new believer will become "acquainted with the sacred writings, which are able to make [him] wise for salvation through faith in Christ Jesus." (2 Tim. 3:15) As the Bible informs us, the Scriptures are holy, and are to be viewed as such. If we are to acquire an accurate or full knowledge, to have the correct mental grasp of the things that we carried out an exegetical analysis on, it must be done with a prayerful and humble heart. It is as Dr. Norman L. Geisler said, "the role of the Holy Spirit, at least in His special work on believers related to Scripture, is in illuminating our understanding of the significance (not the meaning) of the text. The meaning is clear apart from any special work of the Holy Spirit." What level of understanding that we are able to acquire is based on the degree to which we are **not** grieving the Holy Spirit with our worldview, our preunderstanding, our presuppositions, our theological biases. In addition, anyone living in sin will struggle to grasp God's Word as well.

No interpreter is infallible. The only infallibility or inerrancy belonged to the original manuscripts. Each Christian has the right to interpret God's Word, to discover what it means, but this does not guarantee that they will come away with the correct meaning. The Holy Spirit will guide us into and through the truth, by way of our working in behalf of our prayers to have the correct understanding. Our working in harmony with the Holy Spirit means that we buy out the time for a personal study program, not to mention the time to prepare properly and carefully for our Christian meetings. In these studies, do not expect that the Holy Spirit is going to miraculously give us some flash of understanding, but rather understanding will come to us as we set aside our personal biases, worldviews, human imperfections, presuppositions, preunderstanding, opening our mental disposition to the Spirit's leading as we study.

The Work of the Holy Spirit

The following is adopted and adapted from Douglas A. Foster of Abilene Christian University.

Christian Publishing House's understanding of the Holy Spirit is **not** that of the Charismatic groups (the ecstatic and irrational), but rather the calm and rational. The work of the Holy Spirit is inseparably and uniquely linked to the words and ideas of God's inspired and inerrant Word. We see the indwelling of the Holy Spirit as Christians taking the words and ideas of Scripture into our minds and drawing spiritual strength from them. The Spirit moves persons toward salvation, but the Spirit does that in the same way any person moves another—by persuasion with words and ideas:

Now we cannot separate the Spirit and the Word of God, and ascribe so much power to the one and so much to the other; for so did not the Apostles. Whatever the word does, the Spirit does, and whatever the Spirit does in the work of converting, the word does. We neither believe nor teach abstract Spirit nor abstract word, but word and Spirit, Spirit and word. But the Spirit is not promised to any persons outside of Christ. It is promised only to them who believe and obey him.[144]

The Holy Spirit works only through the word in the conversion of sinners. In other words, the Spirit acting through the Word of God can accomplish everything claimed to be effected by a personal indwelling of the Spirit.

longtime preacher Z. T. (Zachary Taylor) Sweeney, in His book *The Spirit and the Word: A Treatise on the Holy Spirit in the Light of a Rational Interpretation of the Word of God*, writes after examining every Scripture that might be used by advocates of a literal personal indwelling of the Holy Spirit,

In the above cases, we have covered all the conceivable things a direct indwelling Spirit could do for one, and have also shown that all these things the Spirit does through the word of God. It is not claimed that a direct indwelling of the Spirit makes any new revelations, adds any new reasons or offers any new motives [other] than are found in the word of God. Of what use, then, would a direct indwelling Spirit be? God makes nothing in vain. We are necessarily, therefore, led to the conclusion that, in dealing with his children today, God deals with them in the same psychological way that he deals with men in inducing them to become children. This conclusion is strengthened by the utter absence of any test by which we could know the Spirit dwells in us, if such were the case.[145]

Christian Publishing House is defined by our rejection of Holiness and Pentecostal understandings of the Holy Spirit. The Holy Spirit transforms a person, empowering him through the Word of God, to put on the "new person" required of true Christians: "So, as those who have

---

[144] Alexander Campbell, The Christian System (6th ed.; Cincinnati: Standard, 1850), 64.

[145] Z. T. Sweeney, The Spirit and the Word (Nashville: Gospel Advocate, n.d.), 121–26.

205

been chosen of God, holy and beloved, put on a heart of compassion, kindness, humility, gentleness and patience."—Col. 3:12.

Ephesians 4:20-24 English Standard Version (ESV)

[20] But that is not the way you learned Christ!—[21] assuming that you have heard about him and were taught in him, as the truth is in Jesus, [22] to put off your old self, which belongs to your former manner of life and is corrupt through deceitful desires, [23] and to be renewed in the spirit of your minds, [24] and to put on the new self, created after the likeness of God in true righteousness and holiness.

Colossians 3:9-10 English Standard Version (ESV)

[9] Do not lie to one another, seeing that you have put off the old self with its practices [10] and have put on the new self, which is being renewed in knowledge after the image of its creator.

DIGGING DEEPER How Are We to Understand the Indwelling of the Holy Spirit?

Edward D. Andrews

1 Corinthians 3:16 New American Standard Bible (NASB)

[16] Do you not know that you are a temple of God and *that* the Spirit of God dwells in you?

Before delving into the phrase, "indwelling of the Holy Spirit," let us consider the words of New Testament scholars Simon J. Kistemaker and William Hendriksen, who write,

> The Spirit of God lives within you." The church is holy because God's Spirit dwells in the hearts and lives of the believers. In 6:19 Paul indicates that the Holy Spirit lives in the physical bodies of the believers. But now he tells the Corinthians that the presence of the Spirit is within them and they are the temple of God.

> The Corinthians should know that they have received the gift of God's Spirit. Paul had already called attention to the fact that they had not received the spirit of the world but the Spirit of God (2:12). He teaches that Christians are controlled not by sinful human nature but by the Spirit of God, who is dwelling within them (Rom. 8:9).

> The behavior—strife, jealousy, immorality, and permissiveness—of the Christians in Corinth was reprehensible. By their conduct the Corinthians were desecrating God's temple and, as Paul writes in another epistle, were grieving the Holy Spirit (Eph. 4:30; compare 1 Thess. 5:19).[146]

First, it must be said that I am almost amazed at how so many Bible scholars say nonsensical things, contradictory things when it comes to the Holy Spirit. Commentators use many verses to say that the Holy Spirit literally **(1) dwells in** the individual Christian believers, **(2)** having **control over** them, **(3) enabling them** to live a

---

[146] Simon J. Kistemaker and William Hendriksen, *Exposition of the First Epistle to the Corinthians*, vol. 18, New Testament Commentary (Grand Rapids: Baker Book House, 1953–2001), 117

righteous and faithful life,[147] with the believer **(4) still being able to sin**, even to the point of grieving the Holy Spirit (Eph. 4:30).

Let us walk through this again, and please take it slow, ponder whether it makes sense, is reasonable, logical, even Scriptural. The Holy Spirit literally dwells in individual believers, controlling them so they can live a righteous and faithful life, yet they can still freely sin, even to the point of grieving the Holy Spirit. Does this mean that the Holy Spirit is not powerful enough to prevent their sinful nature from affecting them? The commentators say the Holy Spirit now controls the Christian, not their sinful nature. If that were true, it must mean the Holy Spirit is ineffectual and less powerful than the sinful nature of the Christian, because the Christian can still reject the Holy Spirit and sin to the point of grieving the Holy Spirit. If the Holy Spirit is controlling the individual Christian, how is it possible that he still possesses free will?

Let us return to the phrase of "indwelling of the Holy Spirit." Just how often do we find "indwelling" in the Bible? I have looked at over fifty English translations and found it once in the King James Version and two in an earlier version of the New American Standard Version. One reference is to sin dwelling within us and the other reference is to the Holy Spirit dwelling within us. The 1995 Updated New American Standard Version removed such usage. We may be asking ourselves, since "indwelling" is almost nonexistent in the Scriptures, why the commentaries, Bible encyclopedias, Hebrew and Greek word dictionaries, Bible dictionaries, pastors and Christians using it to such an extent, especially in reference to the Holy Spirit. I say in reference to the Holy Spirit because some scholars refer to the indwelling of Christ and the Word of God.

Before addressing those questions, we must take a look at the Greek word behind 1 Corinthians 3:16 "the Spirit of God **dwells [οἰκέω]** in you." The transliteration of our Greek word is *oikeo*. It means "'to dwell' (from *oikos*, 'a house'), 'to inhabit as one's abode,' is derived from the Sanskrit, *vic*, 'a dwelling place' (the Eng. termination −'wick' is connected). It is used (a) of God as 'dwelling' in light, 1 Tim. 6:16; (b) of the 'indwelling' of the Spirit of God in the believer, Rom. 8:9, 11, or in a church, 1 Cor. 3:16; (c) of the 'indwelling' of sin, Rom. 7:20; (d) of the

---

[147] Millard J. Erickson, *Introducing Christian Doctrine* (Grand Rapids: Baker Book House, 1992), 265–270

absence of any good thing in the flesh of the believer, Rom. 7:18; (e) of the 'dwelling' together of those who are married, 1 Cor. 7:12-13."[148]

Thus, for our text, it means the Holy Spirit dwelling in true Christians. The TDNT tells us, "Jn.'s μένειν [menein] corresponds to Paul's οἰκεῖν [oikein], cf. Jn. 1:33: καταβαῖνον καὶ μένον ἐπ' αὐτόν [descending and remaining upon him]. The new possession of the Spirit is more than ecstatic."[149] What does TDNT mean? It means that John is using meno ("to remain," "to stay" or "to abide") in the same way that Paul is using oikeo ('to dwell').

When we are considering the Father or the Son alone, and even the Father and the Son together, we are able to have a straightforward conversation. However, when we get to the Holy Spirit we tend to get off into mysterious and mystical thinking. When we think of humans and the words *dwell* and *abide*, both have the sense of where we 'live or reside in a place.' However, there is another sense of 'where we might stand on something,' 'our position on something.' Thus, in English dwell and abide can be used interchangeably, similarly, just as Paul and John use *meno* "abide" or "remain" and *oikeo* "dwell" similarly. Let us look at the apostle John's use of meno,

1 John 4:16

[16] So we have come to know and to believe the love that God has for us. God is love, and whoever **abides [meno]** in love abides in God, and God **abides [meno]** in him.

Here we notice that God is the embodiment of "love" and if we **abide in** or **remain in** that love, God then **abides in** or **remains in** us. We do not attach any mysterious or mystical sense to this verse, such as God literally being in us and us being in God. If we suggest that this verse, i.e., God being in us, means his taking control of our lives, does our being in God also mean we control his life? We would think to suggest such a thing is unreasonable, illogical, nonsensical, and such. Commentator Max Anders in the *Holman New Testament Commentary* says, "This is the test of true Christianity in the letters of John. We must recognize the basic character of God, rooted in love. We must experience that love in our own relationship with God. Others must

---

[148] W. E. Vine, Merrill F. Unger, and William White Jr., *Vine's Complete Expository Dictionary of Old and New Testament Words* (Nashville, TN: T. Nelson, 1996), 180.

[149] Gerhard Kittel, Geoffrey W. Bromiley, and Gerhard Friedrich, eds., *Theological Dictionary of the New Testament* (Grand Rapids, MI: Eerdmans, 1964–)

experience this God kind of love in their relationships with us." (Walls and Anders 1999, 211) Our love for God and man is the motivating factor in what we do and not do as Christians. John is saying that we need to remain in that love if we are to remain in God and God is to remain in us. We may be thinking, well, is it not true that God guides and direct us? Yes, however, this is because we have given our lives over to him.

1 John 2:14

14 I write to you, fathers,

because you know him who is from the beginning.

I write to you, young men,

because you are strong,

and the word of God **abides [*meno*]** in you,

and you have overcome the evil one.

Here we see that the Word of God abides or remains in us. Does this mean that the Word of God is literally within our body, controlling us? No, this means that our love for God and our love for his Word is a motivating factor in our walk with God. We are one with the Father as Jesus was and is one with the Father and he is one with us. Listen to the words of Paul in the book of Hebrews,

Hebrews 4:12

12 For the word of God is living and active, sharper than any two-edged sword, piercing to the division of soul and of spirit, of joints and of marrow, and discerning the thoughts and intentions of the heart.

Is the Word of God literally living, an animate thing? No, it is an inanimate object. Is our Bible literally sharper than a sword? No, if we decide to stab someone with it, it would look quite silly. Is the Word of God literally able to pierce our joints and marrow? No, again, this would look silly. If we literally hold the Bible up to our head, is it able to discern our thinking, what we are intending to do? What did Paul mean? The Word of God does these things by our being able to evaluate ourselves by looking into the light of the Scriptures, which helps us to identify the intentions of our heart, i.e., inner person. When we meditatively read God's Word daily and ponder what the author meant, we are taking into our mind, God's thoughts and intentions. When we accept the Bible as the inspired, inerrant Word of God, take its counsel and apply its principles in our lives, it will have an impact on our conscience, the moral code that God gave Adam and Eve, our mental power or ability that enables us to reason between what is good and what is bad. (Rom 9:1) Then, our inner voice is not entirely ours, but is also God's Word, empowering us to avoid choosing the wrong path.

1 John 2:24

²⁴ Let what you heard from the beginning **abide [*meno*]** in you. If what you heard from the beginning **abides [*meno*]** in you, then you too will **abide [*meno*]** in the Son and in the Father.

Those who had followed Jesus **from the beginning** of his three and half ministry cleaved to what they had heard about the Father and the Son. Therefore, if the same truths are within our hearts, our inner persons, our mental powers or abilities, we too can **abide** or **remain [*meno*]** in the Son and the Father. (John 17:3) It is as James said, if we draw close to God through his Word the Bible, he will draw close to us. (Jam. 4:8) In other words, God becomes a part of us and we a part of him through the Word of God that is "living and active, sharper than any two-edged sword, piercing to the division of soul and of spirit, of joints and of marrow, and discerning the thoughts and intentions of the heart."

In John chapter 14, we see this two-way relationship more closely. Jesus said, "Believe me that I am in the Father and the Father is in me, or else believe on account of the works themselves." **(14:11)** He also said, "In that day you will know that I am in my Father, and you in me, and I in you." **(14:20)** We see that the Father and Son have a close relationship, a relationship that we are invited to join.

All through the above discussion of the Father and the Son, we likely had no problem following the line of thought. However, once we interject the Holy Spirit, it is as though our common sense is thrown out. Christians know that the Father and the Son reside in heaven. They also understand that when we speak of the Word of God, the Father and the Son dwelling in us, it is in reference to our being one with them, our unified relationship, by way of the Word of God. However, when we contemplate the Holy Spirit, it is as though our mental powers shut down, and we enter the realms of the mysterious and mysticism. However, we just understood John **14:11** and **14:20**, i.e., how Jesus is in the Father, the Father in Jesus, and their being in us. So, let us now consider the verses that lie between verse **11** and **20**.

Jesus Promises the Holy Spirit

John 14:15-17 English Standard Version (ESV)

¹⁵ "If you love me, you will keep my commandments. ¹⁶ And I will ask the Father, and he will give you another Helper, to be with you forever, ¹⁷ even the Spirit of truth, whom the world cannot receive, because it neither sees him nor knows him. You know him, for he **dwells [meno]** with you and will be in you."

First, do we not find it a bit disconcerting that all along when looking at John's writings as to the Son and the Father abiding **[meno]** in one another, in us, and us in them, the translation rendered **meno** as abiding, but now that the Holy Spirit is mentioned, they render **meno** as "**dwell**"?

Do these verses call for us to; drive off the path of reason, into the realms of mysteriousness and mysticism talk? No, these verses are very similar to our 1 John 2:24 that we dealt with above; but will quote again, "Let what you heard from the beginning **abide [meno]** in you. If what you heard from the beginning **abides [meno]** in you, then you too will **abide [meno]** in the Son and in the Father." In 1 John 2:24, we are told that if the Word of God that we heard from the beginning of being a Christian, **abides [meno]** in us, we will **abide [meno]** in the Son and the Father. In John 14:15-17, if we keep Jesus' commands, the Holy Spirit will **dwell**, actually **abide [meno]** in us. In all of this, the common denominator has been the Word of God, because it is what we are to take into our minds and hearts, which will affect change in our person, and enable us to abide in the Father and the Son, and they in us, as well as the Holy Spirit abiding in us.

The Holy Spirit, through the spirit inspired, inerrant Word of God is the motivating factor for our taking off the old person and putting on the new person. (Eph. 4:20-24; Col. 3:8-9) It is also the tool used by God so that we can "be transformed by the renewal of your mind, so that you may approve what is the good and well-pleasing and perfect will of God." (Rom 12:2; See 8:9) *The Theological Dictionary of the New Testament* compares this line of thinking with Paul's reference at Romans 7:20, to the "sin that dwells within me."

The dwelling of sin in man denotes its dominion over him, its lasting connection with his flesh, and yet also a certain distinction from it. The sin which dwells in me (ἡ οἰκοῦσα ἐν ἐμοὶ ἁμαρτία) is no passing guest, but by its continuous presence becomes the master of the house (cf. Str.-B., III,

239).[150] Paul can speak in just the same way, however, of the lordship of the Spirit. The community knows (οὐκ οἴδατε, a reference to catechetical instruction, 1 C. 3:16) that the Spirit of God dwells in the new man (ἐν ὑμῖν οἰκεῖ, 1 C. 3:16; R. 8:9, 11). This "dwelling" is more than ecstatic rapture or impulsion by a superior power.[151]

How does the Holy Spirit control a Christian? Certainly, some mysterious or mystical feeling does not control him.

Paul told the Christians in Rome,

Romans 12:2 English Standard Version (ESV)

2 Do not be conformed to this world, but be transformed by **the renewal of your mind**, that by testing you may discern what is the will of God, what is good and acceptable and perfect.

Just how do we **renew our mind**? This is done by taking in an accurate knowledge of Biblical truth, which enables us to meet God's current standards of righteousness. (Titus 1:1) This Bible knowledge, if applied, will enable us to move our mind in a different direction, by filling the void, after having removed our former sinful practices, with the principles of God's Word, principles that guide our actions, especially ones that guide moral behavior.

Psalm 119:105 Lexham English Bible (LEB)

105 Your word *is* a lamp to my feet

and a light to my path.

The Biblical truths that lay in between Genesis 1:1 and Revelation 22:21 will transform our way of thinking, which will in return affect our mood and actions and our inner person. It will be as the apostle Paul said to the Ephesians. We need to "to put off your old self, which belongs to your former manner of life and is corrupt through deceitful desires, and to be renewed in the spirit of your minds, and to put on the new self, created after the likeness of God in true righteousness and holiness. . . ." (Ephesians 4:22-24) The force that contributes to our acting or behaving in a certain way for our best interest is internal.

---

[150] Str.-B. H. L. Strack and P. Billerbeck, *Kommentar zum NT aus Talmud und Midrasch*, 1922 ff.

[151] Gerhard Kittel, Geoffrey W. Bromiley, and Gerhard Friedrich, eds., *Theological Dictionary of the New Testament* (Grand Rapids, MI: Eerdmans, 1964–), 135

Paul told the Christians in Colossae,

Colossians 3:9-11 English Standard Version (ESV)

9 Do not lie to one another, seeing that you have put off the old self with its practices **10** and have put on the new self, which is **being renewed in <u>knowledge</u>** after the image of its creator. **11** Here there is not Greek and Jew, circumcised and uncircumcised, barbarian, Scythian, slave, free; but Christ is all, and in all.

Science has certainly taken us a long way in our understanding of how the mind works, but it is only a grain of sand on the beach of sand in comparison to what we do not know. We have enough in these basics to understand some fundamental processes. When we open our eyes to the light of a new morning, it is altered into an electrical charge by the time it arrives at the gray matter of our brain's cerebral cortex. As the sound of the morning birds reaches our gray matter, it arrives as electrical impulses. The rest of our senses (smell, taste, and touch) arrive as electrical currents in the brain's cortex as well. The white matter of our brain lies within the cortex of gray matter, used as a tool to send electrical messages to other cells within other parts of the gray matter. Thus, when anyone of our five senses detects danger, at the speed of light, a message is sent to the motor section, to prepare us for the needed action of either fight or flight.

Here lies the key to altering our way of thinking. Every single thought, whether it is conscious or subconscious makes an electrical path through the white matter of our brain, with a record of the thought and event. This holds true with our actions as well. If it is a repeated way of thinking or acting, it has no need to form a new path; it only digs a deeper, engrained, established path. This would explain how a factory worker who has been on the job for some time, gives little thought as he performs his repetitive functions each day, it becomes unthinking, automatic, mechanical. These repeated actions become habitual. There is yet another facet to be considered: the habits, repeated thoughts and actions become simple and effortless to repeat. Any new thoughts and actions are more difficult to perform, as there needs to be new pathways opened up.

The human baby starts with a blank slate, with a minimal amount of stable paths built in to survive those first few crucial years. As the boy grows into childhood, there is a flood of pathways established, more than all of the internet connections worldwide. Our five senses are continuously adding to the maze. Ps. 139:14: "I will give thanks to you, for I am fearfully and wonderfully made. . . ." (NASB) So, it could never be overstated as to the importance of the foundational thinking and behavior that should be established in our children from infancy forward.

Paul told the Christians in Ephesus,

Ephesians 4:20-24 English Standard Version (ESV)

20 But that is not the way you learned Christ!— **21** assuming that you have heard about him and were taught in him, as the truth is in Jesus, **22** to put off your old self, which belongs to your former manner of life and is corrupt through deceitful desires, **23** and to be **renewed in the spirit of your minds**, **24** and to put on the new self, created after the likeness of God in true righteousness and holiness.

How are we to understand being **renewed in the spirit of our minds**? Christian living is carried out through the study and application of God's Word, in which, our spirit (mental disposition), is in harmony with God's Spirit. Our day-to-day decisions are made with a biblical mind, a biblically guided conscience, and a heart that is motivated by love of God and neighbor. Because we have,

- Received the Word of God,

- treasured up the Word of God,

- been attentive to the Word of God,

- inclining our heart to understanding the Word of God,

- calling out for insight into the Word of God,

- raising our voice for understanding of the Word of God,

- seeking the Word of God like silver,

- searching for the Word of God like gold,

- come to understand the fear of God, and have found the very knowledge of God, which now leads and directs us daily in our Christian walk.

Proverbs 23:7 New King James Version (NKJV)

7 For as he thinks in his heart, so is he. "Eat and drink!" he says to you, But his heart is not with you. [Our thinking affects our emotions, which in turn affects our behavior.]

Irrational thinking produces irrational feelings, which will produce wrong moods, leading to wrong behavior. It may be difficult for each of us to wrap our mind around it, but we are very good at telling ourselves outright lies and half-truths, repeatedly throughout each day. In fact, some of us are so good at it that it has become our reality and leads to mental distress and bad behaviors.

When we couple our leaning toward wrongdoing with the fact that Satan the devil, who is "the god of this world," (2 Cor. 4:4) has worked to entice these leanings, the desires of the fallen flesh; we are even further removed from our relationship with our loving heavenly Father. During these 'last days, grievous times' has fallen on us as Satan is working all the more to prevent God's once perfect creation to achieve a righteous standing. This has prevented some from entertaining the hope of eternal life. – 2 Timothy 3:1-5.

When we enter the pathway of walking with our God, we will certainly come across resistance from three different areas (Our sinful nature, Satan and demons, and the world that caters to our flesh). **Our greatest obstacle** is **ourselves**, because we have inherited imperfection from our first parents Adam and Eve. The Scriptures make it quite clear that we are **mentally bent toward bad**, not good. (Gen 6:5; 8:21, AT) In other words, our natural desire is toward wrong. Prior to sinning, Adam and Eve were perfect, and they had the natural desire of doing good, and to go against that was to go against the grain of their inner person. Scripture also tells us of our inner person, our heart.

Jeremiah 17:9 Lexham English Bible (LEB)

⁹ The **heart *is* deceitful** more than anything else,

and it *is* disastrous. Who can understand it?

Jeremiah's words should serve as a wakeup call, if we are to be pleasing in the eyes of our heavenly Father. We must focus on our inner person. Maybe we have been a Christian for many years; maybe we have a deep knowledge of Scripture; and maybe we feel that we are spiritually strong, and nothing will stumble us. Nevertheless, our hearts that are deceitful and desperately sick can be enticed by secret desires, where if one fails to dismiss them, he eventually commits a serious sin.

Our conscious thinking (aware) and subconscious thinking (present in our mind without our being aware of it) originates in the mind. For good, or for bad, our mind follows certain rules of action, which if entertained one will move even further in that direction until they are eventually consumed for good or for bad. In our imperfect state, our bent thinking will lean toward wrong, especially with Satan using his world, with so many forms of entertainment that simply feed the flesh.

James 1:14-15 Updated American Standard Version

¹⁴ But each one is tempted when he is carried away and enticed by his own desire.[152] ¹⁵ Then the desire when it has conceived gives birth to sin, and sin when it is fully grown brings forth death.

1 John 2:16 Lexham English Bible (LEB)

¹⁶ because everything *that is* in the world, the desire of the flesh and the desire of the eyes and the arrogance of material possessions—is not from the Father, but is from the world.

Matthew 5:28 Lexham English Bible (LEB)

²⁸ But I say to you that everyone who looks at a woman to lust for her has already committed adultery with her in his heart.

1 Peter 1:14 Lexham English Bible (LEB)

¹⁴ As obedient children, do not be conformed to the former desires *you used to conform to*[153] in your ignorance

If we do not want to be affected by the world of humankind around us, which is alienated from God, we must again consider the words of the Apostle Paul. He writes (Rom 12:2) "Do not be conformed to this world, but be transformed by the renewal of your mind that by testing you may discern what is the will of God, what is good and acceptable and perfect." Just how do we do that? This is done by taking in an accurate knowledge of Biblical truth, which enables us to meet God's current standards of righteousness. (Titus 1:1) This Bible knowledge, if applied, will enable us to move our mind in a different direction, by filling the void with the principles of God's Word, principles that guide our actions, especially ones that guide moral behavior.

Psalm 119:105 Lexham English Bible (LEB)

¹⁰⁵ Your word *is* a lamp to my feet

and a light to my path.

---

[152] Or "own *lust*"

[153] This is an understood repetition of the earlier verb "be conformed to"

The Biblical truths that lay in between Genesis 1:1 and Revelation 22:21 will transform our way of thinking, which will in return affect our mood and actions and our inner person. It will be as the apostle Paul set it out to the Ephesians. We need to "to put off your old self, which belongs to your former manner of life and is corrupt through deceitful desires, and to be renewed in the spirit of your minds, and to put on the new self, created after the likeness of God in true righteousness and holiness. . . ." (Ephesians 4:22-24) The force that contributes to our acting or behaving in a certain way for our best interest, is internal.

Bringing This Transformation About

The mind is the mental ability that we use in a conscious way to garner information and to consider ideas and come to conclusions. Therefore, if we perceive our realities based on the information, that surrounds us, generally speaking, most are inundated in a world that reeks of Satan's influence. This means that our perception, our attitude, thoughts, speech and conduct are in opposition to God and his Word. Most are in true ignorance to the changing power of God's Word. The apostle Paul helps us to appreciate the depths of those who reflect this world's disposition. He writes,

Ephesians 4:17-19 Lexham English Bible (LEB)

[17] This therefore I say and testify in the Lord, *that* you no longer walk as the Gentiles [unbelievers] walk: in the futility of their mind [emptiness, idleness, vanity, foolishness, purposelessness], [18] being darkened in understanding[mind being the center of human perception], alienated from the life of God[not Godless, but less God], because of the ignorance *that* is in them [due not to a lack of opportunity but deliberate rejection], because of the hardness of their heart [hardening as if by calluses, unfeeling], [19] who, becoming callous, gave themselves over to licentiousness, for the pursuit of all uncleanness in greediness.

Hebrews 4:12 Lexham English Bible (LEB)

[12] For the word of God *is* living and active and sharper than any double-edged sword, and piercing as far as the division of soul and spirit, both joints and marrow, and able to judge the reflections and thoughts of the heart.

By taking in this knowledge of God's Word, we will be altering our way of thinking, which will affect our emotions and behavior, as well as our lives now and for eternity. This Word will influence our minds, making corrections in the way we think. If we are to have the Holy Spirit controlling our lives, we must 'renew our mind' (Rom. 12:2) "which is being renewed in knowledge" (Col. 3:10) of God and his will and purposes. (Matt 7:21-23; See Pro 2:1-6) All of this boils down to each individual Christian digging into the Scriptures in a meditative way, so he can 'discover the knowledge of God, receiving wisdom from God's mouth, as well as knowledge and understanding.' (Pro. 2:5-6) As he acquires the mind that is inundated with the Word of God, he must also,

James 1:22-25 English Standard Version (ESV)

²² But be doers of the word, and not hearers only, deceiving yourselves. ²³ For if anyone is a hearer of the word and not a doer, he is like a man who looks intently at his natural face¹⁵⁴ in a mirror.

²⁴ for he looks at himself and goes away, and immediately forgets what sort of man he was. ²⁵ But he that looks into the perfect law, the law of liberty, and abides by it, being no hearer who forgets but a doer of a work, he will be blessed in his doing.

---

¹⁵⁴ Lit *the face of his birth*

Bibliography

Anders, Max, and Steven Lawson. *Holman Old Testament Commentary - Psalms: 11*. Grand Rapids: B&H Publishing, 2004.

Andrews, Edward D. *A BASIC GUIDE TO BIBLICAL INTERPRETATION Understanding the Correct Methods of Interpretation*. Cambridge: Christian Publishing House, 2014.

—. *FOR AS I THINK IN MY HEART—SO I AM: Combining Biblical Counseling with Cognitive Behavioral Therapy*. Cambridge: Christian Publishing House, 2013.

—. *PUT OFF THE OLD PERSON WITH ITS PRACTICES And Put On the New Person*. Cambridge: Christian Publishing House, 2014.

Apranawa, Widy S. H. *THE LORD IS SAVIOR: FAITH IN NATIONAL CRISIS A Commentary on the Book of Isaiah 1–39*. Grand Rapids: wm. b. eerdmans publishing co., 1990.

Arndt, William, Frederick W. Danker, and Walter Bauer. *A Greek-English Lexicon of the New Testament and Other Early Christian Literature*. 3rd ed. . Chicago: University of Chicago Press, 2000.

Arnold, Clinton E. *Zondervan Illustrated Bible Backgrounds Commentary Volume 4: Hebrews to Revelation*. Grand Rapids, MI: Zondervan, 2002.

Baker, William, and Paul Carrier. J. *James-Jude: Standard Bible Series*. Cincinnati: Standard Publishing, 1990.

Barclay, William. *New Testament Words*. Louisville: Westminster Press, 1974.

Blomberg, Craig L., Mariam J. Kamell, and Clinton E. Arnold. *Zondervan Exegetical Commentary on the New Testament: James*. Grand Rapids: Zondervan, 2009.

Brand, Chad, Charles Draper, and England Archie. *Holman Illustrated Bible Dictionary: Revised, Updated and Expanded*. Nashville, TN: Holman, 2003.

Bratcher, Robert G., and Howard Hatton. *A Handbook on the Revelation to John*. New York: United Bible Societies, 1993.

Bromiley, Geoffrey W. *The International Standard Bible Encyclopedia (Vol. 1-4)*. Grand Rapids, MI: William B. Eerdmans Publishing Co., 1986.

Bromiley, Geoffrey W., and Gerhard Friedrich. *Theological Dictionary of the New Testament, ed. Gerhard Kittel, vol. 4*. Grand Rapids, MI: Eerdmans, 1964-.

Campbell, Alexander. *The Christian System (6th ed.;*. Cincinnati: Standard, 1850.

Comfort, Philip W. *New Testament Text and Translation Commentary*. Carol Stream: Tyndale House Publishers, 2008.

Easley, Kendell H. *Holman New Testament Commentary, vol. 12, Revelation*. (Nashville, TN: Broadman & Holman Publishers, 1998.

Elwell, Walter A. *Baker Encyclopedia of the Bible*. Grand Rapids: Baker Book House, 1988.

Erickson, Millard J. *Introducing Christian Doctrine*. Grand Rapids: Baker Book Hous, 1992.

Gangel, Kenneth O. *Holman New Testament Commentary: Acts*. Nashville, TN: Broadman & Holman Publishers, 1998.

Harris, Robert Laird, Gleason Leonard Archer, and Bruce K Waltke. *Theological Wordbook of the Old Testament*. Chicago: Moody Press, 1999, c1980.

Holloway, Gary. *The College NIV Commentary: James & Jude*. Joplin: College Press Publishing Company, 1996.

Hort, F. J. A. *The Epistle of St. James*. London: The Macmillian and Company, 1909.

Kaiser, Walter C, and Moises Silva. *Introduction to Biblical Hermeneutics: The Search for Meaning*. Grand Rapids: Zondervan, 1994, 2007.

Keener, Craig S. *The IVP Bible Background Commentary: New Testament*. Downer Groves, IL: InterVarsity Press, 1993.

Kistemaker, Simon J. *NEW TESTAMENT COMMENTARY: Exposition of James and the Epistles of John*. Grand Rapids: Baker Books, 1986.

Kistemaker, Simon J., and William Hendriksen. *Exposition of the First Epistle to the Corinthians, vol. 18, New Testament Commentary*. Grand Rapids, MI: Baker Book House, 1953–2001.

Lea, Thomas D. *Holman New Testament Commentary: Vol. 10, Hebrews, James.* Nashville, TN: Broadman & Holman Publishers, 1999.

Louw, Johannes P, and Eugene Albert and Nida. *vol. 1, Greek-English Lexicon of the New Testament : Based on Semantic Domains, 2nd edition.* New York: United Bible societies, 1996.

Maier, Paul L. *Josephus the Essential Works.* Grand Rapids: Kregel Publications, 1988.

McReynolds, Paul R. *Word Study: Greek-English.* Carol Stream: Tyndale House Publishers, 1999.

Moo, Douglas. *The Letter of James: Pillar New Testament Commentary.* Grand Rapids: William B. Eerdman's Publishing Company, 2000.

Mounce, William D. *Mounce's Complete Expository Dictionary of Old & New Testament Words.* Grand Rapids, MI: Zondervan, 2006.

Packer, J. I, and M. C Tenney. *Nelson Illustrated Manners and Customs of the Bible.* Nashville, TN: Thomas Nelson, 1980.

Pratt Jr, Richard L. *Holman New Testament Commentary: I & II Corinthians, vol. 7.* Nashville: Broadman & Holman Publishers, 2000.

Ramm, Bernard. *Protestant Biblical Interpretation: A Textbook of Hermeneutics, 3rd rev. ed.* Grand Rapids, MI: Baker, 1999.

Reese, Gareth. *New Testament Epistles James and 1,2,3 John.* Scripture Exposition Books: Moberly, 2007.

Richardson, Kurt. *The New American Commentary Vol. 36 James.* Nashville: Broadman & Holman Publishers, 1997.

Robertson, A.T. *Word Pictures in the New Testament.* Oak Harbor, MI: Logos Research Systems, 1933, 1997.

Rooker, Mark F. *The New American Commentary, vol. 3A, Leviticus.* Nashville: Broadman & Holman Publishers, 2000.

Stein, Robert H. *A Basic Guide to Interpreting the Bible: Playing by the Rules.* Grand Rapids: Baker Books, 1994.

Sweeney, Z. T. *The Spirit and the Word (: , n.d.), 121–26.* Nashville: Gospel Advocate, 2005.

Terry, Milton S. *Biblical Hermeneutics: A Treatise on the Interpretation of the Old and New Testaments.* Grand Rapids: Zondervan, 1883.

Thomas, Robert L. *Evangelical Hermeneutics*. Grand Rapids: Kregel Publications, 2002.

Vincent, Marvin. *Word Studies in the New Testament*. Bellingham: Logos Research Systems, 2002.

Vine, W E. *Vine's Expository Dictionary of Old and New Testament Words*. Nashville: Thomas Nelson, 1996.

Virkler, Henry A, and Karelynne Gerber Ayayo. *Hermeneutics: Principles and Processes of Biblical Interpretation*. Grand Rapids, MI: Baker Academic, 1981, 2007.

Whiston, William. *The Works of Josephus*. Peabody, MA: Hendrickson, 1987.

Wuest, Kenneth S. *Wuest's Word Studies from the Greek New Testament: For the English Reader*. Grand Rapids: Eerdmans, 1997, c1984.

Zodhiates, Spiros. *The Complete Word Study Dictionary: New Testament*. Chattanooga: AMG Publishers, 2000, c1992, c1993.